I Can Dance

My Life with a Disability

Laurie Hoirup

I Can Dance
My Life with a Disability

Copyright © 2012 by Laurell L. Hoirup.

Umbach Consulting & Publishing
6966 Sunrise Blvd., #263
Citrus Heights, CA 95610
916-733-2159
ken@umbachconsulting.com

ISBN: 978-1-937123-01-7

Library of Congress Control Number: 2011938900

This memoir encompasses the author's recollections and reflections. Some names and details have been changed, and conversations recreated approximately.

Cover design by Jeannie Ruesch, www.willdesignforchocolate.com

Printed in U.S.A.

1/9/2012

To Steve & Linda,
With Much Awareness!

Laurell Horup

I Can Dance

Contents

Acknowledgments and Dedication

I want to acknowledge those who played a major role in my development and support, both past and present, and who continue to make my life what it is today.

First and foremost is my mom, Dottie, who brought me into this world, raised me to be the person I am today, and continues to support me throughout all of my endeavors.

Of course, there is my dad, Bill, providing me with love, support, and understanding, and who taught me the true meaning of family, being the best father anyone could ask for.

Also my children, Chad and Jillian, whom no one ever expected me to have, each loving me, always being there when I need them, and teaching me that motherhood does not require an able body, but the ability to love and the desire to nurture.

Most importantly, JR Hoirup, my husband, partner, best friend, lover, and soulmate, who accepted me for who I was, supported me through the good and the bad, raised my children as his own, and provided me with all of the love any woman/wife could ever expect or want. Were it not for him, I don't know that this book would have ever become a reality or my life be as fulfilled as it is.

My friends are too numerous to name, but they know who they are and the role they have played in making my life what it is. I love you all.

To my mentor, friend, and now publisher Ken Umbach, my thanks for having the faith in the merit of my story and the willingness to take a risk in publishing it.

My acknowledgments wouldn't be complete if I didn't include the Northern California Publishers and Authors (NCPA) and the California Writers Club (CWC), whose members encouraged, supported, inspired, and provided me with the knowledge to follow through with my dream. Thank you, one and all.

I dedicate this book to my grandchildren:

Michael Damien, grandma's first, who brings me joy with every smile, pride with every accomplishment, and complete contentment every time I hear him say, "Grandma!"

Then there are my two grandchildren to be, one due in April and the other in May. Though I may not know them yet, they will know they were in my heart and included in this dedication.

Lest I forget, I dedicate this book also to any of my other grandbabies who may come in the future, for all are truly Laurie's Legacy!

Laurie Hoirup
Sacramento, California

Foreword by Catherine Campisi

It is my pleasure to welcome you to *I Can Dance*. In addition to telling Laurie Hoirup's life story, *I Can Dance* provides valuable lessons and insights for people with disabilities, parents of children with disabilities, and service providers. Leading by example, Laurie makes clear how the expectations and actions of parents affect the development of a child with a disability and shape the child's responses to the many challenges people with significant disabilities face in living a fun and self-fulfilled life.

I Can Dance resonates deeply with me as a person with a significant physical disability since childhood. As a professional with over thirty years of experience in disability services and rehabilitation, I appreciate that Laurie's memoir offers real life examples and crystallizes key concepts used in counseling, teaching, and serving persons with disabilities.

Laurie tackles the major milestones of her life with candor, humor, and personal reflection. From the years of her infancy and childhood, we learn about the diagnosis of her disability and its impact on her family as well as her challenges and success playing with friends, attending school, and doing chores. In the teenage years, we follow her search for acceptance and relationships and the exploration of her sexuality. As she goes off to college, we learn about living independently, including arranging and managing caregivers, dealing with low academic expectations, and learning to guide and lead one's own life. In adulthood, we share Laurie's journey into marriage, pregnancy, parenthood, love, and work.

Throughout the book, we have the opportunity to develop new insights for ourselves and others as we read how Laurie faced personal challenges, including the progression of her disability, with creativity, determination, and humor.

I Can Dance is a "must-read" for several audiences!

- For parents, of ALL children, but especially those with disabilities, the book offers valuable approaches to child-rearing to support the development of an empowered, resilient child.

- For persons with disabilities, "over 18, please," the book offers hope, humor, and encouragement that disabilities, no matter how significant, are not a barrier to living a full and rewarding life.

- For doctors, nurses, teachers, counselors, and other service providers, *I Can Dance* candidly describes how *your* actions help or hinder the lives of the persons with disabilities you serve. By example, it warns against stereotyping people on the basis of their disabilities, and instead urges you to listen and work with them. It shows that much more is often possible for persons with disabilities than you ever imagined!

- To all audiences, *I Can Dance* shows that living a full — and self-fulfilled — life is not about walking, taking care of one's personal needs, or being without a disability. It makes clear that living such a life is about developing and using creativity, determination, and resilience. Most of all, Laurie shows that, with these traits, you too can dance!

I commend Laurie on her willingness to share so much of herself and her story, and I encourage you to read *I Can Dance* in appreciation of its message in support of seeing *abilities* in *every* individual.

Catherine Campisi, Ph.D.

Director, California Department of Rehabilitation (Retired)

Disability Advocate

Introduction

I hope that the principals and the teachers and anyone else who ever denied employment to me or to anyone with a disability will read this book and learn from it. There is much to be learned by all of us, and perhaps this memoir will start people on their way.

I have accomplished a great many things for someone with a severe disability. I climbed a tree, I went to slumber parties, I danced, I dated, I made love, I got married, I got divorced, I had children, I raised my children, I lived beyond 18 months, I lived beyond 10 years, I lived beyond 20 years, I lived beyond 50 years, I saw my children grow up, I had grandchildren, I got sick, I survived, I got a job, I got a really *good* job, I bought a car, I bought a house, I am loved, I am respected, and my life has been worth living.

I owe all of this to my parents, my friends, my children, my husband, my colleagues, my extended family, my in-laws, my doctors, my dentists, my nurses, and everyone who has ever played a part in my life, regardless of how small. To all of you, I say thank you.

To those others who only provided me with barriers and obstacles, doubt and no expectation, I can only say I hope you will come over to the other side and provide support and understanding to anyone you meet in the future who may have a disability.

I want my story to stand for something, to teach something, to enable readers to understand we are all human beings with unique qualities and differences, and yet we all have similar needs, desires, and goals. May this memoir be the tool to accomplish these things for many.

About the Book

I Can Dance is about my life as an individual with a physical disability and about the people and experiences that have enabled me to live my life. As you read the book, you will understand the meaning and significance of the title. I wish to be a role model for other individuals with disabilities, to show them anything is possible, even with a severe disability. At the same time, I hope to enlighten health care providers, who too often are unaware of the full range of life lived by people with disabilities, especially those with serious, obvious disabilities. I hope to explode myths and raise expectations.

I share my successes, failures, insecurities, parents, childhood, teen years, school experiences, education, sexuality, marriage, children, divorce, employment, the love of my life, and anything else I believe will allow others to experience my life.

The purpose is also to teach family members and friends of individuals with disabilities what it means to be in their lives and the important role they play.

The story starts in the present, then looks back to my beginning. It moves forward again to the present, including the two years I was actually writing my story.

I Can Dance includes specific details in some instances—dates, places, and names—while remaining very general in others, depending on the intended message. In many chapters, I acknowledge the most important people from my life, and I often include *a message specifically for them.*

I Can Dance is about living with a disability for the majority of my life and how I navigated throughout my life. Perhaps there is a sequel down the road, but for now, this is my story.

This is Laurie's Legacy.

—Laurie Hoirup

1. In the Beginning

If someone had told me that one day I would be working for the famous bodybuilder, actor, and governor Arnold Schwarzenegger, I would have laughed out loud. Never in my wildest dreams might I have imagined me, someone who has virtually no muscles and uses a wheelchair, working for the actor who portrayed Conan the Barbarian and the Terminator. Being married and having children and grandchildren was also beyond imagination. Life takes many strange turns, and working for the celebrity governor was certainly one of them.

"Chief deputy director" sounded so official, so important, and almost unbelievable to me. Though I had known for several months about this promotion, I was still astounded at becoming the new chief deputy director of the California State Council on Developmental Disabilities (SCDD). It seemed to take forever to happen, and to think, just a few years ago I was unemployed.

I always knew if given the chance, I could prove my ability to work, but more importantly to lead. I strongly believed in myself; I was intelligent, had a great deal of common sense, a good sense of humor, and was very much a people person. I had all of the right ingredients for success and yet, I didn't get my first full-time job until I was 45 years old. How sad is that?

It wasn't because I didn't have the skills necessary for employment; in fact, some might say I was overqualified. I held a bachelor of science degree in communication disorders/speech pathology, a master of science degree in rehabilitative counseling, a clear professional teaching credential in elementary education, and a CLAD (cross-cultural, language, and academic development) certificate, which meant I was certified to teach children with English as a second language.

It's still a little mind-boggling to me that I didn't get a job for a better part of my life, especially with all of my education. Even more remarkable is the journey that brought me to where I was on that day, March 10, 2008, the official start date of my new position.

Just how could that be? How could someone with so much training and knowledge have such difficulty in finding work, particularly in a field in such high demand? Well, I'm about to take you down a somewhat disturbing path, when one considers the country we live in, the freedoms we have long enjoyed, and the compassion we believe most of our fellow Americans possess.

You will come to understand why it took me so long to become employed. More importantly, you will have a window into the life of someone who is not so very different from yourself, and yet, very unlike anything you have probably ever experienced. You are about to see life through the eyes of someone with a severe disability. It is my hope that some major life lessons will emerge from this unusual journey.

I've always heard it's best to begin at the beginning, which was the day I was born, March 14, 1956, 52 years almost to the exact date before I became chief deputy director. Of course, most of what I relay here are secondhand stories, shared with me, usually by my mother, Dottie Nelson. She is an incredible lady, whom I credit with many of my successes (my looks too, as I am a younger, identical version).

My mother's pregnancy was fairly normal, except she gained almost 75 pounds and lost most of it within three weeks after my birth. Now that's pretty shocking, just one of the many extraordinary things about her. She experienced no labor, unheard of with the firstborn, as most first-time moms will attest.

In the evening, while she was home alone, her water broke, which no one had bothered to tell her about. Alarmed, she called her doctor. Instructed to go to the hospital, she willingly obliged, still without labor.

A few hours later, while lying in bed waiting for something to happen, she had one major contraction, moaned like an old steer, and was whisked away to the delivery room. She recalls having one more severe pain, which we can only assume was my head presenting itself, and then she fainted. It wasn't until the next morning that she was aware of having given birth.

I was about average at birth, born at 1:46 a.m., weighed 8 lbs. 7 oz., a fairly big girl, and for all intents and purposes, I was a healthy, bouncing baby. But while most mothers are thrilled at the sight of their newborn infant, my mother took one look at me, with a head full of black hair, olive-colored skin, and squinty black eyes, and said, "That's not my baby, she looks like an Indian or Eskimo baby."

The nurse, somewhat in disbelief, double-checked our wristbands and assured my mother I was indeed, her baby. Not completely convinced, my mom laid me down on the bed, opened my blanket and took a long look. Then she saw my father in me, describing me as having his exact build, which I'm not so sure is a good thing when you're a baby girl. At least, she was convinced we were related and made claim to me. Talk about a rocky start . . .

She named me Laurell (pronounced *lor-RELL*) Lynn L——, as one of her dreams was I would go to college some day and have luggage with the triple "L" monogram. My first name isn't found in a book of names, because it's so uncommon. She added the extra "L" to Laurel, because Laurel reminded her of "Laurel and Hardy" and she didn't like the connection.

She also, didn't care for the name "Laura," as there was a girl from her high school days with that name who wasn't a very nice girl, if you know what I mean. So, her fix was to add the extra "L" and make up my name.

Oh, about that luggage thing, well her dream never did become a reality. As a matter of fact, when I graduated from college, I reminded her I did so, never having had any luggage, let alone any with a triple "L" monogram.

A week before I got married, I again brought it to her attention. Now, even if I went back to school, she had lost all chances of her dream coming true because my last name was changing. I tried to find a guy with a last name beginning with "L," but with no success. Sometimes, things are just not meant to be, but I had fun razzing her.

The remainder of my babyhood was fairly uneventful. I achieved all of the common milestones. I excelled when it came to crawling, both on a flat surface and going down stairs head first, never getting tired or falling. I sat without support, rolled over from stomach to back and to my stomach again, and could pull myself into a standing position with no difficulty. I even walked around, as long as I had something to hang on to. Nothing special to write home about or get overly excited for, just the usual things new parents tend to marvel over.

Perhaps my beginning was not my birth at all, but rather, when I was first diagnosed with a disease. Entering toddlerhood, I had a problem. I never took more than eight steps unassisted and always landed in a sitting position. I was falling down more than routinely goes with learning to walk, but my mom believed it was due to my young age. I was around 12 months old.

Little did she know these were the early signs of weakening muscles in my spine and pelvis. She took me to a doctor when I was 18 months old (I'm sure she was hoping it would work itself out) and I was diagnosed with amyotrophic lateral sclerosis (ALS), better known to most as Lou Gehrig's disease.

This diagnosis brought with it some extremely harsh news: I wasn't expected to live for more than a year at best. She was devastated, as any mother would be. As if things weren't bad enough, she was also separated from my father at that time, going through this all by herself.

Being on her own in a state of grief, she concluded she did not want to live without me. Grief does strange things to common sense, even to the most intelligent of souls. Her next move wasn't the brightest thing she'd ever done, but certainly understandable.

In a daze, she took me home, put me down for a nap, turned on the gas, and lay down herself, figuring we would go together. Thank God, within a few minutes she was asking herself, "What if the doctors are wrong?" She came to her senses, turned off the gas, and I am here to tell the tale.

The doctors *were* wrong. A few months later, at the Illinois Research Hospital, a new doctor suspected I might have muscular dystrophy (MD), not quite as life-threatening as ALS, but not having a great prognosis either. (MD is an umbrella term covering some 40 different neuromuscular diseases, but used as a single diagnosis at that time.)

ALS weakens the entire body, resulting in death in a very short period of time. Muscular dystrophy, on the other hand, leads to extreme weakness, but over a much longer time. Some similar neuromuscular diseases can progress even more slowly, allowing a better prognosis with a longer lifespan.

At the age of two, I underwent a muscle biopsy, a surgery (my first of many) to remove a piece of muscle for testing to confirm I had MD. The back of my right calf was used for the procedure. The incision scar is barely visible today. Like the faded scar, I have no memories of the operation. Pictures of me afterwards are the only evidence it ever occurred.

On my second birthday, March 14, 1958, my mother received confirmation of my diagnosis with mixed emotions. I definitely had MD (better than ALS), but was not expected to live much beyond seven or eight years. For the second time in my young life she was faced with my impending death. However, this time the prognosis did not make her think about taking our lives, but rather how to make the best of the years we had together, and perhaps once again, to prove those doctors wrong.

Maybe this was really my beginning. It was the start of my life with a disability, of my identity taking shape, and the path to appointment by Governor Schwarzenegger as the chief deputy director of SCDD.

I am sure that at some point, most people ponder what life has presented to them, and I was no different. I find this to be especially true as I am reaching a mature age. What I contemplate most at this stage of my life is how God managed to choose my mother to be the mom of a child with a disability.

She certainly proved to be the perfect choice, strong in character, as well as physically, with a great deal of common sense, probably more than most, calm in the face of a crisis, determined, fun-loving, excellent sense of humor, a wonderful listener, and a fantastic teacher.

All of those qualities helped me to become the person I am, and I know many of my accomplishments are due to her. I believe turning off the gas was the most critical decision she ever made, and the true beginning of my wonderful life!

2. My Mom, My Hero, My Friend

Telling your life story without mentioning the other major player over and over again is somewhat difficult. This became very apparent to me in just trying to identify my beginning. I didn't want to discuss my mom so early in my life's account, but I can't see any way to avoid it. She is a strand of gold running through my world. Now, this is not to say we didn't have our differences.

Like any mother and daughter, we had our share of disagreements. There are still things from my youth we do not see eye to eye about, and that's okay. We are not the same person and we won't always see things the same way. We are, however, best of friends: two women who can tell each other anything. Even as a teenager, I could talk to her about any topic.

I was raised in a very open and loving environment. I could ask my mom anything, never fearing her reaction. She never got angry or told me I didn't need to know about those things. The lines of communication were always open. My friends knew about the great relationship we had, and I often went home to her with their questions, ones they could not ask their own parents.

One time — mind you I was an only child with no siblings — my friend, who had an older brother, wanted to know what a "wet dream" was. Naïvely, I went and asked my mom. She looked quite taken aback and said she never expected that kind of question out of me, but in her calm manner, she explained what it meant.

I have plenty of examples of the wonderful communication existing between my mom and myself, but before I share those stories, let me tell you a little bit about her history.

She was the youngest of three children, having an older sister and brother. She was born October 16, 1931, as Dorothy W. H——. According to my grandmother, my mom was a very inquisitive, active child (a nice way of calling her a terror) who turned Grandma's hair gray before her

8

time. My grandma used to say she wished my mom had nine kids just like herself, but instead she was blessed with one little angel (remember, this was my grandma talking and every grandmother thinks of her grandchildren as little angels).

My mom would describe herself as being a tomboy growing up. She never liked playing with girlie things, and most of her friends were boys. As a teenager, she was interested in sports, and in boys only as friends.

She was as tough as any of them. When they tried their hand at smoking cigars, she was the only one not to get deathly ill and turn green. She could win any fight and I heard she used to beat up a boy every day on the way home from school just because she could. Both versions of my mom's youth paint a similar picture; she has always been strong of character and very willful, which today we call independent.

She grew up physically strong as well, and looked exactly like my grandmother: dark hair, olive complexion, sharp Czechoslovakian features, with a nice figure. Nothing extraordinary about her appearance, but very attractive, nonetheless. It's funny, I would describe my grandma the same way, and even myself. We were carbon copies of one another.

I would say we were as close as any two people can be. I looked up to her, and hoped I would grow up to be just like her. She was someone I trusted and knew I could count on at all times. I was made to feel safe and secure throughout my childhood, something every child deserves. She instilled in me the confidence I carry today.

She taught me to be strong in the face of adversity and to be a risk-taker, knowing you can't grow if you don't take risks, and she truly wanted me to grow. She did not tolerate self-pity in my life, and her strong family values were ever present.

One day, while looking through a book with pictures of babies growing *in utero*, came her beautiful explanation of pregnancy and childbirth. A few months later, I told her I understood how a baby grows in your tummy and how it is born, but what I couldn't figure out, is how the baby got there in the first place.

I was sitting at one end of the couch watching TV and she was sitting at the other end, sewing a shirt. She slowly put the shirt down, as if thinking about what she was going to say. Then using her index finger and thumb, brought them together and made a circle, explaining this was the opening of the woman's vagina, where the baby came out of.

With her other hand, she took her extended index finger and told me sperm was created and stored in the man's penis, and when a man and woman were ready to have a baby, the man's penis became hard, so as to enter the woman's vagina. She went on to demonstrate this by placing her straight index finger into the circle she had created.

Of course, she emphasized this particular act was one of love, occurring after marriage, and was actually called making love. I remember this day and this conversation like it was yesterday.

Our open communication continued well beyond childhood. When I was away at college and wanted to go on birth control, I knew I had to talk with her, not because of any rules, but because how she felt mattered to me.

I wasn't sure how to approach the subject, so I hinted and she was quick to pick up. She responded by saying, "I am not condoning you have sex before you get married, but I am also not foolish enough to believe it will never happen. Though I want to be a grandma someday, now is not the time and it is a good idea for you to go on the pill."

One of the most frank and open conversations we ever had was during one of our two-hour trips home from college. We were discussing sex and love and I flat-out asked, "Mom, have you ever had an orgasm?"

She was somewhat shocked and said, "Why would you ask such a thing?" I replied, "Well, when I was younger you said certain things were bad or wrong and I can't imagine you doing those things, though I think they are an important part of making love."

She explained that when I was 15, there were things she didn't think I was ready for, but she never intended to give me the idea anything was bad or wrong. On the contrary, anything between two consenting adults is fine. Then I was shocked with her reply, "To answer your question, yes I have, how about you?"

It was absolutely wonderful to be able to have that type of conversation, that type of communication with someone you love and trust. It really is a shame more kids and parents can't talk so openly. At the time, I remember thinking, if and when I ever had children, I was going to be as open and honest with them as my mom was with me, and I promised myself not to forget.

I learned about advocacy from her at a very young age. When I was five years old, ready for kindergarten, the only Special Ed classroom around was about 40 minutes away. It was a self-contained K-8 classroom with one teacher and two aides. Every day, mom would drive me there, picking me up a few hours later.

The aides would play games, color, or read to me while I was there. My mom was anything, but happy with this scenario. The next thing I knew, she was at the school board, yelling about how she could PLAY with me at home.

She was driving me that far because she wanted me to have an education. Soon a tutor was coming to our home every day after school, teaching me at whatever level I was capable of doing. This was my first introduction to advocacy.

After four years of having a home tutor, I was more than ready to go to school with my friends. I loved my mother dearly, but I was bored being home all day. When the kids finally got home from school, my tutor arrived. My school day began while everyone was at play and ended at dinnertime when everyone was in for the night. I really missed my friends.

It wasn't just a simple request to get me into school, but instead required another trip to the school board with a bit more hollering. Once again, my mom prevailed and I began fifth grade in school just like all the other kids. Advocacy at its finest!

Those first few years of actually going to school provided me with a much greater education than one would have imagined. I was exposed to many more children than just my neighbors and I experienced everyday life, as other children do.

Mom's tactics for bringing me together with my classmates didn't involve any yelling at all. One of the earliest incidents from sixth grade involved sports. Most of the girls were cheerleaders, and since, I couldn't be a cheerleader (back then a disability often interfered), my mom became the cheerleader team mom. This meant we went to all of the games and I became a natural part of that scenario.

Mom also went on field trips as a chaperone. She often drove groups of us kids to other school activities and our house soon became a hangout for both my middle and high school crowd. What she couldn't take me to, she brought to me. She was a true pioneer for inclusion (keeping with the mainstream).

I previously mentioned she was calm in the face of a crisis, which is pretty evident considering she had to cope with my potentially passing away throughout the entire course of my youth. She also did well with everyday crises.

One day, I was down by the tree house playing with my friends. I must have been about six years old. When I came home for lunch, mom asked me what I'd been doing. I told her I had climbed the tree and played in the tree house with everyone else.

She asked how I accomplished such a feat. I explained the kids had tied a rope around my chair (light weight aluminum similar to an airline aisle chair) and hoisted me up to the tree house. I am sure her heart was in her throat, but my very smart mom never showed her fear. Instead, she calmly stated, "I don't think tree climbing is such a good idea and you probably shouldn't do it again." I said, "OK" and went on with my play, never the wiser.

One day while we were at the lake, I was out of my chair sitting on the edge of the pier (I was about eight years old). Without telling her that I had learned to roll over and float at summer camp, and with no warning, I yelled, "Watch, Mom!" as I threw myself forward into the water.

Again, she must have died a thousand deaths not being able to get to me quickly. Then I bobbed up and said, "See what I can do!" With a look of horror on an ashen face, she managed to muster up a smile and said, "That's great honey!" I would've choked me had I been the mom.

Like other kids, I had my daily chores, and like other kids, I hated them. It took an hour to push myself around the living room in my manual chair and dust the furniture. My mom could've completed the task in

10 minutes, but she made it clear this was my job. I also had to scrub the bathroom sink and do the dishes.

My doing the dishes resulted in my mom doing twice as much work as if she had done them herself. She would wash all the glassware, pots, and pans, and then set up a bar stool for me to be able to reach the sink. Although she could have finished much more quickly, she knew the importance of my having chores.

What she did was to give me something to complain about along with my friends and be able to relate to their experiences. I should note here though, one day my elbow slipped on the suds causing me to fall face first into the water, quickly bringing my dishwashing days to an end. Had I been smarter, I would have slipped much earlier in that career.

Sometimes I would come home from school in tears after being teased. Mom would tell me to learn to deal with it because I would have to deal with that sort of thing my whole life. Yet, one day my friend was crying because the girls had made fun of her and my mom jumped all over them. I asked, "Why did you yell at the kids when they made fun of Marian, but never when they teased me?"

Her answer was the same. I had to learn how to cope because that was going to be part of my life and probably not so much for my friends. I'm not sure I really understood what she was trying to get across, but I certainly learned to be thick skinned when it came to being teased.

I could go on and on with stories to show my mother's nature, but many of those memories are more appropriately shared in another place, in another chapter. What I can tell you is that you will never find a more perfect mother for a child with a disability.

All of the attributes I have listed about her still ring true today. She continues to be one of my very best friends. I count on her for support and understanding and I look forward to her words of praise. All of these things bring warmth and happiness to the very depths of my soul.

Mom, a message of love and thanks for being the best mom in the world, for being you and for making me the person I am today. I love you, Mom!

3. Early Childhood Memories

I don't have too many vivid memories of my early childhood. I don't think many children do before the age of five, but I have a few that stand out because of a traumatic incident or an exceptionally meaningful event. I was told about other events.

When I was two years old, I had a name change. It was not connected to any specific event, but was still important. It wasn't actually a formal name change; rather, I acquired a nickname.

While at a horse race, my mom bet on a horse named "Missy EL," because there had been a misprint changing the name to "Missy LLL." Remember my birth name left me with triple "L" initials. The horse won and from that day on, she started calling me Missy, which later was shortened to "Miss." I am honored to have been nicknamed after a winning racehorse.

One of my memories is of having chickenpox when I was about three years old. I had to wear footy pajamas the whole time, so I couldn't scratch. It was awful.

I also contracted the measles a year later and had to stay away from the sun for a couple of weeks. As a child, there was no immunization against measles and the belief was you could go blind if exposed to sunlight. One of my mom's friends lived in our apartment complex and her kids got measles the same time as I did.

Their apartment was basement level. They turned a walk-in closet, into a small bedroom with no windows. The three of us girls spent the next two weeks together in our little cubbyhole. They say "misery loves company," and we were definitely miserable. I wish I could forget.

On a more positive note, I can see myself in a beautiful lavender chiffon dress from my Auntie Marilyn, a gift for my third birthday. The short cap sleeves, snug bodice, and full layered (flouncy) skirt made me feel like a movie star all dressed up. It was a dress any little girl would love to have!

I have pictures of myself wearing the dress at my party. I remember the feel of the dress and how pretty it was, one of many wonderful memories about my Auntie Marilyn.

My Auntie Marilyn played a major role in my early childhood. She was my mom's older sister and had the same appearance as my mom, grandma, and me, though she was a bit heavier. As I mentioned earlier, we could have been cloned. We all had dark hair, dark eyes, high cheekbones, sharp features, round face, and same body type. There was no denying we were related.

She wasn't married during my early childhood, nor did she have any children of her own to spoil, so, she spoiled me rotten. I loved the attention she lavished on me and the relationship we had.

She bought me the most expensive dresses and the most incredible toys, and she always took time to play with me. One of the best times I ever had was going to her house for a few days and having a tea party every day. She had the perfect tea set and we used real food. She always made me feel like a princess.

We would go for long outings to the dime store, where I was always allowed to pick a toy for us to play with later in the day. My favorite dime store toy was a realistic looking vacuum cleaner, which was Barbie doll size and actually had real suction.

There were also the numerous outfits she added to my Barbie collection, none of those off brands, just the Barbie label fashions. She surrounded me with the best. Having a disability may have played a role, but I really don't think so. She would have spoiled me regardless.

Barbie was the ideal toy for a little girl in a wheelchair. Small enough to handle and dress, she was the perfect means for me to act out any and all fantasies, both current and future. I could be and do anything I wanted to through Barbie.

One Christmas, when I was almost four years old, Auntie Marilyn went all out, buying me a "Chatty Baby," the latest talking baby doll on the market. A few months later, for my birthday, she gave me a beautiful doll buggy for my new baby. It was incredible, and could've been used for a real infant.

It was nothing like a toy, differing from the real thing only in terms of height, low enough to be pushed by a child. The buggy was hidden in a back room of my grandma's house, and when she pushed it out to me, I felt like a real mom. Chatty Baby and this elegant doll carriage made me feel like a very lucky mom at that.

On my fifth birthday, my Auntie Marilyn really outdid herself. She bought me a 100 percent silk dress. It was black and white with red trim, the most beautiful dress I ever saw, and the feel was heavenly. My mom had a cow about her spending so much money on that kind of a dress for a five-year-old child, but oh how I loved it. As I see it, she was refining my taste for the best.

My memories about my auntie weren't all based on expensive gifts and such. She and I had a wonderful relationship that would have existed with or without the toys, clothes, and other gifts. She spent hours with me, reading, playing games, taking me to the park, anything to make me happy. I loved being with her. My mom said it took her a week to get me back in line after I visited either my aunt or my grandmother.

My grandmother was another wonderful memory-maker from those early years. I loved to go and stay with her, as well. She always had pea-nut butter cups waiting for me (my favorite candy). She usually cooked my favorite meal: pork roast and dumplings. I would get to help her make the dumplings. Mine were always miniature size, making them taste especially good.

She also made the most incredible French toast for breakfast, using just a half of a piece of bread, so I could hold it in my hands to eat rather than using a fork. Each slice was crispy on the outside, soft on the inside, and perfect for dipping into the syrup. Both the dumplings and French toast were a perfect match for my small hands. I loved cooking with my grandma!

Holidays not spent together meant getting money in the mail, with no holiday ever forgotten, regardless of how insignificant. For a child, getting money is a big deal. Add that to food and you have a great foundation for happy memories. But like Auntie Marilyn, my relationship with grandma was much more than food and money. My grandma was my second mom, and how I loved her!

Most of all, I remember how wonderful I felt when she held me close, and how good she smelled. Grandma would give me long bubble baths and trim my toenails with the greatest of care. Afterwards, we would snuggle until I was warm and cozy. I sure looked forward to bath time at her house. I can still see her claw-footed tub, which added to the ambience of the whole event. To this day, I am back in her arms whenever I see one of those old-fashioned bathtubs.

I always felt as though her place was set up just for me. The back porch was my personal playroom, with all of my toys and a TV. On some warm evenings, I would let my grandpa use it. Grandma also had a huge pantry I used to hide in. I loved pretending it was a secret fort, and it was always cool inside.

My early skill of crawling soon transitioned to scooting around on my butt, which was also short-lived. My basic mode of mobility on the floor was the use of my arms and elbows pulling the rest of my body along. This worked well through about the age of six, until I ended up with severe rug burns on both elbows and became too weak to drag myself around.

Grandma and Grandpa lived on the second floor, and the stairs going up to their place looked like mountains to me. When we reached the top, the warmth and excitement I felt as her big door opened was like heaven. I have nothing but magnificent memories of visiting with them.

An unpleasant memory (kind of like the chickenpox, but more traumatic), is when I fell backwards off a tricycle. I didn't have a chair to sit on outside and I wanted to be where the other kids were, so I chose to sit on a tricycle. It's kind of like being a woman and what we go through to look beautiful, even if it's painful.

I was barely balanced, holding on for dear life, when one of my playmates decided to pull on the handlebars to give me a ride. I flipped over backwards. Luckily, I just ended up with a goose egg instead of a concussion or a broken neck. At least I was able to be outside with the other kids.

Another horrible event was when the medical profession tried to figure out exactly what my disability was. Though I had been diagnosed at the age of two with muscular dystrophy (as a result of a muscle biopsy, which I thankfully cannot remember), by the age of five I was considered too active for that diagnosis.

I underwent an electromyogram (EMG, a test to determine muscle activity) to confirm my diagnosis. That test uses needles hooked up to electrodes stabbed (I'm sure they have a better word, but it felt like I was being stabbed) into the muscles along my leg and arm.

When I calmed down, the line on the machine would go straight; if I cried, the line would get all jumpy. There was much pain and many tears, which I'm sure created a wildly, jumpy graph. There had to be a better way.

My second muscle biopsy was at the age of six. This time, the test was to determine the effects on my muscles if there was no protein in my diet, and to reevaluate my diagnosis. The ordeal began over Thanksgiving, and all I could eat for dinner was cranberry sauce. No turkey, no mashed potatoes, no gravy, no stuffing; what a stupid test! I was miserable and starving.

I was off of the diet the morning I was going to the hospital for the surgery. My wonderful grandma made sure there was a helping of everything for breakfast. I couldn't wait to dig in. As before, a piece of muscle was removed from my calf. Though I am not sure what they learned, I know it wasn't worth it.

The results of the biopsy changed my diagnosis to progressive muscular atrophy, one of the 40 diseases under the MD umbrella, with a somewhat longer life expectancy than previously expected. One good thing came about, I guess.

After the surgery, I was dying of thirst (because of the ether anesthetic), but every time I took a sip of water, I would vomit. As a result, I wasn't allowed to have fluids for what seemed to be an eternity, which made me feel worse. It was like crossing the desert with no water. I was finally given some juice, which I had to nurse slowly. Thankfully, it stayed down. It was the best juice I ever had!

No one likes to cause pain for another, especially when it is their own child. I am sure my mother believed all of the medical stuff causing me pain was necessary for my well-being. I am also positive it was the same when they decided to put me in leg braces at the age of two. I know she believed it was best for me.

When I first started using the braces, I could get around pretty well, but only for about a year or so. Then I began to have difficulty holding my body upright, so a hip brace was attached to the full-length leg braces.

Eventually, a body corset was added as well, for more support. My mother was told she needed to keep me walking for as long as possible to keep my strength up, and by golly, that's exactly what she did.

There was a time near the end of my using braces, where I just couldn't stand up. She didn't believe me, or perhaps she didn't want to believe me because that would indicate I was weakening. She slapped me on my bottom and told me to stand. I cried and fell down. She smacked me a second time and told me to stand. I cried and fell down again. She swatted me again and told me to stand.

To me, this seemed to go on forever, but I'm sure it probably only lasted a few minutes. Ultimately she did win and I did stand, even if for just a brief amount of time. I believe this is when she realized braces were not going to be an option for me for very much longer.

By the time I had reached this stage, getting my braces on was as horrible as trying to stand. The contractures in my knees were such that my dad would have to use all of his strength to press down on my knee to extend my leg, in order to get it into the brace and then lock it straight.

I can still hear myself screaming at the top of my lungs because it hurt so badly. It was as though the muscles were being torn apart. The pain never really went away once I was standing; my legs were just kind of numb. Between the pain and the weight of my full-bodied contraption, the braces were for the most part useless. We finally abandoned them for a wheelchair.

I'm not sure of my exact age at which this all occurred, but I do know I was standing for my fifth birthday, but did not have the ability to stand when I turned six. I had worn the leg braces from the time I was two until about the age of 5½, which is when I got my first manual wheelchair.

I was so little that I couldn't reach both of the wheels at the same time. I would lean way over to one side and push one wheel and then way over to the other side to push the other wheel. I didn't get very far, very fast, but I was mobile, unlike with my braces and crutches, for which I didn't have the strength to hold my body up and move.

The wheelchair did not signify getting worse to me; it provided me with much more independence and freedom. I could get around the house on my own, I wasn't in pain, and I could get out of my chair if I wanted to. It's easy to see why I was actually happy about this transition.

I would get tired and want to take a nap or sit somewhere else. I was able to throw myself from my wheelchair onto the couch, rolling over to my back to sleep or watch TV. Even though I remember this, I find it difficult to imagine how I accomplished such a feat. But at that time, I was also able to put on my own socks, my shirt and various other things that seem so unrealistic to me now.

I mentioned wearing a cloth body corset with my braces. That was because I started getting a curvature, or scoliosis, of my spine. Sadly, when the leg braces went away, the cloth body corset was unable to hold me up. So it was decided I should use something that offered the stabilization I needed.

I soon began to wear a hard plastic body jacket/brace that did provide me with the necessary support. My body brace was like a second skin. It didn't bother me to wear it, but the fitting procedure was terrible.

In order to get my body straight, they would put a harness type strap around the back of my head and under my chin, which basically cupped my face. Then the top of it would be attached to a hook in the ceiling and I would be hoisted up until my bottom was about an inch off the chair.

While I was hanging by my head, my body was wrapped with plaster casting material over a snug undershirt type material. Once it dried, it would be cut up the middle and removed. The whole process only took about 10 minutes, but it was long enough for my jaw to lock into place.

With all of my weight hanging from my jaw, it was quite painful to get my mouth to open and usually took about an hour or so. It only got worse as I grew bigger and heavier, but I have to admit, the brace did slow my scoliosis from worsening.

Once the brace was completely dried, it was coated with plastic and trimmed and padded around the edges with leather. There were Velcro straps attached in the front for opening and closing. What a process!

On a more pleasant note, we bought our new house during that time, which was a really wonderful thing! It meant having friends from a very early age who would get to know me and understand my disability, what I could and couldn't do.

Having friends to grow up with is one of the best things for any child with a disability. It allows getting beyond the oddity and fear, and provides a sense of normalcy for everyone concerned.

One of the most "normal" things I ever did was to climb a tree. I know I brought it up once before, but it really does warrant a second mention. There I was, five years old, hanging out with a few other neighborhood friends ranging in age from five to eight years old. They wanted me to be part of what they were doing, and I wanted to be part of what they were doing.

There was a big old tree at the end of our half-acre of property, about a block from the house, and the neighborhood kids had built a tree house in it. It was really no more than a bunch of boards making a platform with rails around the sides. I used to sit below and they would yell down to me about whatever they were doing up there.

I'm not sure whose idea it was (though it was probably Pete), but somehow we came up with a plan to tie a rope around my chair and hoist me up to the tree house. I was thrilled! I really felt like one of the gang and it was worth every risk I took. I must also say it was a much better experience being hoisted into the tree house than being hoisted for my brace fitting.

I believe most of my memories are around events that helped to shape who I am today, especially those involving my taking risks. I think risk-taking is a good thing, as long as it is shared with common sense. I trust I had a sprinkling of both, and each brought me to where I am now in my life.

4. Elementary Evolution

In the last chapter I described myself as standing for my fifth birthday and using a wheelchair by my sixth. What I didn't mention was that I was standing in our rented apartment for my fifth birthday party and sitting in a small chair in the living room of our very own house for my sixth! At the time, I did not recognize the magnitude of what owning a house meant, but now I believe it helped to build my character.

I want to explain why I described myself as "using" a wheelchair by my sixth birthday, but was specific about "sitting" in a regular chair for my party. When I was younger, I sat on regular furniture other than at school, getting carried from place to place as needed. The significance of this will become apparent.

I would sit on a bar stool at our breakfast bar, where we generally ate most of our meals, for mealtime (same bar stool from the doing-the-dishes story), on the couch when watching TV or socializing, and of course, be in my bed for sleeping. Though I received my first wheelchair at around the age of 5-½, it was hardly ever used at home. Mostly, the wheelchair stayed at school because we didn't have a vehicle for transport back and forth and it would have been too heavy for my mom to lift in and out of the car. In addition, the chair wasn't very "outside friendly." It was more practical to leave it at school.

I also think my mom knew this would play a major role in how I saw myself, which at the time was not as someone with a disability. Not that having a disability was bad—it just wasn't a part of my early development.

It was good that things worked out this way. I felt like everyone else using the same furniture, and that was important for my self esteem. My wheelchair and I never actually bonded or became one, because we were rarely together, which was also a good thing, at least for that time of my life.

I Can Dance

Our house was on a quiet street in a small town in the Midwest. I am amazed I still remember the address after all these years. It was a two-bedroom, one-bath ranch-style with an attached garage, the last house on a dead-end street. My room was really big, or so I remember it, and we had a huge backyard.

At the far end of our half-acre yard stood a huge oak tree (the infamous tree house location). Railroad tracks ran along the side of our house, which some would consider a drawback. I somehow learned to ignore the blaring of the horn during the night and on hot summer days when all the windows were open. Nonetheless, it was our house, I had my own big room and it was wonderful!

I especially loved the lilac bushes that lined our street. I must've brought lilacs to my mom at least every other day. There were eight houses on our block and most of our neighbors were families. Everyone looked out for one another and they all kept a close eye on me, providing a good, safe place for me to be raised.

The house next door had the same design as ours and was vacant when we first moved in. Then one evening a small station wagon pulled into the driveway. Kids kept piling out like from a phone booth stuffed with as many people as can fit in it. All told, the car held two parents and seven children ranging in ages from 4 to 16 years. More astounding, they moved into a two-bedroom house.

There were four boys and three girls. From oldest to youngest, it was Butch, Bill, Lee, Nick, Pete (the one from the tree house), Diane (Cookie), and Venus (Corky). Believe it or not, there were three older siblings who didn't live at home. That's probably a good thing, since they surely would not have all fit in the car.

The attached garage was quickly transformed into the boys' room/dorm, while the girls shared one of the original bedrooms and their parents made claim to the other. Over the next few years, two more boys would be added to the brood, but luckily, a few of the older ones, also boys, moved out, keeping things in balance. Little did I know how much each would contribute to my development.

Of all the kids in the family, Cookie, Corky (their nicknames until middle school), and Pete had the greatest influence over me because we were together so much of the time. Cookie and Corky were my primary playmates throughout grade school. Cookie was a year older and a grade ahead, while Corky was a year younger and a grade behind. We were great friends and they never seemed to notice or care that I had a disability.

No matter what we played, they found a way for me to participate. When we spent the night together, either at their house or mine, they did all of my care, even when we were only eight and nine years old. I loved talking through our open bedroom windows on summer nights, as we never tired of one another.

In the summer, they would pick me up in the morning and we'd be off to play for the day, only stopping at home for lunch. Sometimes we played at the other neighbors or we walked to the little store in town when we had money to spend.

We often spent hours at the tree house or down at the creek fishing and staying cool under the bridge. Whenever we left the perimeter of our block, one of the older siblings came along for oversight. Oh, and on rare occasions we were in the backyard pulling weeds, as this was a summertime chore for my friends.

Friends help friends and I was no different. However, pulling weeds was especially challenging for me. The only way I could manage was to have Cookie sitting behind me, while I hung onto the weed, throwing my weight backwards, falling into her lap and having her push me back up to pull another. It took a bit longer this way, but we were working together. We were quite the pair!

Halloween is another time that really represents friendship and teamwork. Though usually too cold for me to go trick-or-treating, it was one of the best holidays of my childhood. Pete, Cookie, and Corky went trick-or-treating together, and they would always take a bag for me, returning with it as full as their own.

The evening began at my house, where we dressed up in our costumes, which was fun in and of itself. I was charged with answering the door all evening and passing out candy, while the three of them were out trick-or-treating for us.

Upon their return, we would revel in our treasures, stuffing our faces until we couldn't eat any more. Candy and homemade treats were no cause for worry back then. I absolutely loved sharing Halloween with them.

Their older brothers and sisters often babysat for me. They liked being at our house because, as I was an only child, things were a lot calmer than at their home with all of their siblings. Pete, however, was the only one of the older kids (about five years older than me) I ever convinced to play Barbie. He was a great Ken!

I owe so much to this family because they each contributed to my feeling of normalcy, of inclusion, of acceptance. Their understanding and willingness to treat me equally helped me to develop into the self-accepting person I am. I like me and I credit them for playing a big part in making that happen.

The house was the link to these relationships. Homeownership provides a mindset of belonging and staying put for a long time. The years spent together as neighbors made us very close. The house, being located in small-town America, contributed to those close relationships and a safe environment for growing up.

The house also made it possible to have pets, which every child should experience. My Black Labrador, "Baby," was the beginning of our family of Labradors, and his offspring, "Muffin," was with me through college. My pets taught me responsibility and to care about someone besides myself, which doesn't come easy in early childhood. How I loved my dogs!

Being in the last house on the dead-end street enabled us to have parties, barbecues, and plenty of room to grow. We eventually remodeled to a three-bedroom, with a family room and a laundry room (built out of the old garage), and had a new big garage, perfect for family get-togethers and such. It really was a wonderful place and I thank my mom for making it possible.

I was re-diagnosed again at about the age of eight from progressive muscular atrophy to progressive spinal atrophy, another of the 40 diseases under the MD umbrella, less severe than progressive muscular atrophy. Don't ask me why, but supposedly it had something to do with my activity level and slow progression of the disease. I can't say the new diagnosis made any difference one way or the other.

Beginning around the age of eight I was excited to go to camp. I attended two camps each summer. The first was a weeklong camp for children with some type of muscle disease, making it easy for me to relate to them. For the first few years, MDA (Muscular Dystrophy Association) camp was held in Michigan and eventually in Illinois, which was a bit closer to home.

It was usually very cold through the night, as our cabins weren't heated. Getting up in the morning and putting on my cold brace was almost torture. Each of my attendants over the years would sleep with my brace in the bottom of their sleeping bag so it was warm and snuggly in the morning. Talk about sacrifice.

Peacock Camp, only a few miles from our home, was three weeks long and was for children with all types of disabilities. It was there that I first learned how to fingerspell from a roommate who was deaf. I've never forgotten how.

I taught my classroom buddies this skill and we sometimes used it to cheat on multiple-choice tests. I know, shame on me for abusing this wonderful ability, but what can I say, I was just a kid.

Camp was a fantastic experience! My parents got a much-needed and deserved break, and I learned I could survive without my mom forever at my side. It went a long way in teaching me to be independent. I looked forward to those special times, and always with tears, hated to see them come to an end.

I first learned to float on my back as part of my swimming test at camp and was able to scare my mom half to death with that jumping (falling) off the pier incident at the lake (Chapter 2). I was able to ride horses, play sports, go to dances, and do all the things children do. I continued going to camp until I was 16 years old, which says a lot. Camp truly was one of the best times of my life!

By now, you can see I didn't spend much of my time staying home and sitting around the house. You're probably wondering how I got around to outside activities at home and out in the community, since my wheelchair wasn't usually with us. I had a very unusual kind of a wheelchair, which we called my "stroller."

My "stroller" wasn't anything like a baby stroller. It was named after its inventor, a man by the name of Hogue who had a son with a disability. He designed a special chair for him, which quickly became available for all children, and thus my "Hogue Stroller" came into being.

The Hogue Stroller was unique, made of aluminum and operated much like a dolly. The chair had to be tilted back on rear wheels (no front wheels), which balanced the weight of the person sitting in it, making pushing simple for anyone (even a child). The design included a very high back with lawn-chair webbing and a curved handlebar like that of a grocery cart.

If the chair fell out of somebody's hand, my head would hit the webbing instead of the ground. The foot pedal stuck way out in front, preventing the chair from tipping forward and the wheelbase was fairly wide, so it couldn't tip over sideways very easily. Go-cart tires made the ride smooth and were very durable.

This chair enabled me to be outside with the kids, who were about the same age as me, going from neighbor to neighbor to play, to the fort down the street in the bushes, down to the creek, or to the infamous tree house. I was in this stroller when I climbed the tree to the tree house. It was a remarkable device and didn't look at all like a wheelchair!

The stroller was also great for camping and hiking, fitting into narrow places, light enough to lift over obstacles, and even good for taking naps. All I would have to do is have someone lay the chair back on the ground and I had a lounge chair.

As I outgrew my stroller, at around the age of 11, my mom looked for the adult size. Regretfully, Mr. Hogue's son had passed away and a larger model was never designed. So my mom, who always knew how to fix a problem, went to a local welder with a similar design and had one made to our specifications.

Like magic, we had an adult-size version of the Hogue Stroller, which we called a "Lorry," partly because my name was Laurie and part-ly, because one definition of a "Lorry" is a push/pull vehicle for trans-porting goods by road. I guess I could consider myself goods and I was being transported, so it was the perfect name.

Going to school, as for most children, had its high points and its lows. I've already talked about my first few years of elementary school, first through fourth grade being spent at home with a tutor, but I can't stress enough how badly I wanted to go to school with my peers.

As I said before, I would be home all day with my mom, and God knows I loved her (still do), but I longed to be with my friends in school. When school finally ended in the late afternoon, my friends would arrive home to play and the tutor would show up to my house shortly thereafter, staying for about two hours.

So, while the neighborhood kids were outside having a good time, I was inside learning. Though I loved my tutors, Mrs. Infield and Mr. Roeder (I can't believe I remember their names after all these years), I hated not being able to go out and play.

By the time the tutor left, the sun had already set and the darkness was accompanied by dinnertime, meaning everyone had gone in for the night. This left me only the weekends to see and play with my friends.

So, why didn't I go to school like everyone else? We had no Special Ed class in our small school, meaning there was no aide to assist if I had to use the restroom or needed help in some other way. Also, during the cold winter season, my health was at risk (or so they believed).

Therefore, the school district decided, I would be better off kept at home for my education. By the end of fourth grade, I was strongly rebel-ling! Thank goodness my mother was my greatest advocate and actually took the time to listen to what I had to say. One more trip to the school board and her advocacy won out again! I was going to school!

I was elated to begin fifth grade in school with all of my friends! Even though I had visited school many times during my first four years of elementary school when I had my tutor, it was always for parties, pic-tures, and special events. Now I was really part of the class. Once again, I was like everyone else.

My friends took turns staying in with me at recess when cold weather set in and the eighth grade girls would assist me in using the restroom, as many of them had babysat for me over the years. I remained at home with the tutor for the coldest winter months, December, January, and February, because of the health risk, but this was so much better than staying home all the time.

The major health risk for me was getting a cold and the inability to cough, which could then easily lead to pneumonia. Respiratory failure was probably the number one cause of death for people with my disease. It was imperative that we be cautious, but at this age, I felt invincible like my peers.

For a while, I was strong enough to cough and make it productive, but as my scoliosis increased, so did weakness in my chest muscles. I very quickly became a diaphragm breather. My parents also learned about a "manual cough."

A manual cough is a process in which someone else presses against my diaphragm as I cough. First I inhale and then at the same time I cough, they push in and up on my abdomen, providing me with the added "oomph" to cough up any secretions. It still took me 10 coughs to the average person's one, but I got the job done.

I've also, never described how I used the restroom, which is something many people are certainly curious about, so I should probably take this opportunity to address the question. I potty trained fairly early because for the most part, all my mom had to do was put me on the potty chair and I stayed put until I went. Not that she left me there very long, but she was able to get me to sit for awhile.

Once I was trained, using the restroom was fairly typical. Unlike many people with disabilities, I had full bowel and bladder control, which certainly made my life easier. Initially, I was small enough for my mom to lean me over her one arm, take my bottoms down with her other hand and sit me on the toilet. I was able to balance on the toilet well into adulthood. For wiping, she would again bend me over her arm, leaning me forward far enough to reach behind and clean me.

As I got bigger and heavier, with others doing my care, the process

29

changed. I would be lifted out of my chair, laid down (bed, couch, floor), bottoms (pants, pajamas, or whatnot) taken down by rolling me from side to side, and then carried to the toilet. Wiping was the same as before, leaning me forward far enough to clean me.

When I was done, I would be carried back to wherever I was lying down, and again rolled back and forth from side to side to get my bottoms up. The whole thing took about 15 minutes, probably 10 more minutes than the average person, which is why it was good I only went to the restroom three times a day.

As for privacy, getting carried to the toilet with my bottoms down was a little tricky if there wasn't an adjacent bathroom, but we always found a way. Once in a while it meant asking others to close their eyes or being covered with a towel. Sometimes I was embarrassed, but usually not.

Bathing also had a process. During these younger years, just as I was small enough to carry to the toilet, I was also easy to handle in the bathtub. Putting me in and out presented no problems for my mom, and it was the easiest place to bathe me. Washing my hair was another story, since I couldn't actually stand under the shower for rinsing.

Hair washing generally occurred in the kitchen sink. I was short enough to lie on the counter top, agile enough to cross my legs like an Indian while my head lay comfortably back into the sink. Initially, mom rinsed my hair with a cup, but eventually she added a spray nozzle to the faucet, making things much easier.

Fifth grade was a wonderful year for me. I had a lot of close friends, I made the honor roll, went to my first slumber party and my first roller skating party, and overall had a really good time. That was also the year my mom and Bill got married, the icing on the cake.

My dad (Bill) is a remarkable man. It's one thing to accept someone else's child to raise, but to accept a child with a disability is a whole other issue. Not only did he do it, he did it with love, compassion, and understanding! Bill is an incredible father, and I will tell you more about him in the next chapter.

One day in the fifth grade, we girls were all in the bathroom during recess. I was leaning forward in my wheelchair, when one of my friends stepped on the little bars that stick out to enable someone to tip the chair back. As the wheelchair tipped backwards, my body fell backwards, knocking the wheelchair right out of her hands. My head hit the marble floor with a big thud.

I was unconscious for a few seconds, and came to with Cookie (my dear friend) slapping my face (I told you we were together a lot). My mom came rushing to the school and raced me to the emergency room, driving with one hand while keeping my head from touching the seat with the other. Luckily, I only had a big bump on the back of my head with no concussion. I really am hardheaded.

The young lady who tipped me over felt bad, but truth be told, there were a number of times I either sprained an ankle or hit my head on the wall because my friends were small like me, so carrying or handling me often resulted in bumps and bruises.

Come to think of it, even my mom sprained my ankles many times throughout my youth, usually as a result of falling on the ice and her landing on my feet. Like I said earlier, I was carried most everywhere I went other than in school, which increased my chances of getting hurt.

One major injury occurred while my mom was carrying me down the stairs of a friend's house from the kitchen to the door outside. The stairs turned and went down to the basement. As my mom stepped sideways to open the door, a throw rug hanging over the steps to the basement began to slide. She rode the rug like a surfboard down the stairs, trying her best to hold on to me, as I was slipping down the front of her and out of her arms.

Thankfully, our friends had been collecting newspapers. As I flew from my mom's arms, I landed with my head on the newspaper pile, which really cushioned my fall. However, it didn't stop my tooth from going up into my lip, resulting in stitches, nor did it prevent me from fracturing my upper arm.

For someone who wasn't involved in a lot of physical activities, I certainly saw my share of physical injuries! I didn't even get to miss school because of them. I was already in a wheelchair, so there was no point in staying home. Luckily, I really liked school, so it didn't bother me.

People always ask me why I would go to a roller skating party since I couldn't roller state. I explain that not all of the kids are skating at the same time. As a matter of fact, a lot of socializing goes on at these parties. I loved just hanging out with my friends and being part of the group. I really am a social butterfly and that's probably where it comes from.

During the intermission, I was allowed to go out and run around the rink in my wheelchair (of course, someone was pushing me) and I sure had fun! The same is true for ice skating parties and such, though I never went out on the ice.

One really funny story about snow and ice was when my mom and Bill decided to take me snowmobiling. I was all bundled up in my snow-mobile suit and boots, ready to go. I sat in front of Bill while we rode around the neighborhood in the snow. It was quite invigorating and I really was thrilled.

However, when we were done, they asked if I had a good time and what I thought about snowmobiling. They were shocked by my reply. When I sat on the snowmobile with my legs straddling the seat, I stepped down into the snow. For the first time, I felt the snow crunch beneath my feet. I told them how excited I was about stepping in snow, making the snowmobile ride kind of anti-climactic.

My folks said had they known stepping in the snow was going to be the most exciting part for me they wouldn't have bothered with the whole snowmobile ordeal. They would have just taken me outside and put my feet in the snow. What can I say? The crunching snow felt cool!

My twin cousins were also born when I was 10 years old. My Auntie Marilyn, who had spoiled me from the time I can remember, was finally blessed with children of her own, two beautiful little girls. Just as with everything else, she did all in her power to share the experience with me.

The twins didn't show much interest in my disability until they were about five years old. They concluded I couldn't walk because I didn't know how, so they decided to teach me in their wonderfully childish way. They were adorable.

They took turns explaining how to put one foot in front of the other very carefully because it takes a long time to learn how to walk, and repeated the process many times. I was touched by how, at such a young age, they wanted to help me. They were great little girls and grew up to be wonderful, compassionate, caring women.

The worst thing about elementary school (along with the broken arm) was the sixth grade. It wasn't all bad, just most of it. Some new kids moved into town and we were excited about having new classmates. To my dismay, they weren't quite as accepting as my peers who had grown up with me over the years.

And so it began . . . the avoidance, the teasing, the hurtful remarks. I especially remember when they walked around with stiff legs and arms chanting "Robots in a Wheelchair" (which never made sense, but was terribly hurtful nonetheless), and the many days of going home in tears. These were the times mom would say get tough and get through it. It was a rough year for me.

To make matters worse, I got lice that year from the little girl my mom babysat, which only added fuel to the fire, giving my classmates one more thing to ridicule me for. It's amazing how cruel children can be, and yet, now that I'm grown, I find it more astounding how cruel adults can be. I didn't much like sixth grade.

Most of my elementary school years were positive, and sixth grade lasted only nine months. When it was over, middle school began, along with which, came a bit of maturity and camaraderie. I had survived and life would go on. My parents were there for me through the good and bad, which made all the difference in the world. *Thank you, Mom and Bill, for all of your love and support.*

5. My Dad Bill, Family Man

Mom's being single left us on our own for a few years. She dated some, but not very much that I remember. She worked hard to take care of me and keep a roof over our head. Baby-sitting and housecleaning during the day allowed her to be with me for my tutored years. Once I began school, she arranged her schedule to be free in the late afternoon and early evening. At night, she worked at a bowling alley after I went to bed, so I never had to miss her.

Her workplace, Beach View Lanes, is where she met my dad, Bill. He would usually stop in after work to have a beer, as the bowling alley was attached to a bar, and he often stayed for a few hours.

I wasn't surprised they met. Living in a small town surrounded by other small towns usually meant there weren't a lot of patrons in the bowling alley or the bar. They would sit and talk for hours when things were slow. My mom didn't drink, but she would nurse a Pepsi while Bill had his evening allotment of Hamm's.

One night after work, my mom, the assertive woman she is, asked him if he would like to go for a drive, since it was such a beautiful evening outside. He was kind of shy, but agreed. They passed a drive-in movie and he got all excited because *The Sons of Katie Elder* was showing, and it was one of his favorites.

He suggested they go see it, and my mom immediately thought this was a come on, but felt she could handle him. To her surprise and perhaps her dismay, all he did was watch the movie. He never tried to hold her hand or put his arm around her. For that matter, he never even offered to buy her popcorn. However, when all was said and done, he did ask her out to dinner, and so began their relationship.

While dating, they often hung out with Bill's best friend/roommate Dickey and his girlfriend Jeanie. My mom was 10 years older than Bill and Dickey. My mom was 34, Bill and Dickey were both 24, and Jeanie was only 21. My mom often joked about finding him a younger woman and marrying him off.

When people met them and heard about the ten-year age difference, most believed Bill was the older. He was quiet and reserved and mom was a spitfire. It didn't hurt that she was in great physical shape and did not look at all her age. I was never surprised by this perception.

On one occasion, they all went out dancing at a nightclub and she was the only one of the four who was asked for an ID. That must've made her feel pretty darn good. I know I thought it was very cool that my mom was not only smart, but attractive as well. It sure is easy to see why Bill fell in love with my mom.

I wasn't allowed to meet him right away, as I usually didn't meet many of the guys she went out with. Finally after dating for a few months, she decided the time had come and I was excited. We went to spend the day at his place and watch some football. Upon our arrival, I was immediately at ease with him.

Later in the day, mom had some errands to run and he agreed to babysit while she was out. Though I was only nine years old, I felt safe. He was a kind and gentle man, and he had a really cool dog. I figure, anyone who likes animals is usually a good person.

One of my fondest memories of that day is tomato soup. It doesn't sound very exciting, but it was the best I ever had. I got hungry and he didn't have much available to fix for dinner in his "bachelor pad," but he did have a lot of soup. He prepared it with milk, and to this day that's the only way I will eat tomato soup.

After dinner, I was comfortable enough to curl up in his lap while we did the *TV Guide* crossword puzzle together. Like the tomato soup, I still love crossword puzzles. I had such a good time getting to know him and I really enjoyed myself.

In no time at all, I knew I liked him a whole bunch. I also knew he cared for my mom a great deal, and soon we were going out a lot as a family. I hadn't known what I was missing. Though we weren't officially a family, it still felt good.

Art was my genetic father, but he was never really a dad to me. I don't think he understood anything about being a family. He had difficulties from the beginning in accepting that he had fathered not only a daughter instead of a son, but a daughter with a disability. He took a real blow to his ego, and he was such an egotistical person. I didn't know that at my young age, but I figured it out fairly quickly. How wonderful it was, then, to have Bill in my life.

One day mom told me Bill had asked her to marry him. She jokingly told him maybe the second Tuesday of next week. I couldn't believe she hadn't said yes. I made her promise if he ever proposed again, she would accept. Luckily for the both of us, he did ask again, and I am happy to say she kept her word, though I'm sure she would have done so, regardless of her pledge to me.

I was 10-½ years old and in the sixth grade when they got married. Several of my school friends came to the wedding and I stayed with them while my parents went away for a few days. The wedding was beautiful and marked the beginning of a very healthy lifestyle, adding a great deal to my secure nature.

For the first time in my life, dinner meant family time: sitting together at the table sharing our day. Weekends were often spent camping, going to rodeos or stock car races, having picnics, visiting friends, or snowmobiling, and life was good. I had never experienced most of those activities until we became a family. I think the operative word was "family."

Initially, Bill wasn't comfortable with my calling him "dad," which is odd. It might have been because he was only 24 years old and I was ten, or maybe it was just too much, too fast. Whatever the reason, I called him "Bill" for about a year, at which point he wanted me to start calling him "dad," but by then it was too late. He was "Bill" to me, unless I was trying to butter him up or something, but he was always my "dad."

Bill's half-brother, Tom, was only four years older than me, and though he was my uncle by definition, by age, he was more like my brother. We got along great, and as with Bill, whenever I was with him I felt safe and secure. He never had a problem with my disability and accepted me for who I was. There was a great deal of wisdom in those two brothers.

As I entered my teens and Tom got a little further along in his, we took a strong interest in each other's friends. We got along as though we had grown up together (without the quarreling). That was one more benefit of the "Bill" package and another addition to the family thing.

Tom was as important to me as any brother and certainly played an important role in my life. I loved him very much. Sadly, he developed brain cancer and lost his battle after just one year. He was only in his mid-fifties when he was taken from us. I was devastated, as was Bill. This was one of my greatest losses.

Getting back to Bill, what can I say . . . he was a great dad! From the beginning, he assisted my mom with my personal care, which was especially helpful, since I was bigger and heavier by that time. He actually continued with my care until I left for college and I was never embarrassed or anything. However, during "that time of the month," he left my restroom care to mom, and who could blame him?

I could also talk to him about anything. He was good to my mom and I loved seeing her so happy. I just knew he would always be there for me and my mom. That kind of security does wonders for your self-esteem and development of a strong character. My mom was certainly the person who built my foundation, but she and Bill together gave me the love and guidance necessary for a healthy adolescence. It sure is easy to see why my mom fell in love with Bill.

Now, though things seemed to be wonderful and their marriage seems to have been made in heaven, life can never go along without some type of ripple in the pond. For our family, that ripple was brought on by my becoming a typical teen, along with Mother Nature (the weather), and let's not forget my disability.

High school brought the usual problems most teenagers experience with a stepparent, but our average problems became exaggerated because of my disability. When Bill said no to something I really wanted to do, I didn't care if it was in my best interest, it just wasn't fair.

It never seemed to fail; the weather always interfered with my plans. Either a big dance I had been looking forward to for weeks or a party everyone was going to (and most assuredly, included whichever young man I had a crush on at the time) would be over before it even began. The snow would start to fall, the wind would be blowing, and of course the chances of my getting sick were too great to take the risk, so I would not be allowed to go.

I would get so mad! After all, this was my life and if I wanted to take the chance with my health, I should have been allowed to do so. I was a young adult and I certainly could judge what was best for me. How dare this man, who wasn't even my real father, try to tell me what to do or make my decisions for me!

This man came to my defense on so many occasions and yet, it didn't matter to me. One time he picked me up from my friend's house after spending the night and saw I had a hickey. Tim, my girlfriend's cousin who was there on vacation (a real cutie, I might add) was just playing and we weren't really doing anything. Bill knew my mom was against hickeys and it wouldn't make any difference to her.

Bill did all of my care for the next week, keeping my mom at bay and she never found out about the hickey. He also helped me to hide my smoking habit when I first started. You would think I'd realize by all of this, he really wasn't out to get me, but instead did everything he could to show me how much he cared.

I still resented his telling me no, which only grew worse with each dance or party I had to miss. I would cry and carry on and I am ashamed to say, more often than not, put my mother in the middle of the whole situation. I would go to her and plead my case, ranting and raving about how unfair Bill was being to me. Even worse, I would point out to her he wasn't my real father and she should be the decision-maker about my health and welfare.

I'm sure she was miserable during this period. She loved Bill and wanted to agree with him. After all, he was right, but there was that everpresent piece of motherhood that nags at your heartstrings when your offspring are in pain. Your instincts are to make it better, which caused her and Bill to argue many a time over this subject. Surprisingly, she didn't win very often and my attempt to play one against the other didn't have much success.

I understand what I did was wrong, but I also know all kids do it. I recognize what a terrible thing I did, to even suggest Bill was not my real father, since he was really the only father I ever knew. I realize it is fairly typical for stepchildren to go through this phase at some point with their stepparent, but that is no excuse for my behavior. However, my youth and immaturity do provide me with some defense and justification.

Not that any of this makes it okay—just typical. When being a teenager is combined with being a stepchild, and then a disability is thrown into the mix, you are left with a bombshell just waiting to explode, as ours often did.

The bomb really ignited when our family moved to Arizona at the end of my junior year of high school. My parents decided to relocate where it didn't snow and the wind would be warm, leaving no reason for restricting my activities, at least not based on the weather. In addition, I planned to attend Arizona State University and this would ensure my residency, making the costs manageable.

Everything about the move was about me and for me. I knew this, but it didn't make it okay. The big day arrived and our new journey began. I was absolutely miserable. My world was falling apart! I was leaving all of my dearest friends and family who had been with me my whole life. Spring Grove was the only home I knew and everyone accepted me and my disability.

It's funny how life can change so dramatically—not that there was anything funny about this. My resentment continued to grow and Bill was the target of that resentment. I didn't blame my mom at all, even though I'm sure their decisions were made together.

We first landed in Camp Verde, Arizona, starting our new life in a small travel trailer. A few weeks later, we settled in Cottonwood, Arizona, in a larger travel trailer, and within a few months progressed to a three-bedroom mobile home. None were very accessible, but I still wasn't using my wheelchair at home, so it worked out. I must admit there were some good things about the move.

The high school was brand new and very accessible. The weather was certainly perfect, as it was never cold enough to prohibit me from going to places I wanted to go. To my surprise, everyone accepted my disability as well. I made friends quickly, dated, and for the most part everything was good. There was still however, an edge between me and Bill, but it came to a head rather quickly.

It was raining outside and a bunch of us were hanging out at the park. We also happened to be drinking (hard to believe, huh?). Bill came to pick me up a little earlier than I had expected because of the rain, and when he found I had been drinking, I expected all hell to break lose. I figured I'd be grounded for life, or at least until I moved out on my own. To my welcome surprise, his reaction was just the opposite.

We drove home in silence, making things considerably uncomfortable. I was really sweating it, imagining any number of terrible scenarios. When we finally got home, my mom was in bed asleep and we started talking (no yelling). At first, we discussed alcohol and he was actually giving me pointers on the right way to drink, if I was going to continue to do so.

He advised me to never mix alcohol, to stick with whatever I started out drinking. If it was beer, then I should only drink beer; if hard alcohol, stay with hard alcohol; and if wine, well you get the idea. He also said to never drink water after drinking wine, no matter how thirsty I felt, because I would be drunk all over again.

Most importantly, he let me know I could call him any time, without fear of being in trouble, if my friends were too drunk to drive or because I was uncomfortable with how much they had to drink. Whatever the reason, he just didn't want me riding in a car with someone driving drunk. Two valuable lessons: how to drink and avoid the chance of getting deathly ill, and just how much Bill really loved me.

His calm and understanding demeanor opened the door to one of the best conversations we ever had. He talked about how much he cared about me and never wanted to see me sad, but he wanted me to understand my health was a major concern for him and my mom. They never wanted to lose me, and they only did what they felt was best for my well-being. They never wanted me to miss out on anything if at all possible, and that is why they decided to move to Arizona.

I opened up to him about my fears, my hopes, and my dreams, and he sincerely listened to me. We really communicated and it was wonderful. I think for the first time he began to see me as a young adult, and not for the first time, but certainly for the rest of my life, I knew he was my real dad!

I don't know if this chapter can even begin to tell you how much I love you, Bill, but I hope it gives you an idea of how much you mean to me, what an important role you have played in my development, and how thankful I am you decided to stop in at Beach View Lanes for a beer after work one day. I love you, Dad!

6. Middle School, Maturity, and Me!

Middle school varies from school district to school district. It can range from sixth, seventh, and eighth grades to seventh, eighth, and ninth grades, and in some cases only seventh and eighth grades. In my case, we did not have a middle school in our small town, as our elementary school wasn't nearly large enough to call for a second school.

Our elementary school was kindergarten through eighth (K-8), but for my purposes, I separate seventh and eighth grade from my elementary school years. They were very different for me, and I have many more memories of those two years than of the others. I was 11 to 13 years old, and I considered myself quite mature.

I mention maturity because for the most part my friends and I started to mature. I'm not talking about in the physical sense, though that happened as well, but emotionally; we all grew up a little bit, which helped a lot in regards to my disability. All of the teasing seemed to disappear, mysteriously just going away. It was really kind of weird. Not that I'm complaining, because I was never so thankful about anything in my life as I was about that.

Also, by the seventh grade I was tired of staying home during the winter months. I convinced my mom I would be fine and she decided to give me a chance. I am pleased to say I completed the seventh grade without getting sick, even during the coldest months. However, my mom did warn my friends to stay away from me if they were sick, and they honored her wishes. Part of the maturity thing was for them to understand why she made the request.

One thing they weren't very mature about was the new addition to our school. For most of my years in elementary school, we were doubled and tripled up in classrooms because there were so few of us. There were only four classrooms and they were assigned as needed.

First, second, and third grades shared one of the classrooms; fourth and fifth grades were together in the second room; and sixth, seventh, and eighth were in the third. The only classroom not shared was kindergarten because that was the largest group and only went half day.

The summer after seventh grade, our school population had grown and every class needed its own room. An addition was built with an upstairs and a downstairs, creating a tri-level school. That was very exciting for all of us, especially for those who had been there forever (actually only six years).

The upstairs would house the upper grades, with the first through fourth grades remaining on the main level, which was the old part of the school. The lower level would be home to the kindergarten, a real cafeteria, a huge library, and a media center. There was no elevator to navigate the three floors.

It didn't take long before someone realized I was an eighth grader and couldn't get upstairs. Logical solution: keep the eighth graders on the main level (old part of the school) with the first, second, and third grades. That wasn't very popular with the eighth graders, though the fourth graders loved the opportunity to move upstairs with the big guys and occupy the brand-new part of the school.

My peers were not happy with me at all! It was obviously my fault they were stuck with the little kids and the old, boring part of the school. I wasn't very happy either. I couldn't even eat with my peers, though one of them was allowed to stay with me in the classroom during lunch time. What a lawsuit I would have if this happened in today's world.

Well, you certainly can understand why they weren't happy and why they blamed me, but soon their maturity kicked in and they got over most of their anger and disappointment. I, too, learned to deal with the situation, and like the teasing, it only lasted for a short time of my life.

However, even though the teasing had stopped and the anger had dissipated, I was now faced with a whole new set of dilemmas. Along with middle school and maturity, come hormones and an interest in the opposite sex. This stage is naturally awkward for kids anyway, but when you add a disability into the mix, oh my . . . it gives "awkward" a whole new meaning.

43

I'm sure the first dance every young person goes to is a kind of initiation into the dating world, or at least a precursor to that world. I had been around all of my classmates for a long time, and I didn't see myself as someone with a disability. I participated in everything my friends did, and though some of the ways I took part were slightly different, I still considered myself to be one of the gang. I wasn't at all prepared for my first dance experience and what I was going to learn.

It was a Saturday night, around 7:00 p.m., when I arrived at the school gym. I was dressed up, with a touch of makeup (lipstick was all my mother would allow me to wear at that age), anticipating a wonderful evening of dancing and socializing. I had butterflies in my tummy, hoping the young man I had a secret crush on would be the first to ask me to dance.

As the night wore on, song after song, each of my girlfriends got asked to dance more than once and by more than one young man. Sadly for me, that was not the case. Luckily, at this age, it's okay for girls to dance with girls, because that's who I was dancing with. I tried to be positive and keep my hope alive; after all, I was having a good time socializing and dancing with my friends, but deep down inside, I really wanted to dance with a boy.

I was gaining a whole lot of experience in the art of flirting, trying to seduce someone into popping the question (no, not the big question, just the dance question). As the clock neared 10:00, and the band played its final song, the harsh reality that no one wanted to dance with me became all too apparent.

I managed to hold back the tears until I reached the girls' restroom, but behind those doors, the floodgates opened. My heart was breaking. What was wrong with me, why didn't anyone want to dance with me? My mom arrived a few minutes later, and in her reassuring way, she made me feel a little bit better.

On the way home she explained how difficult it was for boys at this age to ask any girl to dance, let alone a girl in a wheelchair. It wasn't because they didn't want to dance with me, but rather, they had their own self-esteem issues going on. They wanted to be cool.

Since I could only dance in my wheelchair from the waist up, I could imagine this might be difficult for someone to accept, especially if they are trying to be cool. I guess I understood what she was saying, but it didn't make things any easier.

One saving grace for me was fast dancing was the style. All I had to do was wiggle my body and move my arms. Dances such as the "Monkey" and the "Jerk" were pretty easy to do with just arm movements, but nevertheless, it was still different than dancing with a girl who stood up and danced like everyone else.

She did go on to say it would probably take just one boy to break the ice and ask me to dance and she was sure the rest would follow. I went to bed saying my prayers, asking God to please let her be right. Lo and behold! Her motherly wisdom proved to be right, and that's exactly what happened. *Thank you, God!*

Our second dance was held in the basement of the Catholic school (the one other school in our small town) just a few weeks later. I went to this dance with much lower expectations and certainly more understanding of what my fellow classmates were probably experiencing.

I still got dressed up, did my hair and makeup (again just lipstick) and went to the dance determined to have a good time. Dancing with my girlfriends and more socializing would suffice. I saw it as more opportunity to hone my flirting skills.

It just so happened one of my friends had an older brother in the same grade as we were (in those days, you got held back if you didn't pass all the subjects). For whatever reason (maybe she paid him or something), he asked me to dance. I was so surprised and happy! Like many others throughout my life, he will never know the importance of that dance to my development and self-confidence.

As predicted by my mom, the other boys started to ask me to dance and I was elated! I am happy to say throughout my two years of middle school, we had a lot more dances and I was never faced with this dilemma again. Well, not until I was old enough to start clubbing. My mother sure was a genius!

Along with middle-school age comes hormones, better known as puberty and all that goes with it. Interest in the opposite sex is but one piece of puberty, though a pretty major piece. Usually it is one of the most painful of all of the components, for rarely does the one you are interested in feel the same way about you.

My first crush was on a boy named David and my guess is he never knew. It was probably best, because his family moved away some time during the seventh grade. Had he reciprocated, I most assuredly would have been left with a broken heart. I figure one less broken heart to deal with, the better. Besides David, I wasn't interested in many boys during this time, but no worries, the day arrived.

Now as for all the physical changes, there were many. My breasts began to grow and my mom was in sheer denial. I bugged her and bugged her to buy me a bra and she kept saying I really didn't need one. She finally gave in, I'm sure just to shut me up, but proved my point, because the bra she brought home, to my delight, was too small!

Now mind you, she bought me a double-A cup size, not much bigger than a training bra. What I actually needed was an "A" cup, which isn't huge or anything, but it sure made me feel good that I was bigger than she thought. To be quite honest, an "A" sounded pretty darn big to me even if it wasn't huge.

It is important to picture my plastic body jacket, which went above my breasts and was flat as a board on the outside. I'm not surprised that she didn't think I needed a bra. After all, they were well hidden. Of course, enlarging breasts are usually accompanied by menstruation, as in my case.

I have always been good with dates and this one is especially unforgettable. In my mind, I was now a "woman." On Thursday, May 9, 1968, I was feeling sick, so I stayed home from school. I was lying in bed watching the Newlywed Game, which came on at one o'clock in the afternoon. At the commercial (which was about 1:15 p.m.), I used the restroom and learned why I wasn't feeling well.

I had begun to menstruate and I just kept thinking, "Wow, now my body could actually have a baby." Not that this was something I wanted to run right out and do, but the fact I could was totally amazing. It never even crossed my mind that I might not be able to have a baby because of my disability.

As excited as I was to be having my period, in just a few short months, I was not very excited anymore. Menstruating was nothing but a pain and I did not like it at all. Thankfully, I wasn't one of those girls who had bad cramps or other PMS side effects, but I hated it even without those things.

Not too long after starting my period, I became very interested in using tampons. My mother was strongly against the whole idea and my very forward-thinking grandmother helped me convince her. My grandmother totally understood that sitting all day on a sanitary napkin was probably not the most comfortable thing in the world, so she became my "tampon advocate."

My mom finally gave in (how could she not after getting pressure from both her mother and her daughter?) and agreed to let me use them. Her only stipulation was one of my friends had to help me out. This seemed to be her usual requirement for anything new I tried.

One of my best friends, Marian assisted me my first time. She helped me to position my body, lying flat on my back, using the back of my hand against the applicator of the tampon, which enabled me to push it into place. I had a little difficulty at first, but each try got easier, which is probably the case with most girls' first attempts.

I soon learned about a tampon without a traditional applicator. The tampon was on a cardboard stick, and it was much simpler for me to push with the back of my hand getting the tampon in place. I grabbed the stick between my thumb and my hand to pull it out, leaving the tampon behind. I put my thumb through the string loop to remove the tampon when I needed to change to a new one. I do my own menstruation care. Very cool!

Tampons provided me with a fair amount of independence during my time of the month (though I did need assistance with positioning) and I appreciated all the independence I could get. Obviously, my friends could not be there during every menstrual cycle and though my mom wasn't totally supportive in the beginning, she quickly adjusted, giving me whatever assistance I needed.

It was also around this same time, I first started shaving my legs and got my ears pierced. My ears were done in a very unique way. I was at a friend's house and decided to be brave. Carole froze my right ear and did the piercing. Not so bad, other than hearing the layers of skin pop as the needle went through.

Then she realized she was late for work. She thought our other friend was going to stick around to do my second ear, but found out the next day no one had pierced my other ear. She came right over to complete the project. I am probably the only person who ever got their ears pierced on two different days.

Now my mom, in her very predictable manner, only agreed to allow me to do both, with her usual stipulation. One of my friends would have to assist me with the shaving of my legs and the cleaning of my ears, as well as changing my earrings. Mom wanted no part of either.

So it became a pattern; I would try something new and my friends would initially help me out. Eventually the time would come when they weren't available and my mom would have to step in. Once in awhile she complained, but was always there for me. These specific events were the initial stage of my friends doing a big part of my care.

Having friends who could actually do my care allowed me a great deal of freedom and independence. I never looked at it in those terms, we were just friends hanging out together and part of being my friend meant helping me out with certain things. I did, however, grow to realize just how important it was.

Most of my friends started out just helping me to use the restroom as young as eight and nine years old. They progressed to undress-ing/dressing, and in time showering and washing my hair. Some did more than others, but for the most part, my close circle of friends learned to do the majority of my care, if not in middle school, certainly by early high school.

Bathing and washing my hair transitioned to showers once my friends were doing a big part of my care. We used an old padded kitchen chair from a yard sale to shower me on. It was tall enough to put me closer to the shower head and made it much easier to put me in and out of the tub, as well as to bathe me.

One of the events most affected by my friends' ability to do my care was the infamous "slumber party." Anyone who has ever been a young girl or the parent of a female child knows of the importance of the slumber party.

Just as the first dance is a precursor to dating, the slumber party becomes the initiation into social acceptance. Anyone who is anyone is asked to the party, leaving only the severest outcasts without an invitation.

Thanks to my friends' compassion and acceptance, I was made part of the "in crowd," providing me with another invaluable experience for my self-esteem and identity. In addition to slumber parties, their care made field trips possible for me without always having to bring my mom along. This was one more support to my ever-growing independence.

I attended one slumber party, which I'm sure very few, if any, of my friends will admit to participating in. We harmlessly turned the evening into a precursor to "making out." Just to be clear, in my generation, the term meant a whole lot of kissing, nothing more, and is what I mean here.

In my mom's day, "making out" meant having sex. One day she overheard my friends and me talking about "making out," and she quickly asked for a definition. She was relieved to find out we were talking about what she referred to as "necking." Interestingly, today, its meaning has reverted back to her era: having sex.

It's amazing how things return to what they once were. The clothes my mom wore when she was a teenager became popular again when I was in college and again when my daughter was in high school. Much of the music from back then is popular today. Things really do come full circle.

The slumber party turned into what I call a practice kissing party. None of us had really experienced a kiss from a boy, let alone making out. We were all quite concerned about the notion of being kissed and not knowing what we were doing. I'm not sure whose idea it was, but soon, we were paired off and kissing.

We took turns making the first move like being the boy. We tried to make the kisses long (no French kissing; I don't think we were even aware of French kissing at that stage), with our heads moving and whatever else we thought we had seen in the movies. It really was quite innocent and what I consider to be typically experimental for kids, which is exactly what we were.

However, many of my peers obviously experienced a great deal of guilt over this because a few years later when the subject came up at another slumber party, no one could remember ever having done that. Amazing how quickly they conveniently forgot. Perhaps I just had a dream . . . not!

At another slumber party, one of my friends brought a shoebox wrapped as a present (must've been a birthday slumber party) filled with alcohol. Not a lot. I mean, how much can you fit in a shoebox? There was one can of beer, a half-filled bottle of vodka, and a jar of whiskey. However, for young girls, it doesn't take much to get drunk, especially since we were mixing the alcohol, as we all wanted to try everything.

We decided to hold a séance. What started out as a simple attempt to make contact with the dead, turned into quite an extravaganza! My friend had recently lost her sister in a car accident and we foolishly tried to make contact with her. Soon we were trying to make contact with other lost family members. Having had too much alcohol, many of my friends ended up in tears.

Of course, there were those who just got sick from the alcohol, too. My parents had gone out for a few hours, figuring we'd be doing silly girl things, and came home instead to a bunch of girls crying and being sick. Needless to say, they weren't exactly pleased. I didn't host another slumber party for quite some time.

One of my first field trips with friends and no mother was a "college day," and we used the stroller for my mobility. We were all very excited about going to a college campus. Everybody took turns pushing me. I had told them the doctor suggested that the unique way of tipping back and pushing my stroller made use of certain chest muscles, which would surely promote breast enhancement.

This excursion was too funny, because soon they were fighting over who was going to push me. Debi said, "I need it more because I have no boobs" and Marian pointed out Debi had a boyfriend and didn't need to worry, and so it went. Everyone wanted a turn at pushing me wherever we went. I felt so popular . . . but I wasn't what they were after, they were just using me to get bigger boobs! What really needed to happen was for me to be pushing myself.

I talked about going to camp in my elementary years and what a fantastic experience I had, but I want to address it again. I can't emphasize enough the importance of having time away from my family and friends and all I gained from attending. Exposure to other people with disabilities was very enlightening.

Though for some time, I was more interested in the teenage counselors than in the people with disabilities as friends, I learned a lot. This was my first introduction to the disability world as a community. I still hadn't crossed the bridge of identifying myself with a disability, but I was headed in that direction.

Whether or not I saw myself as someone with a disability wasn't the issue. Instead, and more importantly, I broadened my world to see others and their struggles. I learned about compassion, I saw people give of themselves to provide others with some wonderful experiences, and I learned I could survive independently of my family.

I continued going to camp for many years, all through high school. I made many close friends, with and without disabilities, and camp truly was one of the best times of my life. Again, I would encourage any parent of a child with a disability to send them to camp. This was probably the beginning of my identity as having a disability. It was a healthy beginning surrounded by inclusion and acceptance.

Graduation came all too soon and marked the end of my middle school years. I was about to embark on the next leg of my life's journey. By coincidence or fate, whichever you choose to believe, I received my first power wheelchair a week before that eventful ceremony.

For the first time in my life, I was able to get around completely under my own power, and how appropriate that should occur on the very day I was heading into a whole new stage of my life.

My parents had the event all worked out. I was already up on a stage for the ceremony, waiting for my class to come in. I walked up to the podium (rolled, but you know what I mean) to get my own diploma, and at the end, Bill and Tom lifted me down, so I could march out with my class. I was so excited and never felt more like one of the gang. Why didn't we think about putting in a ramp? Today, more and more schools provide for those access needs.

Graduation from middle school marked an end and a beginning: the end of childhood and the beginning of adolescence. It was exciting and scary, at the same time. My power wheelchair also marked an end and a beginning: the end of my dependence on others for my basic mobility and the beginning of a world of mobile independence.

I now had the freedom to go where I wanted to go. I could turn around when I heard a noise or see who was entering a room. I could walk alongside of my friends rather than having them behind me, move from one place in the room to another without assistance, choose where I wanted to sit without having to plan and ask someone to put me there, and just be mobile like everyone else.

A new identity was beginning to take shape, from dependently non-disabled to independently disabled and the transition was so subtle, I didn't even see it happening. I doubt any of my peers or family did either. I was getting a little further along on that bridge, and high school would bring me yet even further. My journey was certainly beginning to change course.

7. Freshman: Frantic, Frustrated, but Free

Though middle school ended in May, something really exciting happened the summer after my graduation: I became a big sister! Sadly, mom and Bill didn't have a baby, but rather my biological father and his wife gave me a little brother. Arthur Thomas L—— was born on August 1, 1969. Pretty exciting, huh?

I always wanted a sibling. Tom was like a brother, but Artie was a blood brother, not an uncle. I didn't get to see him much during his youth, but somehow we maintained a connection. Once I was older, I saw him more and today, we see each other a lot, because we both live in Sacramento. I love him dearly!

I also started high school in August and now I was a big sister like so many of my other friends. High school usually comprises 9th through 12th grades: freshman, sophomore, junior, and senior years. Most of them draw from several elementary schools, as was the case in our community.

Richmond Burton Community High School (RBCHS), about five miles from where we lived, drew from two public elementary schools and one private school. It wasn't a huge high school, but certainly bigger than my grade school. My class size jumped from 24 students to roughly 80, and in a small town, that's a big jump.

RBCHS had two floors and was equipped with a freight elevator, enabling me to get to all of my classes without any major adjustments. (Thank goodness, I didn't have to relive the eighth grade upstairs dilemma.) Because it was so much larger than my previous school, I had my fair share of getting lost while looking for my classes that first year, all part of being a freshman, I guess.

The freight elevator also came in handy for football games. The weather was usually too cold for me to attend our home games, but because I was able to get upstairs, I could watch from one of the big windows and remain warm. I was allowed to have one friend stay with me indoors and we would join the others in the gym after the game for the dance that always followed. At least I was there.

It's funny how in the eighth grade you feel like such a big shot and then you are quickly demoted to the bottom of the barrel the first year in high school. I felt like the lowest of all life forms. I lived for the day I would be on top again. It would be a while, but the day would come.

Once again, there was no Special Ed classroom, resource room, or instructional aide available. My friends escorted me to my classes, assisted me with the elevator, and helped me with the restroom. You would think a teacher would have this role, but not back then. Students with disabilities have no idea how good things are today as compared to my high school years.

Around that same time, I started training my body to use the restroom only early morning, late afternoon, and bedtime. That way I didn't have to rely on people very often. This skill proved to make all the difference in the world in terms of my future employment endeavors (though it ultimately led me to develop kidney stones, as well).

I couldn't take the bus to school because accessible vehicles were rare. Today, I could be rich over such lack of access. But things worked out for the best. No one liked riding the bus, and since we were going to the same place, many of my friends rode along with us. Carpooling was great for maintaining friendships and encouraging new ones, as well as being part of the "in crowd."

My mom had a big car for holding lots of kids, but there was certainly no way to transport my very heavy power wheelchair back and forth each day. Therefore, my wheelchair was housed at the high school in the teacher's lounge, and it was charged every night.

In the morning, mom would run in, bringing my chair to the top of the four steps at the entrance. Then she would carry me up the steps into school, to my chair and my mobility independence. The end of the day was the same, carrying me out to the car and returning my chair to the teacher's lounge. If there was a special event outside of school on the weekend, we would bring the chair home, but most of the time, not.

This created a good balance for me; I was independently mobile at school, but I sat on the couch to watch TV, at the breakfast bar for meals, and so on and so forth. I still used my stroller for outside activities, as it fit in most people's cars and was easy to use for camping, upstairs events, and other non-accessible activities. I loved my power wheelchair, but we had not yet become one. It still wasn't part of my identity, just a tool to make my life easier.

Getting carried in and out of the school, for the most part, never bothered me. However, in the dead of winter, mom insisted on covering my face with a blanket so I would not breathe in the cold air and get sick. Now, that embarrassed the heck out of me. I felt like a baby, as that's what mothers do with their babies in the cold. I hated for my friends to see me.

I'm not sure they ever noticed or cared if they did. However, I know I thought about it a lot. Always having to worry about getting sick was such a pain.

A memorable experience with being carried in and out involved my freshman biology teacher. Mr. Kier was the scariest teacher I ever had, at least to that point. He taught freshman biology and I had him for third period. The fact I remember this demonstrates just how much he affected me. I was terrified after walking into his class on the first day and hearing him say in a very firm voice, "Today you are eighth-graders, and tomorrow you will be freshmen; I expect you to behave as such!" I'm not sure I even knew what he meant, but I did sit up and take notice.

He assigned Chapter 1 to be read with all of the questions and vocabulary completed by the next day. I couldn't believe this was happening on the first day. Even more unbelievable; the next morning entering class, he had us put our books away and take a quiz. Everyone failed! Following the quiz, we were given the same assignment for Chapter 2 and dismissed. We were all in shock.

On the third day, same thing, books away, followed by a quiz, which we all failed again. This wasn't funny and I don't think he was trying to be. After the second quiz we were given the identical assignment for Chapter 3. Upon our arrival on day four, we were ready for the quiz and instead he said, "Today we are going to discuss chapters 1, 2 and 3." I wasn't liking biology or Mr. Kier very much at all.

Another unpleasant biology experience involved learning about blood types. We had to prick our own finger, come up with two drops of blood, and run some tests. I tried several fingers with numerous pricks and could never muster more than one droplet, which dried up before getting a second.

To my dismay, Mr. Kier offered to assist. When he pricked my finger, not only did I get two drops of blood, but the bleeding wouldn't stop. My finger bled through my entire next period of study hall and required a tissue wrap for the full hour. I wasn't bleeding to death, but I was still bleeding. I spent the next few days with some very sore fingertips and an even greater dislike for Mr. Kier and biology.

I share stories of this teacher because they relate to being carried in and out of school. I had often told my mother about this strict teacher who never smiled. Then one day as she was carrying me out to the car, Mr. Kier held the door open for us and smiled as she said, "thank you."

To my horror, she said, "See Miss [Miss was my nickname], he smiles." I wanted to die, or at least dig a hole and jump in, never to be seen by him again. I couldn't believe she said that in front of him. How was I going to face him in class?

Surprisingly, he was quite pleasant the next day. Maybe he thought about what mom said or maybe not, but whatever the reason, the class got progressively better. In the end, he wasn't such a bad guy after all. It probably didn't hurt that I was a good student and did well in his class. I actually learned to love biology and like Mr. Kier. Imagine that!

My other three freshman-year academic classes were Government, English, and French. My government class was my fun class. I would never have guessed that government could be fun. I'm sure it had something to do with the teacher.

Mr. Rittenhouse was a young, new teacher and we related to him quite well. He was the freshman adviser, and being new together nurtured our relationship. He also didn't look too much different from us except for his red hair, which made him stand out from the rest of the teachers; he could be seen for miles. The best part of him was his great sense of humor, making us laugh and making learning fun!

English was divided into three levels. I was placed in the highest of the three. Sadly, the majority of my friends from grade school were in the second level, leaving me among mostly new kids. They accepted me fairly well and the disability never was much of an issue. I did as well as any of them in terms of grades, even better than some, so I proved I belonged.

Being academically equal was helpful in my overall acceptance, but was still something I was concerned with. In elementary school, acceptance was only a problem in sixth grade and dances, but the thought of being left out was much more intimidating now. I'm sure it had something to do with being new and all, but probably more to do with the stage of development I was in.

I learned very quickly that a good sense of humor eliminates barriers and generally puts people at ease. My English class peers were my first experiment in acceptance. By the end of the year, I had become close friends with many of them and was well on my way to mastering the art of being accepted. I was also mastering the art of accepting myself as someone with a disability.

French was disappointing to me. I started out so excited to be learning what I consider the most romantic language of all. Antoinette was my French name for class. I don't remember the teacher's name, probably because she wasn't very good. Most of the time, I felt we were all playing a game of charades.

She would try to act out the meaning of the words and by the time we figured it out, we had forgotten the word. She expected us to do the same when someone didn't understand what we were saying. Physically acting out a word wasn't very easy for me to do and I dreaded having to speak (and trust me, that is so unlike me, if you haven't already figured that out).

Carole, one of my best friends, was also in the class and didn't get along very well with this teacher, either. Perhaps, that influenced my attitude towards the teacher and the class, but whatever the cause, I was really soured on learning French. Needless to say, I did not take a second semester.

The rest of my day was filled with music and study hall. I wasn't required to take PE for obvious reasons, though I often joined the class just for fun. Usually I was the scorekeeper for whatever game was being played, and I learned a lot.

Home Economics was the same way. I couldn't really cook or use a sewing machine, but a lot of my friends were in the class and I enjoyed spending time learning about cooking and sewing, even if I couldn't do the hands-on stuff.

The teachers were very supportive and allowed me to drop in whenever I had the time. Generally, I was okay with the situation, but sometimes I was really frustrated by not being able to do what everyone else was doing. I would have to learn to deal with frustration, as there would be many frustrations throughout my lifetime.

I have mentioned my friends many times, and should introduce them. My very best friends in high school were Debbie B., Carole W., Debi P., Venus L., Diane L. (Venus and Diane alias Cookie and Corky, my neighbors since the age of six), Marian H. (all from elementary school or middle school), and Karen J., whom I met my freshman year. They know who they are.

Marian went on to a private high school, but we remained close friends even though we didn't see each other daily. Of course, they have all gotten married and changed their last names, but this is who they were when they played such an important role in my life.

To this day, I have contact with all but one. I communicate regularly with four of them and occasionally with the other two. I am amazed by how distance and time can take its toll on relationships. I didn't believe I would ever lose touch with these ladies. Maybe this will motivate me to keep closer contact with them.

In any event, I wanted to take this opportunity to thank each and every one of them for their compassion, understanding, and acceptance, intentional or not, and to let them each know my successes today are in part due to their support from my yesterday. *Thank you, guys!*

Other big events from ninth grade were important to my development. Freshman initiation was one of them. Sadly, the tradition has long since been banned in most schools because someone got carried away resulting in illness or injury. For me and my classmates, including the seniors, it was all in fun.

We had to wear really silly outfits; we girls wore frayed shorts, hanging below our knees, long sleeve shirts on backwards with one sleeve rolled up, knee socks on our hands and under rubber galoshes, hair in little braids all over our head, and a pacifier in our mouth, unless we were spoken to. The boys wore shorts with a sheet put on like a diaper, a T-shirt with no sleeves, and the same accessories.

We had to memorize a poem about what freshmen were and recite it whenever we were asked. If we didn't do what we were told by the seniors or we couldn't recite the poem, we were doused with ketchup, mustard, toothpaste, vinegar, or any combination thereof, and we were also smeared with lipstick, oil, and other concoctions created by our Masters, as we were their slaves for the day. We didn't have to ingest anything, and only our pacifier went into our mouth.

This event was unforgettable in its own right. However, for me initiation was another sign of acceptance. I dressed up in the same outfit and got smeared with all of the same disgusting condiments as my peers did.

No one treated me any differently or cut me any slack because of my disability. Matter-of-fact, my wheelchair caught the overflow. I cleaned up rather nicely, but my wheelchair was another story. I was going to smell like garlic and vinegar for some time.

The day ended on a positive note with a "Welcome Freshmen" dance put on by the seniors. The gym was nicely decorated, there were all kinds of goodies and the freshman got in free. I certainly felt like one of the gang and I was now officially a Rocket (our high school team was the Rockets).

This dance was the first of the year, and I was curious as to how things would go. I was pleasantly surprised, as all of my male classmates from middle school continued to ask me to dance, with no real regard to the opinions of the new guys. Their disregard opened the door for the others to follow suit. Dancing was obviously not going to be a problem during my high school career. How cool was that?

Dancing may not have been a problem, but clearly dating was going to be one of those things needing some work. I was only allowed to double date until I was 16 anyway, which for me was my senior year, so I had a while before single dating really entered the picture.

My parents believed the only safe way for me to date was with a friend to protect me in the event my date turned out to be something unexpected. It never came up though, as most of my friends didn't date much this first year of high school either. We usually went to dances, sporting events and other school activities as a group. A few went to a movie or a dance as a couple, but for the most part, dating did not become an issue until my sophomore year.

However, many of my friends attended the homecoming dance with a date. To save face, I went with Tom (Bill's brother, my uncle, more like a big brother). My close friends knew who he was, but the rest of my classmates did not. They just thought he was from another school (which he was).

I could have stayed home, but this dance was important, as one of my best friends was on the homecoming court. I got a lot of practice fine tuning my flirting skills. I learned over time, flirting in combination with a good sense of humor would be my greatest tools for attracting the opposite sex, putting them at ease so as to accept me, disability and all. Oh, my friend was also crowned Queen!

This is also the year I started to have problems with my stepdad, Bill, as this is when I really started socializing with my friends outside of the house. With more and more activities happening at school and away from home, the chances of the weather interfering with my plans increased, creating a great deal of frustration for me. My newly found freedom was often nixed before even beginning.

Bill and I were able to work things out, though it took us another three years. There were actually a whole lot of things I would learn to work out over the next three years, all part of growing up.

Freshman year presented challenges I had never faced before, but I had a great deal of fun in the ninth grade. I was able to carry my own books, take my own notes, feed myself, dance in my wheelchair, and be independently mobile. I looked forward to what the rest of high school had to offer me. I consider high school to be one of the best times of my life.

In high school, all of my needs were taken care of. I didn't have to worry about money or bills, my food and clothing were covered, and my greatest concern was my grades. How could anyone not like high school, even with a disability?

I was really looking forward to my sophomore year. I would no longer be at the bottom of the barrel. I was much smarter now, knowing the ropes of high school. I knew my way around, I had a lot of friends, I knew all the teachers, and best of all, I wasn't a freshman anymore. I was cool, though some might call it smug!

8. Sophomore: Smart, Smug, but Small

Ninth grade, better known as freshman year, was finally behind me. No longer was I the lowest life form on the planet; I actually looked down on those poor kids just coming on board. I was now part of a smarter, more sophisticated crowd, and perhaps, a bit too smug to boot!

I may have been a step above the freshman, but quickly learned being a sophomore was still very small on the scale of power and prestige (unless of course, you happened to be dating an upperclassman, which had a way of elevating you like no other).

Dating my classmates didn't occur very often, but rather I'd go out with someone I would meet at another school through friends. They were usually older than me and not too worried about image. I went to a lot of dances during the tenth grade, but mostly with a group of friends.

Clearly, my classmates and friends were beginning to participate in the whole dating game. Also very apparent to me was that I had not yet mastered this aspect of acceptance. It was obviously going to take some time, perhaps a very long time.   .

I tried to pretend I didn't care, but more than anything I wanted to have a boyfriend. I had a major crush on a young man from another school, which afforded me an easy way to avoid facing the issue on a day-to-day basis and provided me with a good front, but my problem didn't go away.

Having my guy attend a different school allowed me to talk about him without anyone following the relationship too closely. Making excuses as to why he couldn't come to a dance, such as something going at his own school, was easy enough. He was a convenient way to fill my void and have something else in common with my dating peers. However, I knew the truth.

He wasn't exactly imaginary, but he wasn't exactly a boyfriend either. To make matters worse, all of my close friends were really cute with very nice figures and were never hurting for male attention. Now, mind you, I had tons of guy friends, just not romantic ones. I wasn't jealous, well yes, maybe I was a little, but it just wasn't fair. My mom always said, "Life isn't fair."

My dating experience may have been limited, but I had another whole year to experience my power wheelchair and the independence attached. I had it not only for the school day, but very often for evening events as well (dances, football and basketball games, etc.), and I loved it. My wheelchair and I were finally bonding and I was more comfortable with opening up about my disability.

The wheelchair-bonding and identifying myself as someone with a disability occurred simultaneously. That was probably not a coincidence, and came about subtly, with no conscious effort on my part. This major attitude shift did not damage my self-esteem; I still liked who I was, even with a disability.

I rarely dreamt of myself walking. When I did have such a dream, I was always entering the front door of my elementary school and walking down the hallway. I never walked anywhere else.

I interpret this as meaning that walking was never as important to me as it was in grade school, when I so wanted to be like everyone else, running, jumping, playing tag and such. As I matured, my subconscious must have recognized how unimportant walking really was to my self-image, and my self-acceptance increased as well.

My sophomore academic classes included English, Geography, Physical Science, and Shorthand, with study hall and choir completing my schedule. English class was the place where I was most expressive about my disability and where my connection with the disability world began to take hold.

That was due to the research I was conducting, as I started writing papers about SMA (spinal muscular atrophy) and other disability issues. I also credit my teacher, Ms. Shumaker, as she made me comfortable with who I was. Perhaps it was that she was a woman, or maybe not, but whatever the reason, this is where things began for me.

She introduced us to plays and debates. Acting out *Romeo and Juliet* was fun, and I enjoyed trying on different personas. I debated about euthanasia with a football player who didn't want to live if he couldn't play football. How young we were; this was a completely different kind of challenge, one which most of my classmates could not begin to grasp.

The concept of fighting for life, regardless of what life has to offer, was far beyond their realm of comprehension, which is understandable for their age. I, however, learned very early on how precious life is, regardless of the design handed out, and I am thankful for that lesson.

Geography was taught by a gruff man, Mr. Behrens, and I didn't like him at all. I was an A/B student and he gave me a D for an easy subject. My mom talked with him about what I had done or not done to deserve that grade and he said, "Nothing really, I like to start students out low, so they can work to better their grade."

She asked what I could do to improve my grade and he told her I should just keep doing the work I'm doing. How stupid is that? I didn't do anything different, but I eventually got the "B" I deserved. I didn't care much for this teacher in the beginning of the school year and I didn't come around to liking him any better at the end, unlike Mr. Kier and biology.

Physical Science was taught by Mr. Wolpert, whom I liked a lot. He gave me a nickname. He called me "Trouble," and I can't imagine why. He had a good sense of humor, made me laugh, made learning fun, and I very much enjoyed his class.

It's hard to believe I liked physical science more than geography, which used to be one of my favorite subjects. I guess I still like geography, but not Behren's class.

Shorthand was another class I liked because of my teacher. Mr. LaMontangue made learning fun, too. I originally took shorthand because we believed I would have an easier time taking notes when I went to college, especially since my hands often tired so easily. I also liked the class a lot because it was like communicating in a secret code, kind of like a puzzle, and I love puzzles.

Now truth be told, because I have the ability to look ahead, I happen to know I never used shorthand in college, in fact, I had forgotten most of it by the time I got there. In hindsight, I should've taken shorthand my senior year. I certainly would have had more memory of the signs and used it more readily. This is where that line comes from "If I only knew then what I know now."

Study hall continued to be our way to ditch class. We would go from study hall to the library and sit at a table nearest the door to the Commons Area (free area to talk, drink pop, chew gum, eat chips, etc.). That was where we all wanted to be, but weren't allowed until we were juniors.

When no one was looking, we would disengage my wheelchair motors and quietly push me out the door to the forbidden land. Goes to prove, "If there's a will there's a way"! We definitely had the will.

One of my worst experiences during tenth grade (besides the dating thing) was getting my nose broken by an elevator door. If you recall, my high school had a freight elevator, enabling me to get to my upstairs classes.

The design was very different from a passenger elevator, with a spring-loaded wood-slatted gate that lifted up to open. Two metal outside doors came together in the middle, from top to bottom instead of side to side, and were pulled apart by a strap.

From inside the elevator, the gate had to be gently lifted up, so as not to spring back down. Then the strap on the outer doors would be pulled and one door would go up and the other down, opening up the elevator for exit. With an understanding of the mechanics of the freight elevator, you will be better able to appreciate how I broke my nose.

My friend and I were running late for class and hurried on our way. Arriving on the second floor, my friend threw up the gate and pulled up on the outer door strap, and I headed out.

I heard a noise, looked up, and the gate came down right across the bridge of my nose! I saw stars! I was in a great deal of pain, but if I had gotten hit across the top of my skull, I would most assuredly have been killed.

This makes for a very funny story, since most people think about the typical elevator doors when trying to visualize my nose getting broken. Now mind you, I wasn't laughing too much at the time. I was walking around with two black eyes and a swollen nose for weeks. I am thankful to be around to tell the funny story.

Considering all of the injuries I have acquired over the years from my friends, they should throw me a big party or something. I know they never hurt me intentionally, but having a reason to throw a party is a good thing.

The most embarrassing event of the year had to do with my breasts. I persuaded my orthotics (brace) guy to cut down the front of my hard plastic body jacket (brace), which went from above my chest to my lower abdomen, encompassing my entire torso. A brace alteration doesn't sound embarrassing.

As my breasts grew larger, room was made for them on the inside of my brace, but their existence was not apparent on the outside. I wore baggy shirts through all of my freshman year and most of my sophomore year, leaving everyone to believe I was just a flat-chested girl.

By late spring and after many months of pleading, I finally convinced my orthotics man I didn't need the support of the brace so high in the front. I think he felt sorry for me and that is why he agreed to cut away the chest part. Voila, I had breasts! Very nice full breasts I might add.

Now being an overzealous young woman, I wanted to show them off. Who wouldn't? So, the next day at school I wore a tight fitted shirt with a zipper in the front, unzipped as low as I could get away with. I didn't think about the fact that my classmates had seen me one day without breasts and the next day they were there. You can imagine the questions they had.

Most of them believed I had somehow undergone breast surgery, though I'm not sure how I could have accomplished that in just one day. My close friends had to go around educating my fellow classmates. I was developing a pattern of defending my breast size, beginning with my mom and my first bra.

School wasn't the only place I wanted to show off my newfound breasts. There was also my favorite hangout, Baron of Beef, which was about five miles from our house. My fantasy guy lived in the same town, increasing my chances of seeing him. Venus and I frequented the place as often as we could. My parents usually drove us there and we would find a ride home with friends.

I had this really cool purple silk shirt that tied at the top in the front, creating an open circle between my breasts. The no-bra look was just becoming popular and a bra could not be worn with this style of shirt without looking tacky, so I decided to go braless.

I had my friend dress me and put a jacket on me to cover up, which tells you I knew better. Once in the car, my mom said, "Aren't you hot in that jacket?" As she spoke, she reached over and pulled my jacket open and immediately noticed I wasn't wearing a bra.

She got pretty angry and warned me to never try to sneak out of the house again without a bra on or I would be grounded. We were very close to our destination and she did not turn around and take me home, she just let it slide. Boy was I lucky, in more ways than one.

I never tried pushing that rule again because it was too easy to get caught. However, I can't count the times Venus and I walked home late at night because we couldn't find a ride or the ride was only going half way. That was also definitely against the rules!

Luckily, we never got caught. We just spent the night at her house because we could sneak in quietly and go to bed. We would have never been allowed to go there again if either of our parents knew the truth, and I certainly couldn't blame them. I would have grounded me for life if I were the mom.

One night we couldn't find a ride at all. It was very dark with no stars out, but we weren't about to call home. We knew our parents would be angry and our trips would become limited, so we walked. We were both terrified, but somehow made our way home, walking about five miles in the dark, how stupid were we? What can I say, we were young and invincible, or so we thought.

By now, almost all of my friends did most of my care, other than getting me up in the morning and putting me to bed at night, unless we were spending the night together. One of them usually did spend the night sometime during the week and almost always on the weekends, so they did my showers, shaved my legs, washed my hair, etc. It was a much-needed break for my parents.

I was becoming quite independent from my family and it was a good thing. I still had all my teenager rules (the no-bra thing), I continued to be close to my mom, and the struggle with my stepdad hadn't ended, but my disability was not interfering with my independence. I think my sophomore year was right on cue.

Becoming an upperclassman was within reach. There would be power and prestige (and hopefully dates and romance) very soon. Life was going okay, school was doing great, I had a lot of friends, my identity definitely included my disability, and at the same time, my wheelchair and I were becoming one.

9. Junior: Jealous, Juvenile, but Joyful

My junior year was a mixed kind of a year. On one hand, I felt very grown up and on top of the world, yet on the other, I knew the seniors were really in charge and well respected. We juniors were in limbo. We may have been upperclassmen, which held a certain amount of prestige, but not enough to make us gods like the seniors. Still, my junior year was mostly good times.

I was quite comfortable with my disability. I was who I was always going to be. I really felt lost when I couldn't be in my power chair, as I had grown accustomed to my independent mobility. When sitting in a regular chair, I often found myself grabbing for my nonexistent joystick to turn around and look at the noise I heard behind me.

I was finally starting to date. I went to parties. I made out with boys I liked. And I did most of the typical high school things. Everyone was used to my enlarged chest and knew they were real, and my disability was pretty commonplace for all of my classmates. I was accepted for who I was and it felt good.

My junior year classes were English, U.S. History, Bookkeeping, and Algebra, with choir and study hall to fill in the extra slots of the day, as the years before. My English class was mostly literature, which I wasn't too thrilled with. I especially hated having to read *Beowulf.* I despised that book. We did, however, get to read *Romeo and Juliet* again, which was a lot more fun, though the boys may have disagreed.

U.S. History was taught by the same teacher I had for Geography, so you can imagine how much I disliked the course. In addition, we covered all of the information I had learned in Freshman Government, which I considered a complete waste of my time, though I did need to complete it to graduate.

Bookkeeping was with my previous shorthand teacher, whom I liked a lot. We had a simulated checkbook with weekly bills and such, and I had a great deal of fun with this course. It was like being on my own and taking care of myself, and since I had a newfound respect for independence, this just added to it.

Algebra was a fluke. I was excited when I first got to high school and learned math was not a requirement. I couldn't stand my eighth grade math teacher, thought I hated the subject, and therefore didn't take any such coursework.

However, during my sophomore year, I learned I needed two years of math to attend college. So, here I was a junior, along with mostly freshmen taking algebra. How embarrassing was that?

Luckily, the algebra teacher was also my Freshman Government teacher, whom I happened to like a whole lot. As I was the only junior in his class, he treated me as sort of a teacher's assistant. I guess he understood the embarrassment I was experiencing. He was definitely a great teacher.

I finally had a real boyfriend, even if only for few months out of the year, which did wonders for my self-esteem. He wasn't a boy from my high school though many of my friends knew him from the neighborhood. In fact, he wasn't from any school, as he had quit the year before. He was, however, a boy and he seemed to be interested in me, which is what I desperately needed at this stage of my life.

In terms of sexuality, it was still a time when, for the most part, girls didn't have sex with someone unless they had been going steady with them for a very long time, planned on getting married (which often happened due to pregnancy), and no one except maybe their very best friends knew about it.

As a matter of fact, one of my closest friends did get pregnant during her senior year. She had been with her boyfriend for several years and only her closest friends knew. (I happened to be one of them.) She dropped out a few months shy of graduation to get married and become a mother.

That was a good lesson for me. I saw her often, a housewife, missing out on a lot of fun things, and though I was happy for her, I knew I wasn't ready for that life. I always thought about her whenever I thought I was ready to be sexual.

During my teen years, most of us went through stages of sexuality: making out (kissing a lot, with and without tongue), petting (above the waist over and under clothing), heavy petting (below the waist over and under clothing, both partners to one another), and then going all the way (sexual intercourse). Each of these stages occurred at various times throughout a relationship and never with someone new. Well maybe the kissing part, but certainly none of the rest.

This last stage usually took a long time to reach. During my senior year, in a different part of the country, I became aware that some girls went all the way their very first time with a guy. Many were young (12 and 13 years old), which shocked me. Perhaps I was a bit naïve! I was also probably the oldest virgin in town, something I should have been proud of, but chose not to brag about.

Speaking of the stages of sexuality, I have another funny story. My friends and I were talking about French kissing and my mom happened to overhear us. Now, mind you, she was very fearful of my getting a cold, leading to pneumonia, which ultimately would cause my death. Having said that, she came into our group and asked me to promise her I would never French kiss with a boy who had a cold.

I thought this was the funniest thing. I could see me getting ready to make out with some guy I had a huge crush on and just before he started to French kiss with me, I would back off and say, "Excuse me, you don't have a cold or anything do you?" Yeah right, sorry mom, I was going to take my chances when the situation arose.

I will share that I maintained my virginity throughout high school. I did experiment with several of the stages before then, but I believe this was pretty normal development. My mom had told me it was normal to experiment, just as long as I didn't experiment to the point I hurt myself or someone else (I believe she was referencing pregnancy, perhaps disease).

Very wise advice from that very wise mother of mine. She put the ball in my court, which made me seriously think about my actions. I'm not sure if all teens would have seriously thought about their actions, but I was pretty grown up for my age and it worked with me.

What she really taught me was respect. Because of my respect for her, I never wanted to hurt her, and that often kept me from doing things I might have otherwise tried. My mom was pretty open-minded, but not always.

I had a friend who I would say was quite promiscuous. There were rumors about her activity with oral sex, and when my mom got wind of them, I was no longer allowed to hang out with her. We went round and round on this, but she insisted you can get a reputation by association and was looking out for my own good. That was one of those things we never agreed on, but I had to follow her rules.

One thing I believe, though I'm sure others may disagree: it's easier to be a female than a male with a disability in the dating/sexual world, because of the way our society operates. Usually the guy does the driving, makes the first move, puts his arm around you, picks you up and carries you, does the undressing, is the strong one, the protector, etc. I am thankful I am a woman in regards to my disability.

Of course, having a disability and being female does not make you immune from heartache. My family went on vacation while I had my boyfriend and he cheated on me with a girl I knew. He didn't even have the decency to break up in person. I experienced my first broken heart, the first of many.

Though I know guys cheat on girls all the time (and girls on guys), deep inside I believed it was because of my disability, which probably was not the reason at all. I took a while to let that one go.

I didn't like what he did to me. I certainly didn't like being lied to, but I was convinced I loved him and the hurt was unbearable. I didn't believe I could ever love again and since my disability was not going away, how could I even think about taking another chance on love. Shows you how young and immature I really was. But aren't we all during this time?

I spent the remainder of my junior year just being a flirt. I didn't want a boyfriend (or that's what I told myself). I wanted to get myself ready for college. My first meeting with the high school career counselor was during sophomore year, when I found out I needed two years of math. My junior year I let him know I was thinking about attending Arizona State University (ASU).

Reflecting on his response, I am really taken aback. He told me though I was an A/B student in high school, Arizona State was a tough college to get into and I shouldn't get my hopes up about getting accepted. He went on to say I should only expect to get C's and B's at whatever college I went to, because college is a lot harder than high school.

I wondered, did he say that to all the students, or just to me because of my disability? I probably should have been thankful to him because now I was more determined than ever to get accepted to ASU and do well. I guess you could say he was my motivation. (Well, part of it; I don't want to give him too much credit.)

Being a junior is usually accompanied by a driver's license, which for me wasn't going to happen. However, I helped most of my friends study for their Driver's Ed tests and could easily pass the written part. Probably the driving part too, considering all my experience with my wheelchair. Ironically, my parents decided to give me a car on my 16th birthday, as long as I had a driver.

Not only were they giving me a car, but a 1967 Camaro Rally Sport, with a 327 engine and a three speed on the floor. It was an incredibly cool car for a 16-year-old, and for that matter, it was an incredibly cool car for anyone. My friend Debi, to whom I had grown quite close that year, became my driver. Just like that, we were more independent than ever.

My mom spent a lot of hours driving with Debi, teaching her all the things she would have to be aware of while driving with me. Mom had her drive on snow and ice, took her out into the field to show her how to stop on ice and what to do in the event of a spin.

She made Debi drive with a grocery bag full of groceries in the passenger seat until she learned to always put her arm out when stopping fast. Seat belts weren't really in use at that time. Debi and I were presented with my car and the keys on my 16th birthday, which only left a few months before summer, and we were thrilled!

My Camaro, designed for driver and four passengers, had bucket seats in the front and a bench seat in the back. I had been given strict instructions from my parents to have no more than four kids at a time in my car, including the driver and myself. That meant we could only have two other friends with us. I must admit I broke that rule many times over.

We would often have friends sitting on the laps of other friends and, more often than not, we would have somebody straddling the console and stick shift. The real challenging part of all of this was that my dad (Bill) was the UPS driver in our town, and we often crossed paths.

At those times, everyone on the laps of others would duck over sideways and the person on the console would lie back. I am amazed we never got caught and very thankful we never got into an accident.

Another great time I had with that car is the racing we did. My cousin had a Mustang of the same year, the rival car to the Camaro. We were about the same age and he lived a few miles away.

A road connected our two towns, a straightaway not heavily traveled. We would routinely race against one another whenever we had the chance. We each won our fair share of races, and once again I am so very thankful we never got into an accident. God was certainly watching over us.

My Camaro also led to my starting to smoke cigarettes. Many of my friends smoked. In Illinois it was often still cold in March and April, so you couldn't roll the windows down much of the time. I didn't want to be a prude and say no smoking in my car, and yet the smoke was killing me, so I started taking a few puffs off of their cigarettes to help me get used to the smell.

Soon the puffs turned into whole cigarettes. Then I felt bad about bumming cigarettes from everyone, so I figured I would buy a pack of my own, which would last a long time. Well I don't have to tell you where this story goes. In no time at all, I was a full-fledged smoker. How foolish of me, but once again my youth and immaturity shine through.

We had some great times with that car, but they were short lived. I lost Debi as my driver before the end of the school year. It took less than three months. We were so stupid, thinking we wouldn't get caught.

On her boyfriend's birthday we decided to ditch school and go shopping for a gift for him. We thought we were really smart and showed up at her house when we would normally show up after school. No one was the wiser until Debi decided to show her mom what she had bought. Her mom got this puzzled look and said, "When did you have time to go shopping?" Busted! Her mom promptly took her driving privileges away.

Luckily, my mom wasn't too upset with me because we were so close to the end of the year, I had straight A's, and this was the first time I had ever ditched school. I am happy to say I did not lose the car. However, I wasn't too sure what I was going to do about a driver.

Again, luckily for me, by this time my mom was a little more comfortable with me being out and about and left it to my discretion as to whom I would allow to drive my car. Debi still drove a fair amount of the time; she just wasn't my regularly designated driver.

One of the best times of my junior year was my junior/senior prom. This dance was very special and was held at a country club rather than our high school gym. There was dinner, dancing, the crowning of the king and queen, and of course the all-night after-prom parties. Debi was on the prom court, which was icing on the cake.

Not at all surprising, I wasn't asked by any of my classmates, which might be perceived as a bad thing, but instead, I was going with Tom's (my uncle/brother) friend Tony, which was a good thing. I had known Tony for several years and we had hung out a lot.

He had just returned from a two-year stint in the Vietnam War. He was on the front lines and had several medals to prove it. So, while everyone else had dates dressed in tuxedos, my date came clad in a uniform, and boy did we stand out and get everybody's attention. Sure made me feel good!

Up until the actual night, I hadn't been invited to any of the after-prom parties, but all of a sudden, I had several invitations. As though on cue, Tony automatically responded, "No thank you, we have other plans and want to be alone." He made me feel very special and so grown up. Truth be told, we didn't have other plans, but my classmates didn't know that.

My dress was absolutely beautiful and like no other. My friend who had gotten pregnant and quit school made it. I would go to her place several days a week for fittings and such, which gave us the time together I so missed by not having her at school.

The dress was amazing; we took the bodice of one pattern, the A-line skirt of another, the bell sleeve of yet another, and the puffy shoulders from one last pattern for a final creation no one was going to match. She was so creative and such an incredible seamstress.

She could make my shoulders look even and my back zipper look straight, and I really looked like a princess. I don't know if she understood how much it meant to me for her to do this, but in the event she didn't, I will take this opportunity to say *thank you for your friendship, your time, and for just being you.*

Debi, my close friend on the prom court, was popular all through high school, with a great personality and a great sense of humor. She was liked by all.

Some of the others may have been prettier, but only on the outside. They were "stuck up" or conceited, whereas my friend was beautiful both inside and out. She was meant to win.

Sadly, she and her boyfriend had broken up a few weeks before prom and it was too late to get another date. What we thought was an honorable gesture turned out to be a cruel joke. Her ex-boyfriend offered to be her date for the prom, since she was on the prom court, and then as the evening drew to a close, he went and left her there with no transportation. What a jerk!

On a more positive note, she was crowned the queen, a much deserved honor, I might add. My date and I drove her home. Neither one of us went to an after-prom party, but our classmates thought we had bigger and better fish to fry that night, so neither one of us was embarrassed. It's funny how things work out.

As I mentioned earlier, Debi and I had grown quite close in these past few months. We shared the car, we hung out a lot more than before, and summer brought us even closer. We often went on picnics with our whole group of friends and had water fights to keep cool.

We usually ate Kentucky Fried Chicken and drank Pepsi (filling the empty bucket and cans with water). Though I couldn't chase after anyone or run from them, my friends never had problems pouring water over my head, and I never had a problem telling where they were hiding. We came home equally drenched.

During that summer my parents managed to sell our house, and moving became a reality. I had a very hard time with this, as I had lived there since I was five years old. My senior year was no time to make a change. For the few days before we left (August), my parents stayed with friends and I stayed with Debi.

I cried buckets, though I knew the move was in my best interest—
the warmer weather for my health, the residency needed for ASU, and the freedom I would be afforded with a new accessible high school. I was still devastated!

Debi tried to comfort me. On our last night together, we went out with some friends. We tried to get some alcohol to dull the pain, but the only thing we came up with was a few joints of marijuana.

I had never smoked marijuana before. Everyone in the group said getting stoned the first time you try is hard to do, so they were going to make sure I smoked enough. No one coerced me into trying marijuana. It was something I wanted to experience, and that seemed to be the right time.

We went out on this dirt road where kids often went to make out and I had my first introduction to smoking weed. It was also the first time I got a really good look at the northern lights (aurora borealis), which were exceptionally bright that evening. Actually, I'm not sure if they were exceptionally bright or if I was just more aware of them because of being high. Being high was kind of nice. I felt mellow and everything was funny. I felt much more in control than with alcohol. Having a disability, one doesn't want to give up much control. That is why I will never try heavy narcotics or other mind-altering drugs.

I did, however, manage to burn my thumb on the roach (butt of the joint). I wasn't able to bring my hands together while leaning back on the car seat and I couldn't get anyone's attention because they were too stoned. Of course, it wasn't too long before we were all very hungry, so we went to the local hangout for pizza.

While we were there, I tried putting my thumb in flour because I had heard the burning stops, but it didn't work. Then I tried sticking my thumb in a glass of ice water only to come up with a thumb full of paste that still hurt like hell. We filled our tummies, played "Go Fish" with the pictured sugar packets, and had a wonderfully good time before heading back to Deb's.

When we finally got back to her place, reality started to set in and the tears began to flow again. Her dad felt bad for us and gave us each a can of beer, I guess to drown our sorrows. Well it didn't take long to work, because by the time we drank the beer on top of the marijuana we had smoked, we went right to sleep, or more accurately, we passed out.

The morning light came much too quickly, as did the time to leave. My parents showed up with our truck and travel trailer in tow, along with my Camaro. My aunt and one of my friends were going to Arizona with us to help make the transition easier for me, as if anything could make this move easier for me.

The goodbyes were filled with tears and heartbreak. Deb and I promised to never lose touch, and with one final hug (me not wanting to let go), the doors closed and we were on our way to Arizona. I think I cried as far as New Mexico.

This new journey included both excitement and fear. What was this new life going to hold for me? Were people going to accept me and my disability? Would I ever date again? Would I have friends like I have now? So many questions, and luckily for me, I was armed with the necessary tools to move forward and accept new challenges.

My family, friends, teachers and community had all been there for me and perhaps it was time to spread out and share what I had learned to try to make a difference for others. Only time would tell where life would take me and what I would give back.

10. Senior: Superior, Sophisticated, but Scared

We arrived in Arizona during the first week of August and settled in a park in the town where I would be attending my senior year in high school. Arizona State University (ASU), my ultimate destination, was in Tempe, approximately two hours south.

One of the changes I decided to make accompanying this move was to leave my nickname "Missy" behind and start using my birth name, or at least a simpler version. Since no one knew me here, I could be Laurie and no one would know the difference.

For a while, I felt like I had a dual identity, as everyone from Illinois and my childhood continued to call me Missy. It took me some time to learn to respond to Laurie, but the name was so much more grown up. I was pleased with my decision; now I just needed to change my last name, which wasn't going to happen until I got married someday.

As a way to meet people, I started hanging out in a small park downtown with my friend from Illinois, Debbie. In no time at all I started making new friends. One of the first was Ed, a guy who was already out of high school, having graduated the year before.

He was a really nice guy and funny too. As a matter of fact, the first time we met, he had a banana sticking out of his ear. No particular reason, just being silly. We quickly became good friends and started hanging out together a lot.

Along with his silliness, he possessed a sense of maturity and responsibility and quickly took on the big brother role for me and our group. He didn't drink, he didn't do drugs (though he did smoke cigarettes), and he was usually with us wherever we went.

Many of my girlfriends had a crush on him at one time or another, but he and I seemed to maintain a brother-sister relationship, which is the same today. He was one of the nicest guys I ever knew.

Our relationship was also conducive to his providing me with personal care whenever necessary. I never felt embarrassed or at risk. This was just something he did for me. His willingness to do my care allowed me to be more independent from my family, though it took several months into our friendship to occur.

Debbie headed back home after a month or so, and I had very mixed emotions about her departure. I was excited about my new school, my new friends, and the prospect of going to college, but on the other side, I was truly terrified of being alone and on my own in this unfamiliar world.

My risk-taking skills would really be put to the test as I began to explore my new surroundings and opportunities. I thought when I became a senior, I would have mastered everything, boy was I wrong!

My closest friends were no longer a few blocks away. For that matter, they weren't even a phone call away, because back then talking on the phone cost a lot for even a few minutes. I missed their support and understanding, and more importantly, their acceptance of who I was with the disability.

In addition, all of them could take care of me physically, which afforded me a great deal of independence. I wasn't sure how easily I was going to find that again in my new life, though Ed began fairly quickly, but not immediately.

It wasn't too long after Debbie had left when I had my little drinking experience and reconnected with my dad, Bill, having our very meaningful conversation (Chapter 5) and recapturing what we once had. It felt good to be close to him again, to feel protected by him, and to understand his side of things.

That night helped me to accept this move as right, and to be a little less terrified. I also became one step closer to adulthood, realizing no matter how angry I was with my dad, I never stopped loving him.

School began shortly after my friend went home. Luckily, I had already made several friends and wasn't too scared. I was still the only student at my school using a wheelchair, which I thought made me stand out, but no one seemed to notice or care one way or the other.

The school was remarkably accessible, being new and all. Everything was very modern and open, and I required no accommodations, which was cool. The main auditorium was in the center of the building, without walls, and had ramps down to the stage, while the library was on a lower-level with ramped walkways instead of elevators. The school was beautiful, designed to blend into the desert and mountains with the perfect colors.

I quickly became friends with Jeannie, who lived close by. She was a true artist in every sense of the word. She could paint in various media, sculpt, and write, and she was secretly in love with the art teacher. Interestingly, one of my closest friends in Illinois was also a true artist, but not in love with the art teacher, probably because the art teacher there wasn't nearly as handsome.

Jeannie was also into the mystical and magical. We spent many an hour reading through her dream book, analyzing our visions from the night before, and playing the Ouija board, trying to figure out what our future held for us.

We spent a fair share of our free time smoking weed, which seemed to enhance all of the mystical, magical things. Jeannie was also the crazy one in our group. I say that in the kindest way, with a great deal of admiration. She was never afraid to be silly and she had a great sense of humor. Jeannie was one of my friends who had a crush on Ed (after falling out of love with the art teacher). They would have made a great pair with their silliness and all, but they never got together. Some things are just not meant to be.

Jeannie had the hands of an artist (which only makes sense), as she had long, slender fingers. She created a little creature with her hand and fingers, which we called "the beast." She would make it come alive in any scenario.

The beast especially liked to crawl across the table and look at you or crawl up your back and lean over your shoulder. The beast just naturally became one of our gang. He became particularly popular whenever we were sitting around stoned. We each had some version of our own beast, but none like hers, and we always had such fun with them.

Halloween that year with Jeannie was unforgettable. A group of us had gone out trick-or-treating, even though we were all much too old and behaved poorly. She was dressed all in black, with a white face like the Grim Reaper, scary even to us.

We were on a nearly deserted road with one street light and we saw a group of younger kids coming up the street. Jeannie ran out and lay under the street light with her arms across her chest, while the rest of us hid behind some bushes. I know, it was a really mean thing to do.

As the kids approached, you could hear them whispering, trying to figure out what was in the road. As they got closer, Jeannie started to sit up very slowly and when they got right up close, she screamed out. The poor kids dropped their candy and ran. We thought it was pretty funny at the time, though looking back, it probably wasn't one of the brightest things we ever did.

Many of her other shenanigans occurred while I was away at college, when she came to live with me. To my extreme pleasure and surprise, Jeannie quickly learned how to do my care, allowing me to spend many a night at her house and making it possible for her to be my caregiver later on at college.

Another dear friend from my senior year in high school was Peggy. She was very petite and soft-spoken, and had the greatest clothes. Her family was fairly well-to-do and she was always handing down her clothes to Jeannie or me. Going to her house was like shopping at the mall, I always came home with a new bag of outfits. I was so glad we were the same size.

As little as she was, she never had trouble carrying me around or doing my care. She just accepted it as part of being my friend. Whenever we were in a room with a group of people, you would hear them gasp as she picked me up, tossing me higher into her arms, using her knee to bump me up to get a better grip.

One time as we were leaving a party, there were about five stairs from the front porch to the sidewalk. Peggy took one step and we were on the sidewalk. She was sitting on her butt with me sitting in her lap, both of us laughing our heads off. We didn't get hurt and I'm sure we must have been stoned.

Every time I stayed at her house, a couple of times a month, she and I would spend a great deal of time in her bathroom with the window open, as we quickly smoked a cigarette. I believe we called it "hot boxing," taking many hits quickly, one right after the other, and the cigarette would get very hot. Ah, those bathroom memories . . . I wonder if her mother ever suspected. Either that or she thought I had a terrible bladder problem.

Peggy was the first of the group to get a car besides Ed. The day Peggy got her car, we all found a new sense of independence and freedom. Peggy and Jeannie were both sophomores, making them about a year or so younger than me. The freedom of driving didn't come about until halfway through the year, but some is always better than none.

I didn't have my Camaro before then, as I did in Illinois, because I didn't have a driver old enough and whom we had known long enough. Ed drove us around once in awhile, but all he had was a pickup truck and we couldn't all fit. We always seemed to make do though, even without a car.

We would often go to the drive-in with lawn chairs, having my parents drop us off. Eventually we would find some cute guys who would invite us to sit in their car. For the most part, this worked out well. However, on one occasion, Peggy really wanted to be with this guy she liked a lot, who had his own car and was also a sophomore.

The problem: he was with his buddy, who was only a freshman. I finally gave in and agreed to sit with him, thinking all the while, "If anybody at school finds out a senior was at the drive-in with a freshman, I will be a laughing stock." Thank goodness, no one ever found out, but interestingly, this young man became quite a ladies' man throughout the year, dating several upperclassmen. Who knew?

As with many high school friends, Peggy and I didn't have much contact once I was off to college, but I knew she was married and had two daughters. I looked her up once when her girls were young and we had a very nice visit.

Many years later, I heard she had cancer. I regretted not having been in touch more. I was able to reconnect with her one more time before she passed and I was very sad. Her girls were only teens; what a terrible time to lose your mom.

I'm always amazed at how things turn out. Several friends from my youth have passed away, and to think, most people expected me to be gone a long time ago. *Peggy, your daughters will always be in my prayers and I hope you are in a better place. Thank you for your friendship and acceptance.*

Other friends were Tami, Roy, Steve, Keith, Dan, Valerie, and Randy. Each either had a special lesson or story. Tami was the oldest of five kids and her father was a leader in the local Jehovah's Witness congregation. She was only allowed to hang around with me because he believed that having a disability prevented me from doing bad things.

Another girl wasn't allowed to hang around with me at all because her mom was fearful she wouldn't be active enough as my friend. It's funny, the weird things people think about disabilities.

Tami went with me to dances and movies, dated, smoked pot, wore makeup, and read books, everything I learned she wasn't supposed to do. Tami had never told me she wasn't allowed to do those things, so I really wasn't sure what her parents meant by bad things (except for maybe the pot).

Then I found out Tami was abused. Her parents would make her sleep naked on the floor in their room to watch over her. She was routinely beaten and forced to kneel on the kitchen floor, naked, for hours begging forgiveness for having evil thoughts. They left her bruised and even chopped off her hair.

Jeannie and I convinced her to go to the police and she was finally taken away from her father, who was supposed to be a man of God. I hope the things we did together did not bring on her punishment, but rather brought some enjoyment to her horrible youth. Tami's situation was my first introduction to child abuse, knowledge that helped to shape me into the person I am today and to encourage my love for kids.

Roy was also the son of a preacher man, but his family was very loving and giving, which I would expect from a Christian family. Roy was a lot of fun, extremely bright and respectful. I often went to the youth group at his church. His father was a very understanding pastor and knew teenagers well.

One night for an activity, he gave us each a piece of paper and we were to write down all of our sins. Then we were supposed to pray, asking God's forgiveness for each of the sins. One of the guys in our group was well known as a rowdy teenager and it was too funny when the pastor gave him two pieces of paper. We were on the floor laughing, but I guess you had to be there.

Steve became a dear friend not long after school started. He was also an artist and a close friend of Jeannie's. Jeannie and Valerie had a crush on him as well. Too bad for them, Steve was gay. I was the first one he shared this information with, and I was honored. He became my first homosexual friend.

He often confided in me, though I certainly didn't know how to advise him. I did encourage him to be sure, as this wasn't an easy lifestyle, especially back then. I also suggested he try an experienced woman before choosing homosexuality, actually believing it was about choice. I didn't understand the only choice was whether or not to act on his desire—more of my youth and naivety ever present.

This was a very important lesson in my life about acceptance and compassion. I learned that disabled people are not the only group facing discrimination. I couldn't imagine being gay and having a disability, but I know people who are and live quite happily. I guess we all have a degree of prejudice or misunderstanding about something. Steve was one more friend who later became my caregiver.

Keith dated Jeannie, I dated Dan, Dan and Valerie were brother and sister, Steve tried dating Valerie, Steve tried dating Jeannie, Randy dated Tami, and so things went. We were a very happy group of friends. Sadly, I only have contact with Ed and Jeannie and our connection has only occurred in recent months, after many years of no communication.

How easily we lose track of those who were such a central part of our lives. My friends were even more central to my life because of all of the things they helped me do. All of my girlfriends did my care, as did some of my male friends: Ed, Steve, and Dan. You would think with those friendships, nothing would change.

Academically, my senior year included English, Geometry (that second year of math I needed for college), Civics, and Art. Once again, there I was, the only upperclassman in geometry because I thought I could get away without taking any math when I first got to high school. English was required for all seniors and was really no big deal. Civics, however, really pissed me off.

I had taken Government my freshman year, which covered national government along with Illinois government. My junior year I had taken U.S. History, which also covered government. In Arizona, because Government wasn't called "Civics," I had to take it one more time, learning about national government again.

The only new piece of knowledge I gained was about Arizona government, which I can say wasn't very different from Illinois government. Can you tell I was pretty tired of government? Maybe I should run for governor.

Art class was fun. That's where I met Jeannie and Steve. I met Roy and Peggy in geometry and the others I met through these four friends. This was a very simple year for academics, and the only negative thing was the counselor.

Again, I was advised about how difficult of a time I was going to have at college. What was up with in these counselors? It really is amazing that even though I was an A/B student, I wasn't expected to do well on a college level and I am positive that had something to do with my disability.

I learned people don't set very high expectations for people with disabilities. As a matter of fact, I don't think they set any expectations at all, other than to expect you to stay home with your parents until they can no longer care for you, leaving you to finish up your life in a nursing home. That certainly wasn't my plan. It's a good thing by this time of my life, I had become an independent thinker, with independent goals and expectations for myself.

Romance my senior year wasn't nearly as complicated as I had expected. During my first three years of high school, being around everyone who knew me well, no one ever dated me unless they were from another school or new to ours. Starting over like this was kind of the same thing.

Everyone was new, but it still took a few months before I dated anyone from school.

I met Tim just as the new school year began, or should I say my mom met him. She picked him up hitchhiking in our small town (it was pretty safe back then) and invited him to dinner. She thought he was a nice guy and wanted him to meet me. He was from San Francisco, out visiting his grandmother. We met and I was completely smitten with his charm and big-city finesse.

We spent many hours together every day, and he took me to my homecoming dance. We were so bored, though, that we left after about an hour and went to a bar with a pool table and live music. I don't drink now, nor did I then, so I didn't leave my homecoming for alcohol, but rather to go wherever he wanted to be. We talked and danced and I watched him play pool.

This was my first slow dance with someone taking me out of my chair and holding me for the whole song; I was hooked! Like many good things, it was short lived. About a month later, the time had come for him to return to San Francisco and I was devastated, to say the least. My heart was broken even though we had never done any more than kiss (not for lack of my interest). I couldn't figure out why until much later.

Throughout the rest of the year, I did some dating trying to forget about Tim. Sometimes I went out with someone on more than one date and sometimes not. I had a crush on Randy for a while, but he was interested in Tami. I had a crush on Roy, but he was too much like a best friend.

I did go out on a few dates with a guy named Chris, but it didn't really amount to anything. I went out with a few other guys as well, but it was the same. However, none of them seemed to be bothered by my disability. They accepted me as I was, but just no fireworks, so they didn't turn into relationships.

Of course, no relationship meant there would be no sexual relations either, as I was still a Midwestern girl with Midwestern values, and sex did not occur without a commitment involved. No one-night stands for me. I was looking for love.

I was, however, becoming more and more curious about the sexual intercourse part of sexuality. I wondered if I could have sex (go through the physical act), but did not want to have sex with just *anybody*.

I had done my fair share of experimenting with the various stages of sexuality, as well as masturbating, and I knew my body responded appropriately. I had no problem getting aroused or having an orgasm, but what I didn't know is whether or not I could physically have intercourse.

My mental image of intercourse generally conjured up female on the bottom, legs apart and straightened out. My knees and hips were contracted in a 45° angle, so how in the world was this going to work? After conferring with my mother, I learned that more often than not, during sexual intercourse, the woman's legs are bent at the knees and wrapped around her partner. There was hope!

Though my hips were contracted, they were contracted from going straight down and back, but not from side to side. My legs were kind of like those of a frog, so with this new found knowledge, I was fairly confident that when I made the decision to take this next step, things were going to work just fine.

I met another Steve about a month before graduation. He was a hippie with long hair and low-cut, hip-hugger jeans. I was quite intrigued by his air of independence and freedom. He was a free spirit. I was really into independence.

He became my boyfriend after a few parties and makeout sessions and was the first relationship I had since Tim. We did a lot of fun things together over the course of the next few months, and, of course he learned to do much of my care.

He was allowed to go with me to "Grad Nite" at Disneyland as my caregiver, and what a time we had. My mom actually suggested I not wear a bra because it would continuously need to be adjusted after I was carried on and off the rides.

I couldn't believe she was breaking her own rule. She probably did because I would be leaving home in a few short months and making my own decisions. Whatever the reason, it marked an era of "bralessness" from that point on.

We were all searched for drugs before going into the park, but I was able to hide some pot down my body brace, which we thoroughly enjoyed the whole night. Being together all night long and slightly stoned made the trip unforgettable.

About a week before graduation I was given the surprise of a lifetime. A whole group of my friends came from Illinois to help me celebrate. There were five of them, and what fun we had. One night all of us, including Steve, were out partying, when everyone decided to go skinny dipping.

Steve and I wanted more privacy, so we went down the road a bit further to make out. Little did I know, my mom was concerned about the late hour and came looking for all of us, following us for several miles.

She saw the majority of my friends head for the lake, but not Steve and me. Well she continued to follow us and I can't even begin to tell you how horrified I was when she pulled up alongside our car and told me to get my ass home. Luckily, I didn't get into too much trouble, and I'm sure it was because of the company.

Steve and I did a lot of making out and heavy petting, but I didn't decide it was time to make love until my Illinois friends came to visit and one of them encouraged me (which was just the nudge I needed).

Everyone had gone camping, but one of my friends wasn't feeling too well, so we decided to stay home for the weekend. Steve arrived with his friend and I was in my bikini. Even though I had a curvature of the spine, I still had a fairly good figure and good self-esteem. My friend knew of my plans and asked Steve's buddy to go for a ride. Not long after they left, we were in the throes of passion.

We started in the living room on one of the mattresses (for our visitors from Illinois), but quickly went back to my bedroom. Everything progressed normally. I had enough strength to wrap my arms around him, stroke his back and be positioned in any number of ways. It was great until the moment of penetration.

What I wasn't expecting was the feeling of being ripped apart. I was very much aroused, he was taking things slowly, and there was plenty of foreplay, but it hurt like hell. I believe it was because of my never having done anything physical to stretch or such. I had used tampons, but that didn't make any difference.

I remember screaming "stop," which he didn't, and I am thankful he did not, because I might not have ever tried again. I bled quite a bit and he just kept apologizing for hurting me. Even in my painful situation, my common sense told me to throw the sheets into the washer, which was a very good thing, because within moments my parents arrived home.

I was shocked when they pulled into the driveway and couldn't imagine what they were doing back here. They weren't supposed to come home until late Sunday and today was only Friday. Though my bedroom door was closed, mom knocked and walked in, like she usually did. We didn't actually have a privacy policy here.

Thankfully, we were already dressed when she came in. She asked why we were back in the bedroom, to which I replied, "We were just talking." Then she asked where Debi was, to which I replied, "She just went to the store to grab something for her cramps."

Her next question was about where the sheets were, to which I replied, "They're in the washer; Debi got her period and that's why she wasn't feeling well." Not completely truthful, but very quick thinking if I do say so myself. I learned to always listen to my common sense.

She said they were back because the axle on the Jeep had broken and they needed some tools. I'm sure she knew exactly what had just happened, but she never said a word. Well, now I knew I could go through the physical act of intercourse and I was very relieved, though I was a bit concerned about the pain. I wondered if it was normal for all girls.

It took me about a week before I could sit flat with no pain, but I eventually healed. Then we tried again and there was no pain, but no bells and whistles or fireworks either. I wasn't sure if it was worth going through all the pain, but I convinced myself that with a more experienced lover I would certainly find out. I sure hoped that making love would measure up to everything I'd heard.

Graduation was great! We went out for a very nice dinner before the ceremony. The formal procedure was as you would expect, and the next day we had a big party for my parents' friends as well as mine. We finished the celebration with a trip to the Grand Canyon. Everyone enjoyed my special day.

I went to camp in Colorado for a week shortly after graduation, only to find upon my return my first lover had cheated on me and had taken off to who knows where. My second broken heart in just one year, not fun!

This was also, the second time I had left a boyfriend to go on vacation only to find he had cheated on me while I was away. They both broke up with me by leaving, rather than giving me the common courtesy of telling me. What cowards!

The other really sad part is that he lied to me. He told me he was sterile and being the young, naïve teen I was, I believed him and never used birth control. I probably knew better, but didn't want to. No one ever believes they will get pregnant the first time or two and I was no different.

Later in the summer, I went to Illinois to visit with my friends and family and I had a miscarriage, not even realizing I had been pregnant. My mother had done her best to educate me about these things, but young love won out and my emotions were more powerful than my common sense. Not only did I learn I could go through the act of intercourse, but I could become pregnant, as well.

My friend Karen and I went to a rock concert. It wasn't my first, as I'd gone to see the Monkees and a few local groups in previous years, but this was different. We went to see Uriah Heap in a real rock concert, and they were incredible. I was well on my way to becoming a "groupie."

The really incredible part of this concert was that one of the stage crew recognized me from MDA summer camp, as he had been a camp counselor there. He arranged for us to sit on stage and meet the band. When the concert ended, we were invited to go backstage and actually talk with the group.

To add icing on the cake, the drummer and I got very friendly and I made out with him for a while. I guess you could say I was more than well on my way to becoming a groupie, I was definitely there. He gave me an autographed drum stick and even bit into it, leaving his teeth marks. Don't ask me why I thought that was cool.

We were also invited back to their hotel for a party, but I knew where that would lead and wasn't willing to go there. I just enjoyed the moment, the kissing, and the drum stick. I did, however, receive an invitation to attend their next concert in Tempe, Arizona the following summer. I thought that I just might take them up on it.

Summer quickly drew to a close and what an eventful summer it had been, but now the time to head off to college was here. I was going to be living in a dorm and for the first time in my life, completely on my own!

Of course, my mom was heading down with me to help me get settled and would stay until I could find a caregiver. I was very excited about my upcoming journey and at the same time, terrified. This was déjà vu; I had just gone through this same kind of thing last summer. I can only hope things would go as well now as they did then.

11. College Collection

My introduction to college was quite challenging. As a matter of fact, by the end of the first week, I figured compared to what I had just been through, college was going to be a breeze. Registration prepared me for anything.

A few months before college started, I met with the Department of Rehabilitation (DR), as the department was paying for my school: tuition, dorm, food, books, and supplies. After receiving the paperwork from ASU, which accepted me with no difficulties, I completed and mailed everything to my DR counselor, as instructed. (The Department of Rehabilitation has since become the Rehabilitation Services Administration, part of the Arizona Department of Economic Security.)

I thought about mailing copies of my letter of acceptance to the skeptical and discouraging academic counselors at both of my high schools, but decided they weren't worth my time. Having followed the instructions from DR, I arrived at ASU a week early to get settled, and I found nothing but obstacles in my path. Instead of moving in, I raced around in a frenzy trying to get everything taken care of before classes began.

The first problem I encountered was that my dorm, Manzanita Hall, was not physically accessible. As the newest dorm on campus, you would think it would have the greatest access, but sadly, it did not. The elevator was one level up (four steps) from the main floor. With rooms on the third floor and above, I was high and dry. What idiot architect came up with this design?

This dorm was intended for freshmen. I would have been with my peers who were experiencing the same things as I was, which is why I selected it in the first place. I was very disappointed about my inability to get into Manzanita Hall. Luckily, we had arrived early in the day, allowing time for a great deal of scrambling. Amazingly, by end of the day I had a room.

I was placed in an honors dorm, McClintock Hall, housing for juniors and seniors only. I found it funny that here I was a freshman with no GPA, let alone honors, and I was given a room in the honors dorm. At first, I was upset, but it really was a good deal.

The rooms were like suites, with a sitting room and a bedroom. The students here were serious about their grades, so there wasn't a lot of partying. I had access to a lot of mentors and this dorm was centrally located, very close to everything—library, Memorial Union for meals, class buildings, etc.

Taking care of the first obstacle in only one day would indicate things weren't all that bad. Not so: things got worse. The next day I went to pick up my identification card, only to find that I wasn't registered. The DR counselor never sent in my paperwork, so I wasn't signed up for any of the classes I selected.

I spent most of the second and third day getting all of the documents from DR to show my tuition was in fact, paid. I was still left to pick up the classes I wanted and needed, which, I can tell you, was no easy task. I wasn't looking forward to it at all.

At this late stage of the game, the only way to sign up for classes was to go to the department from which the class was offered. If the class was filled, which most of mine were, special permission from the instructor was needed. Since I already had my own seat, I was able to persuade each of them to sign off. My good sense of humor usually helped.

The bigger issue was that the class departments were located in different buildings spread across campus and we were walking to each in about 115° temperatures. Getting around in my wheelchair added to the challenge because I had to find the wheelchair-accessible entrances, which always seemed to be in the back of the building. Finding the elevators proved just as difficult.

Because of the wait time for each signature, I spent the last two days of the week finalizing my registration, leaving only the weekend to find a caregiver before Monday morning class. Mom and I spent our evenings in the lobby socializing with other dorm residents with the hope that one of them would like the job.

We were elated when on the first night of the weekend we met a young woman, Moni, who was quite excited about the prospect. My parents offered to pay her dorm room costs in exchange for her providing my care. After just a few days, mom was on her way home and I was on my way to becoming completely independent from my family (other than the financial support).

Moni and I got along fine; she was someone else I would define as a free spirit. After she got me up and dressed in the morning, we would go our separate ways. I would head for the Union and have breakfast to begin my day. Someone there would serve me and get my food to the table. At the time, I could feed myself.

After eating, I would be off to class, where I was able to take my own notes and such. When I had a break, I would sometimes head back to the room. I could open the door by myself and turn the TV on or I would go socialize at the Union. If the breaks were long enough, I would study at the library.

I would meet Moni midday after lunch, so I could use the restroom. Then, I would be on my own again off to my afternoon classes and dinner at the Union. We were both in our room in the evening doing homework until bedtime. This was our standard weekly routine. On the weekends, I went home, giving her time off.

Shortly after starting college, I decided I should be on birth control. I wasn't seeing anyone at the time, but I wanted to know I was protected if the time should arise. I always did believe in "Better Safe Than Sorry," and this was certainly one of those times.

I wasn't sure how to broach the subject with my mom and truth be told, I didn't need her permission, but we were close and I wanted her blessing. Besides, she would be the one giving me my pill on the weekends. As usual, she surprised me, by agreeing I should be on the pill. She was not condoning my sleeping around, but she wasn't ready to become a grandma in case anything did happen.

On one of my weekends at home, my dad found my packet of pills and went to mom asking why I was on birth control. To keep peace, she told him it was to regulate my period, since I had to have others doing my care. We really did have a unique and close relationship.

95

When I went to the health center to get on the pill, the doctor actually had the nerve to ask me what I wanted it for. I looked at him in utter disbelief and answered pretty matter-of-factly, "So I don't get pregnant."

His reply was more astonishing than his question; he looked at me and said, "I assumed being in the wheelchair, you couldn't do anything like that." All I could bring myself to say was, "Well, you assumed wrong."

I got my prescription and was on my way. I was thrilled to find I was one of those women who were designed to take the pill. I never had any side effects, never gained any weight, and my periods became very short. I loved being on the pill!

I only had one relationship during my first year at college, which was somewhat short-lived. Lasting three months, it was great for my self-esteem and my lovemaking experience. Rick was three years older than me, unlike Steve, who was my age. He took the time to show me what pleased him, as well as taking the time to find out what pleased me.

I had a conversation with him about why someone would want to be with me over a woman who had her full capabilities and I'll never forget his answer; he said he had been to bed with women who were fully capable, but just lay there because they didn't care much about pleasing their partner. What mattered to him most was I wanted to please him, even if there were things I couldn't physically do.

He also told me if I was ever with someone who cared more about what I could do than about being with me, I was with the wrong person. Now I'm not sure if he meant any of what he said, but it was what I needed to hear at that time of my life, and his message was good for my ego.

Rick was also my first experience with oral sex. I bring this up because as he began to pleasure me, all I could think was oh my God, he's going to expect me to do the same thing for him and I didn't have a clue how to pleasure him. I was terrified and didn't enjoy the encounter a whole lot. Somehow, I survived and had a great learning experience. It soon became a wonderful, sexual part of my life.

He was such a good experience for me in other ways. Not only did he share those words of wisdom with me in regards to my fears around my inadequacy, but he also took the time to demonstrate what he wanted me to do to pleasure him by using his mouth on my finger. It was a great way to teach me without embarrassing me. He really was the perfect lover for my early encounters.

At that stage of my life, I was pretty agile and could be positioned in any number of ways for sexual activity. I was able to lie on my back and have my partner put my legs around him, as well my arms, as I did not have that kind of mobility on my own.

I was small and light enough for my partner to roll me on top of himself, though he had to do the actual movement, as I could only lay my head on his shoulder (not enough muscle strength in my neck to hold my head up). I was also still able to lie on my stomach or my side for some variation.

As I wasn't capable of moving myself about to do things to my partner, they had to be versatile and move themselves into positions I could reach them. Kissing their neck or chest required bringing those parts of their bodies to my lips.

Oral sex was another challenge for me because I wasn't able to open my mouth very wide. It required creativity on my part, enhancing my skills with my lips and tongue. There were no complaints I am aware of, and lovemaking seemed to work out fine.

It's funny how protective my dad was about me and men. I guess most fathers are. However, my dad was always encouraging me to go out with someone I'll call "Dan." Bill adored him and was like a dad/mentor to him because Dan didn't have a father. I actually dated him in high school and occasionally during my first year in college.

Well, I finally got tired of hearing how great Dan was and I told my dad he had asked me to go to bed with him. Expecting my dad to blow up and want to kill Dan, I was shocked when he responded, "The little shit is growing up." So much for him being my overprotective father. Too bad I couldn't get him to react that way when it was someone I was really interested in.

Interestingly, as much as my dad thought of Dan, he fell into the category Rick had described to me. He wasn't concerned about what I could or couldn't do in bed, but he was bothered by my disability in public.

Whenever we were out as a group, he would avoid any kind of intimate contact with me, such as sitting together, holding hands, kissing, or anything of that nature. I decided if he was too bothered in public to be affectionate with me then there would be no more affection in private.

One night while partying at Valerie's house, we got fairly drunk or stoned and decided no one should drive. Everyone found a place to lay their head and crash; I took the couch, others were strewn all about and Dan was on the floor.

However, he soon found his way over to me, trying to have his way. I kept telling him no and I explained why, but he wouldn't take no for an answer. He forced himself on me and I was too embarrassed to call out to my friends.

Though I knew I was raped, I could never bring myself to tell anyone because I knew how much my dad cared about him and the hurt I would cause wasn't worth it. I never told anyone until much later in my life.

My mom was so worried about my getting raped in high school, and here I was in college with someone we knew very well when the unthinkable occurred. I wonder if Dan ever thought about what he did to me without my consent. He probably figured since we had slept together in the past, I was just playing hard to get, though I was very clear.

I am happy to say my following college years went by pretty smoothly with none of the obstacles I first experienced. My paperwork was routine now for my tuition and such. My classes were all in place with pre-registration occurring at the end of each semester and my dorm room was established as well. Everything was standard until I decided to move off-campus to an apartment.

The only thing I did have to worry about each semester was my caregiver, which very often was a problem. I usually began each semester with my mother as my roommate until I could find someone else to move in and do my care.

Second semester found me living in the dorm with Moni as my caregiver again, but she was only able to do so for a month. That's when

Jeannie, my friend from high school, decided to join me. She had dropped out of school and was having difficulty at home, so she became my care-giver, and what fun we had.

We spent a great deal of time listening to the radio, since she wasn't old enough to go into any of the college bars, and we developed a friend-ship with one of the DJs. We spent many an hour talking with him during those late-nights on the weekends I was now spending at school, rather than going home all the time.

I had a little refrigerator, a toaster oven, and food for the weekend because the cafeteria wasn't open for use of the meal ticket on Saturdays or Sundays. Jeannie and I became quite the little gourmets with our small, simple kitchen.

I also learned I liked sleeping in more than eating breakfast, so I only used my meal tickets for lunch and dinner and just kept some quick breakfast foods handy in my dorm room.

One shopping experience I will never forget involved Jeannie and her antics. We were in the grocery store, and out of the blue she started dragging her leg behind her, changing her voice to sound like she had an intellectual disability and saying "Laurie, when's it my turn to ride in the wheelchair, you said I could have a turn?"

I was so embarrassed that I headed straight for the door, all the while Jeannie was right behind me dragging her leg and continuing with her question. We laughed so hard when we got back to the dorm, I almost wet my pants. I later made her go shopping by herself for everything we didn't get earlier in the day.

We had a pretty tight group of friends that semester—Moni, Jeannie, Sharon, Roger, Jim, Barbara, Mary, and Mike (Rick was long gone). We were a mellow group, smoked a little weed, drank a little alcohol, but for those of us who were students, school always came first. My grades were very important to me.

After one party at Jim's place, we all went home late into the night and no one had seen Mike. He appeared the next morning with his beauti-ful long hair frizzed and sticking out all over, like he put his finger in a light socket. We asked him what happened and he said he took a shower.

He couldn't find any shampoo, so he used "Janitor in a Drum." He was lucky to have any hair left at all—eyes and skin for that matter.

He obviously had way too much to drink (Jack Daniel's was his preference) or he was doing a whole lot more drugs than weed; it was the funniest thing we'd ever seen. I really did have friends from all walks of life and I often wondered where I managed to find many of them. I was just beginning to get a picture of the bigger world I was living in.

During the spring an outdoor concert was scheduled, to include Uriah Heap, Kiss, Ted Nugent, and Bob Seger. I was so excited as I remembered my invitation from last summer, so I raced right out and got tickets. What a good time I was going to have! This time, I would be brave and join them for a party at their hotel. I was older and could handle myself in such a situation (or so I thought).

To my dismay, three days before the concert Uriah Heap cancelled and there was no refund on the tickets because the other groups were still performing. I was really bummed, but decided to make the best of it and went with a group of friends for fresh air, good music, and a lot of fun.

It was just an open field with no assigned seating, just blankets on the grassy knoll. There were a lot of drugs floating around in Frisbees for the taking. I was never into drugs much beyond weed, so I really wasn't interested. However, the majority of the crowd was, and by early evening things got a little restless.

Thankfully, I had a lot of friends there because everyone started pushing to get closer to the stage and people were actually getting trampled. My friends, as well as some other guys, formed a human fence around me, locking their bodies tight to ensure that no one knocked me over or hurt me in any way. It was quite scary and I decided no more concerts like that one for me again.

I went home for the summer with one year of college behind me, and Jeannie returned home as well. However, I still had four years to go, as I was only taking 12 units a semester, instead of the usual 15 units. I was doing this to make things a little easier and to keep my GPA at a 3.00 or better. Taking five years to graduate, instead of four was okay.

I decided on my course of study fairly early in my college career. I would major in speech pathology, with a minor in special education, receiving a bachelor of science degree in Communication Disorders when I was done with the program.

I couldn't wait to get beyond all of the general education courses and start taking things of interest to me. The most unbelievable part of my coursework thus far, was I had to take Arizona and National Government again!

Not only was this my fourth time through this crap, I had the worst teacher anyone could imagine with the worst testing procedures I ever experienced. He was worse than Behrens, which I didn't think was possible. As I said earlier, maybe I was meant to be in politics.

All his tests were multiple-choice and the answers went something like this: (1) a & b, (2) b & d, (3) a, b, & c, (4) all of the above, and (5) none of the above. I hate this kind of test. I might be sure of one answer or maybe even two, but the various combinations were always difficult for me.

Needless to say, I didn't do very well. Though I had taken the subject several times over, I still managed to get a "D" for my final grade It then took me two years to fix my cumulative GPA. So much for the "taking fewer units" idea.

While home for the summer, I went to Illinois for a month. I loved spending time with each of my friends. I sure miss them a lot. There was always something special to do with each of them.

I attended another concert with Karen, but this time we sat in the VIP box seats because my biological father, Art, had some connections. We saw Jefferson Airplane (or maybe they were Jefferson Starship by then; I don't remember). I do know we had fun.

I convinced one of my friends to come to Arizona to be my caregiver at college for my second year/third semester. Debbie was the same friend who came with me when we first moved to Arizona. I was excited—I was going to have a part of Illinois with me again.

We arrived back at college the week before classes started. I had the same dorm room as the year before and I was very comfortable. My same friends of last year, Moni, Sharon, Barbara and Mary (suite mates), Jim and a few others were still around, and in no time at all, the gang was hanging out together.

During the first week we went to a fraternity party and several friends were playing in the band. There I met Kevin, whom I consider to be my first true love. He was a friend of Jim's and one of the guys in the band, but he sat by himself looking lonely for most of the evening. I felt bad for him and decided to strike up a conversation. That's what I would have wanted someone to do if it was me.

Before the night was over, we were fairly well acquainted and getting along really well. He was shy, which made him even more attractive to me. He wasn't like the fraternity guys, who were aggressive, always trying to get you upstairs to the bedrooms. By the time we got back to the dorm, I didn't want the night to end.

The next few days I continued to probe Jim for any information I could get about Kevin, but he remained quiet and uninformative. I was going crazy trying to figure out how to reconnect with him, but I was at a loss.

A week later, the band was playing at a local bar and we all went to provide moral support. I had no idea Kevin would be there, and I arranged to meet for the evening one of the bouncers I was occasionally dating.

You can imagine my surprise and excitement when I found Kevin helping the band set up in the back of the bar by the dance floor. The bar had three rooms: front room, bar and tables; middle room, pool tables and other games; and the back room, stage and dance floor. This design worked out well for me.

There I was on a semi-date with the bouncer in the front room and making out in the back with the guy I'm really interested in. I spent the evening traveling a lot between rooms and keeping the guys in their respective areas. I didn't want to ruin things with the bouncer if Kevin didn't return the interest.

By the end of the night, Kevin made clear he and I were on the same page. I declined an invitation from the bouncer for an after-hours get-together, happy that I didn't have to rely on my ace in the hole, but a girl's got to do what a girl's got to do.

From then on, Kevin and I were together every chance we had. Making love was incredible! We were each other's third lover. We had very limited experience, but learning and experimenting together brought us each the most pleasure.

Kevin was my second introduction to oral sex, both receiving and giving, and I knew in my heart this special gift was only meant for those I truly loved. I had never felt like this before and I knew he felt the same way.

I was absolutely sure we would spend the rest of our lives together. As my first true love, the love of my life, we had our whole lives ahead of us. I was in heaven. I was so young and had such belief in love, honesty, and forever.

Though Debbie had made other friends, she was feeling left out and abandoned with all my time being spent with Kevin. Before too long, feeling very homesick, she decided to return to Illinois, and I couldn't blame her. I wasn't sure what I was going to do about a caregiver, but then Mary, one of my suitemates, offered to do my care, while remaining in her room with Barbara.

It couldn't have worked out any better for me; now I had the room to myself and Kevin spent most nights with me. I was falling more in love with him day after day, the sex kept getting better and better, and my parents loved him to death too. What more could a girl ask for?

Kevin lived with his brother and sister-in-law who had rescued him from a not-so-great situation, and he felt he owed his life to them. They seemed to like me a lot too. They were excited he was coming out of his shell and having a social life. However, by Christmas, his sister-in-law started doing things to break us up.

She felt we had gotten way too serious, way too fast, and wasn't liking me so much anymore. She wanted him at home more and more, limiting our time together, and she fully expected him to cooperate.

When he did spend the night, she would call early in the morning needing him for one thing or another. She also started having female company over for dinner to meet him. He generally obliged her every request out of respect and obligation. It was, however, making me crazy, and I was becoming very resentful.

By late January we were hardly seeing each other at all. Mary could no longer do my care, so I found a girl, Linda, who liked her freedom, and without Kevin around very much, I needed her more than she wanted to be available. That made my everyday life quite difficult, to say the least.

I should've had Linda during the fall when my friend was here and wanted attention, and my friend from Illinois during the spring when I had lots of attention and free time to give, but things don't always work out like we want. I was a very unhappy girl and my fourth semester was not starting out on a very good note.

By mid February, things were really bad for me and Kevin. His sister-in-law called whenever he did manage to come by, and if he spent the night, her calls always came at the most critical time. Needless to say, our sex life was taking a nosedive. I was feeling neglected, my feelings were hurt and whenever our group got together he wasn't around or had to depart early, leaving me dateless.

During one of those gatherings, one of our group members had a new friend visiting. Joe was from California and very nice. I found out what it was like to have attention again. At evening's end, everyone went to their respective rooms with their partners, leaving Joe and me alone.

We talked for most of the night and then things just kind of happened. I am not justifying my actions, because what I did was the worst thing anyone can do to another person they claim to love. I cheated on Kevin, and I can't begin to explain the remorse and the guilt I was experiencing the minute we were done.

The following morning, when everyone else got up, I was asleep on the couch completely dressed and Joe was on the floor in his sleeping bag. No one knew or even suspected Joe and I had been together.

However, Kevin and I promised to always be truthful with one another, but I must say, it was probably the worst decision of my life to tell him. Well, the cheating was the worst decision, but telling Kevin was second to that.

All I succeeded in doing was hurting him, and that was certainly not my intention. The last thing I ever wanted to do was hurt him. I begged for his forgiveness and promised I would never be unfaithful again, and for the moment he accepted my apology and forgave me.

A month later he was at one of our group parties, which I could not attend, and he cheated on me with a new visitor. Not that I didn't have it coming, but he never told me. I found out from friends, and I was humiliated.

Maybe he was trying to protect me from the hurt, but it just seemed he was being dishonest and our beautiful relationship came to an abrupt end. His sister-in-law had won. She got her way. I, on the other hand, learned one of the most difficult lessons in my young life, and it was all my own doing.

The rest of the fourth semester was somewhat uneventful. I threw myself into my school work and tried not to think about Kevin. I returned home for the summer and met a guy I started dating. He and I, along with a couple of friends, decided to take a road trip back to Illinois.

While on our way there, I discovered my new guy had a violent streak that only got worse once we were in Illinois. Things were so bad that I called my mom. She flew out to my rescue and brought my friend and me back home, leaving the violent bastard on his own. He never actually hit me, but came awfully close. I was definitely afraid for my well-being.

I don't know how I got involved with him, but I'm sure it had something to do with being on the rebound and wanting to be loved. Although my disability was well received as far as dating went, I was never quite confident about acceptance for long-term relationships, Kevin excluded.

I even called Kevin from Illinois for the calming effect of his voice. We remained friends for many years. Of course, I wanted so much more than to be friends. I still loved him with all my heart and prayed for a miracle.

I was much relieved to be back home and starting college again (third year/fifth semester). My caregiver, April, was a friend of my high-school friend Roy. We rented a room in an apartment with another girl. In a very short time, we realized this set up was not going to work because April had a boyfriend, and she and I shared a room.

So we left that two-bedroom apartment for another, where she and her boyfriend would share a room and I would have the other. After a month, her boyfriend disappeared, along with the rent money and the deposit. I guess I wasn't the only one with bad luck when it comes to men. April was devastated and decided to move on with her life, on her own.

Mom and I found another apartment for much less rent, with one very large bedroom. I advertised amongst my classes and soon found a caregiver from my health class, Sue. Once again, I was fairly independent. I came and went on my own. School was within walking distance, as were the stores and bars.

Sue would get me up in the morning, be there to put me to bed in the evening, and we would meet midday for the restroom. My routine became fairly standard and school was my primary focus. I dated occasionally and Kevin continued to drop by and we often made love. Maybe we'd get back together someday. I could only hope.

I was finally taking classes I was interested in and pertained to my major. I really enjoyed Speech Pathology and I was looking forward to the following year when there would be practicum, working with real people, doing real therapy.

By spring of 1976, my parents helped me to buy a house. It was a three-bedroom, one-bath with a carport converted into a living room, leaving the original living room as the dining room with a bigger kitchen. There was also an inside laundry room and storage room.

My house payment was only $200 a month, so we quickly converted the dining room into a fourth bedroom and rented out two of the bedrooms for $100 each. I was rent-free with the ability to provide my caregiver free room and board and I had several hundred dollars provided by DR to live on.

The house was within biking distance from campus and close to a few popular college bars (Minder Binders comes to mind), which made the rooms very desirable. I never had a hard time keeping them rented, which was a good thing.

I Can Dance

The summer after buying the house, I had both rooms rented. The family of one of my roommates owned a house down in Mexico right on the beach. He took different groups of us there on several occasions and we always had a great time. I used my Hogue stroller to navigate the sandy beach. Interestingly, the roommate's last name was also Hogue. Small world.

The beach house had a stocked bar, the closets were full, and minimal packing was needed for a weekend. Each bedroom had a view of the beach or the courtyard, a fireplace, and its own bathroom, with a shower large enough for 10 people. This place would normally cost big bucks, but we enjoyed it for free.

One weekend, six of us (three couples) went down to party and relax. We were about one hundred yards from the beach and we girls were sunbathing topless, figuring no one could see us. However, we saw some guys walking on the beach. We waved and they waved back. We happened to have a pair of binoculars and we found they also had a pair. I learned another good lesson.

I also took my mom, dad, and other family and friends on a weekend trip, and besides the terrible sunburn, we all had a good time. We did some clam digging and made a seafood stew from our catch of the day, which was delicious. One more of the benefits of roommates, especially as I loved to travel.

Jeannie moved back in with me and the good times continued. She did my care through the fall, which began my fourth year/seventh semester. Ed also rented a room from me in the fall. He was going to school to become a carpenter.

One day he brought a friend home from school. It was love at first sight for Jeannie and Reid. Within a month, Reid moved in with Jeannie. Having four other roommates really helped in paying the utilities.

Renters came and went for the one bedroom we had available. One time while showing the room, Jeannie pulled one of her crazy stunts. She answered the door wearing short shorts, an afro wig shoved in her pants, hair sticking out of the legs and over the top and two grapefruits under her shirt, hanging to her belly. As she answered the door, she was scratching at the hair. I can't imagine why we did not get that renter. Just one more of her shenanigans

Kevin continued to drop by fairly regularly and spend the night. Though it had been almost two years since we broke up, we were still sleeping together. Neither of us had a serious partner, just some occasional dating.

He also bought a house a few blocks from mine. You'd think he'd want to live a little further away if he truly wanted to forget me. Who knows? My hopes were still very much alive.

We had a great Halloween party the fall of 1976. I was Cleopatra and Jeannie was a belly dancer, with Reid as her sheik. Ed was a hunter and my friend Debi was a turkey. There were some great costumes, fog filled the room, our pet tarantula sat on a piece of driftwood in the doorway, and we were joined by another party from down the street for a scavenger hunt. It was quite the event.

However, the party ended on a very sour note. Kevin showed up later in the evening while a group of us went to another party, and he slept with my good friend. I wish I could've just been over him, but obviously I was not, because I was very hurt. Maybe he was trying to permanently bring us to an end.

I was well into my major courses by now and had formed a strong study group with my fellow classmates. School was going well; I had finally gotten enough A's and B's to overcome the "D" I got my freshman year and was able to bring my GPA to where it belonged.

I was doing real therapy now with real people, mostly articulation, but some stuttering as well. Dr. Mower was my advisor. He was well known for several books he'd written on articulation. His nickname for me (like Mr. Wolpert in high school) was "Trouble," although I can't begin to imagine why.

One of my other instructors, who taught language acquisition, terrified me with his first true/false/explain exams of the semester. One of the questions read like this: "Whorf [linguist Benjamin Lee Whorf] likens language to a cloak following the contour of thought. True or False? Explain." As you can see, it freaked me out so much some 35 years later I can still remember the question.

Each following semester I took a course from that professor, and the courses got easier and easier for me. I am pleased to report none of my other classes ever traumatized me like that one. I loved my anatomy classes and my major in general. My Special Education courses were about disabilities and were pretty easy for me. College was a lot of fun and an incredible experience.

Spring of 1977 brought a close to my fourth year. Jeannie and Reid moved into their own place and I hired Allison as my caregiver. Nothing else too eventful occurred. Classes continued, now and then a new friend would join our group, Kevin still dropped by and I couldn't say no, though I know I should have. I wasn't dating anyone new or in a relationship, just pretty casual and life was okay.

One Friday afternoon I had a late afternoon class on the third floor. I would often go into the elevator on my own, having someone push the button for me. The elevator went to the fourth floor, the doors opened, and there before me was a floor entirely under construction.

I usually dart out quickly to avoid having the doors close on me, but for some reason I didn't. It's a good thing, because I would've been trapped for the entire weekend. No one would have thought to look for me on that floor. I sat there shaking while the doors closed. About 45 minutes later the elevator got called down. This time I raced out! I would never ride alone again.

By semester's end, I knew I no longer wanted a female caregiver. There was always a problem. Either the lifting became too much, it was their time of the month with cramps, they had to do their makeup or their hair, or they were catty or just moody. Always something. So, in the fall I would hire a male caregiver.

Instead of going to Illinois that summer I went with friends to California. The trip was very eye opening in regards to having a disability. The state had a program called In-Home Supportive Services (IHSS), which paid a fairly good wage to caregivers. California also supplemented the federal SSI amount, so people with disabilities had more money to live on. There was nothing like that in Arizona.

California was a very disability-friendly state and very accessible. So once I graduated, I was going to move to California, especially since Arizona didn't hold anything for me anymore. My parents decided to put the house on the market in early January in hopes it would sell by the time I left in the late summer of 1978.

As I mentioned earlier, my mom always came with me at the beginning of every new semester to find a caregiver if I didn't already have one set up. That fall was no different. I found Mark in just a week. His girlfriend completely accepted the situation, making me very comfortable.

He was a big guy, so lifting me was never an issue, and the semester went really smoothly. I wasn't looking to get involved with anyone, knowing I was going to be moving in the summer, so I spent most of my time focused on school and just hanging out with my friends.

The last days of the fall semester were here, my finals were over and the house was decorated for Christmas. Mark's girlfriend was spending the night and they were in his room for some private time.

I sat on the couch by myself enjoying the light of the Christmas tree, but feeling very sad Kevin and I hadn't managed to work things out. I wanted so much to be in his arms holding him tight.

I had Mark put me to bed around 10:00, and not 15 minutes later, there was a knock at the front door. I knew immediately who it was. Sure enough, when Mark answered, he found Kevin wanting to come in and talk to me. Of course, my answer was yes, and we both knew what that meant.

This night was different from our other lovemaking sessions; we made love most of the night, like when we were first together. We eventually fell asleep in one another's arms from sheer exhaustion and slept well into the morning (he would usually go home after the lovemaking, never spending the night).

I was convinced we were finally going to get back together. This single act was all I needed to assure me we were meant to be. I prayed and prayed we would reunite. He left in the morning and told me he would call soon.

I went home for Christmas break, which was about a month long, and no phone call. I was devastated. I wrote to him professing my love and pointing out he hadn't helped matters by continuing to come around for the last four years. I told him of my plans to move to California, to cut all ties, moving on with my life.

I gave him one month to think about us; if I didn't hear anything, I would accept he didn't feel the same, in which case, my house would go on the market and I would move forward with my plan. I never heard from him and with my heart breaking, I knew I had to get over Kevin.

Before leaving for Christmas break, Mark told me he would not be coming back because he and his girlfriend wanted their own place. He didn't want to leave me without a caregiver, and he had a friend who was very interested in the job. I trusted Mark and was willing to give his friend Sam a try.

I met Sam before heading home for the holidays and we agreed that he would be my next attendant. He was gorgeous and all of my friends wanted to date him, sleep with him, marry him, anything they could. He did sleep with several of them, but he and I were just great friends.

It would be easy to become sexually involved with a male caregiver considering all of the intimate things they did for me, but I knew it could mess up a good caregiving situation. So I made the rule never to get involved with my attendant.

As with any new caregiver, there's a lot of stress, but especially with a male. Sam, however, put me completely at ease our first day together. I came home from class and he suggested cleaning me up in those private areas, as he was sure I must be uncomfortable after sitting all day in the heat. I had been very nervous about how I was going to ask him to do just that.

Architecture was his major, and he had no specific nursing training, but he was a natural for the job. He learned everything very quickly and rarely did I have to show him how to do any part of my care more than once. He was athletic, intelligent and well-rounded. He was just a good person. My disability came in handy for him too; he used me for his accessibility designs for school projects.

The house went on the market in January, sold in just a few weeks, and would be turned over to the new owners a week after graduation near the end of May. I graduated with honors earning a bachelor's degree. However, to work in the field of speech pathology, a master's degree was required. So, I wasn't quite done yet. My California plan included a year off to establish my residency, and then I would go back to school.

I still needed two practicum courses to complete my requirements for admission to graduate school, so I took them at ASU before my move. I got reconnected with my gay friend Steve from high school and he decided to move to California with me. How cool is that! Now I wouldn't have to move on my own.

He also agreed to be my caregiver at ASU for my last two practicum courses. Believe it or not, we were staying in the dorm I first tried to get into my freshman year. There was now a ramp to the level where the elevator is, making the dorm accessible.

However, the dorm was still for women only, so we kept Steve out of sight. He always came in the back, was never seen in the morning or after curfew. I can't believe we never got caught.

During this time, I developed a new problem. I began having trouble balancing on the toilet, which I used for having a bowel movement, though I still used a bedpan for urinating. I hoped it was due to the style of toilet, but whatever the reason, something had to be done.

I acquired a shower/potty chair on wheels to use over the toilet. Now, I had yet one more piece of equipment in my entourage. I didn't like it, but I had to admit it was safer for me and better for my caregiver, not having to carry me so far.

Though I was excited about the future, I knew there would be some unpleasant physical changes due to my disability, which I would have to learn to accept. It was the adult thing to do. Doing what's best is not always what we like best. Another one of life's lessons.

My friends were throwing me a going away party and asked who to invite. Every part of me wanted to say Kevin, but I knew how the evening would go. We would spend the night together and it would only make moving away harder than ever. It had been seven months since I even talked with him and I had to keep it that way.

Then one day as I was coming out of the dorm, he was there delivering a pizza. He was surprised to see me, as I was to see him. I explained my house was sold and I would be off to California very soon. Again, I ached to tell him about the party, but I was determined to protect myself from any more hurt and I held strong. It also took all of my willpower not to order a pizza during my time remaining.

The party was great. All of my best friends were there, with a lot of tears and hugs, and then Steve and I were on our way. My parents had gone out earlier to Sacramento, which is where I decided to settle, and found us an apartment. Steve and I were excited about our new journey and what lay ahead.

So there we were, with the van packed to its max on our "California or Bust" trek.

12. Post Degree, Pre Marriage

Steve and I arrived in California in August 1978. The apartment my parents selected for us was in Rancho Cordova, a suburb east of Sacramento. We weren't thrilled with the apartment complex, and so two months later moved into a duplex with a fireplace and a yard.

Things were pretty much accessible, though there was a small step from the living room to the rest of the house. We had a ramp, so I could maneuver throughout. The duplex had only one bathroom, but it was just the two of us, so we were fine.

My kitchen chair no longer worked in the tub for my showers because I couldn't balance without sides and the padding got old and soggy and duct tape could only do so much. We graduated to a lawn chair.

Before too long, we were the proud parents of a Labrador Retriever. We named her Sierra Vista Carmichael Terra Cotta Sandia. Quite the name for one small puppy; it was our way of compromise.

One of the things Steve and I discussed before moving in together was his getting away from the gay lifestyle and having more straight friends as my roommate. We really were in for quite a surprise and a bit more compromising.

Residency for school was going to take a year, so Steve and I started dancing in our free time. Disco dancing was popular. I often danced in my wheelchair from the waist up to rock 'n' roll, but I hadn't figured out how to do touch dancing like a disco routine.

Steve and I started going to a little bar around the corner to practice every afternoon. There usually wasn't anyone there in the middle of the day and we had the jukebox for music.

We choreographed a dance in which I moved in and pulled out using my control box as though Steve was doing it, and we even mastered an under-the-arm spin. We got quite good and were ready to go public. I wore a white dress with black trim and he wore black pants and a white shirt; we looked very professional.

We went to our first disco, Bojangles, (BJ's). We weren't aware it was a gay bar (actually more of a mixed bar), until we were there for an entire evening, but regardless of the clientele, everyone was impressed and we had a great time.

We started making our first real friends there and spending a great deal of our time. From then on, it seemed no matter who we met or where, they would be gay, and I thought San Francisco was the Gay Capital of the World.

We also volunteered at a nursing home several days a week, visiting, reading and listening. We met a guy playing the flute for several of the residents. We later ran into him at BJ's. His name was Norman, and he would come to play a much bigger role in my life, more than I could ever imagine.

While at the grocery store one day, the guy bagging our groceries struck up a conversation with us and a few nights later we saw him at BJ's. His name was Mike, and yes, he was gay as well.

We also became friends with Rick, Scott, John, and several others we met somewhere other than the bar, and they were also gay. I was beginning to think there were no straight people in Sacramento.

Now mind you, Steve was one of my closest friends and I have no problem with homosexuality, but after a while, we didn't have any straight friends, which wasn't so great for my dating situation. I did manage to meet a few guys who were bisexual, so I did some occasional dating, but for the most part, not so much.

It's funny how things work out. Steve wanted to distance himself from the gay lifestyle with more straight friends and we didn't have any. I wanted to meet someone new and fall in love, but I wasn't meeting any available straight men. Irony at its finest!

I even took my mother to the bar when she came to visit because she loved to dance. I couldn't believe it, there was my mother teaching several gay men how to dance. One of her best friends in her young adulthood was also gay, so she wasn't at all put off. I also, had my own special table at BJ's.

I was friends with the owner and I teased him, saying, "I don't pick up men in your bar, I don't drink alcohol in your bar, and with a new raised dance floor, I don't dance in your bar, yet I add class to your bar." I told him I deserved my own table and I wasn't paying a cover charge, and he agreed. Like I've said, a good sense of humor goes a long way.

I had a great relationship with my gay friends and I used to give them rides on my wheelchair, chiming in with, "Whoever said I couldn't pick up a gay man?" I also told them I was going to get a T-shirt that said, "Come straight to me."

I used to tell them I was going to line them up for speech therapy to get rid of their lisps. They always got a kick out of me and loved my teasing. They knew it was always in fun, no harm intended, and trust me, they gave me a hard time too.

Sacramento had a great muscle disease clinic (associated with the Muscular Dystrophy Association, MDA). The doctors found my records to be anything but complete. They suggested I have a few tests to determine my exact diagnosis. Of course, the one test needed was an EMG (the one with the needles jabbing into my limbs). I reluctantly agreed.

I was diagnosed as having spinal muscular atrophy type 2 (SMA), also known as anterior horn cell disease and Werdnig Hoffman disease (another of the 40 diseases under the MD umbrella). Basically, my brain sends a message to my spine, but there aren't enough cells to carry the message to the muscles. When muscles aren't stimulated, they atrophy (deteriorate).

This disease wasn't nearly as bad as all my previous diagnoses, and actually had a prognosis of a normal life span. I'd have some weakening and loss of function over the years, but for the most part, I could expect to live an average number of years.

I am thankful that it wasn't type 1, which usually results in death before the age of two, and regretful that it wasn't Type 3, with onset much later in life, thus much less disabling for a much longer period of time. At least, I was going to be alive, and technology, along with people, would give me quality of life.

Six months later, I learned from the MDA clinic that I needed back surgery. The curvature of my spine was 145 degrees, with my hip bone up under my arm pit and my lung on the verge of collapse. My spine needed to be fused. Breathing is a very important part of life, so of course I agreed to have the operation.

My mom was very fearful about my undergoing major surgery because of the general anesthesia, but I knew it had to be done if I wanted to be around more than just a few years. The surgery was scheduled for August 1, 1979, six months hence.

Around that same time (January 1979), Steve decided to return to Bible College to try renouncing his homosexuality and living a straight lifestyle. He had been involved with several guys since we moved here and was going through a great deal of conflict as his physical desires clashed with his spiritual beliefs.

Norman (the flute player from the nursing home and bar) became my caregiver when Steve left. He was a health food/holistic medicine kind of guy. So, from February to July I let him practice on me.

I ate all kinds of health foods, took a lot of vitamins, and let him perform different types of massage, which I enjoyed. I met his family and they were very nice. His grandmother was a nurse and I loved her to death.

Norman was bisexual, and we did eventually become intimate. I made it clear to him if we were going to be a couple, there would be no others, as I was not going to risk a disease. He agreed to be monogamous.

I was fearful about my upcoming surgery. (I knew how serious and risky general anesthesia was for me.) I decided to take a road trip to Illinois to see all of my friends, just in case I didn't live through the surgery. I know, very morbid thought, but what can I say, I am a realist. Norman and I went to Arizona to see my parents before heading across the country.

While at my parents' home, I had the most horrifying, humiliating, embarrassing situation I could ever imagine happening. Norman and I were sleeping in my van because my parents only had one bedroom. I had my head lying on his tummy, while he was rubbing my back and I saw something moving in the hairline from his belly button down to his groin. Further investigation concluded he had crabs.

It didn't take a rocket scientist to know that I, too, would have them. I had no choice but to tell my parents, as they were at risk, since we had been using their towels and such. My mom quickly got a prescription from the family doctor and we were all treated in no time at all. Nonetheless, I couldn't get out of there quick enough.

Norman assured me he contracted them before we got together. He swore he hadn't been with anyone else since then. I'm not sure I bought his story, but we were on the road, so I would have to deal with this when I got home.

The trip to Illinois was great, like always. We stayed at everyone's home for at least a couple of days each. I was able to spend time with everyone important to me, both friends and family, and I was more than ready to face the risk of surgery.

Upon our arrival home, Norman got a call from the VD clinic, informing him they had been given his name as a sexual partner to someone who had tested positive for syphilis. Based on that information, he was required to come in and be tested and give all of the names of his sexual partners.

If he came up positive, his partners would be contacted and have to come in for testing as well. I was horrified! First, there was the humiliation with crabs, and now the possibility of syphilis. Luckily, his results were negative and I didn't have to go in, but I decided once I was recovered from my surgery, he was out. As for the intimacy we shared, over and done when he got the call.

Mom had talked with my birth father, Art, and asked him to come out to my place to help with my care after the surgery, so it didn't become too much of a burden on any one person. I was expected to be in the hospital anywhere from four to six weeks and she felt he should be part of it. To my surprise, he came for the operation.

I went into the hospital and met both my medical team and my surgical team. They were very nice. I made it clear I was only to have my blood drawn once a day, so they'd better be sure about what tests they wanted to run each day. I had very long hair, which I put up on top of my head in a ponytail that could be brushed daily, and so my hospital life began.

My memory of the surgery and the time immediately following is somewhat groggy. I know my mother and Bill were there, as well as Art, and Norman came by occasionally. Dr. Benson, my primary surgeon visited me several times a day. Soon I was familiar with my hospital staff. They were like another family.

One of my regular nurses, Susan, and I became good friends. Our friendship continued for many years after my hospital stay until we lost track of one another. I was in the hospital for exactly four weeks, with my surgeries being two weeks apart instead of the six weeks initially predicted.

The first surgery was from the front, on my right side under my rib cage. A Dwyer apparatus, which is like a metal bracket, was placed along my spine with screws going into several vertebrae. A rib was removed and chipped into smaller pieces of bone to go between the vertebrae, to seal as one solid bone.

However, there was a small mishap when the doctor handed my rib to the other doctor: it fell on the floor. They tried putting my rib in the sterilizer, but it turned brown and they decided to remove a second rib instead of using that one. What can I say, doctors are human too.

This first surgery took approximately eight hours. I came out of it quite well and even made a joke when they told me about my rib; I asked if I was going to get an Adam. They looked at me a bit puzzled, until I reminded them that when Adam gave up a rib he got an Eve, and it was only fair that I should get an Adam.

They were quite amused that after such a traumatic event, I still had a sense of humor. It took about two weeks until I recovered enough to undergo the second surgery. It seemed like forever, but was much quicker than anticipated.

My second surgery was from the back and lasted six hours. An incision was made along my spine and two stainless steel rods were inserted. The Harrington rods were placed where my hip and shoulder blade were touching and attached to my pelvic bone and my shoulder blade.

I was only straightened to 70 degrees because that was as much as my spinal cord could stretch. They were fearful it could snap. I healed remarkably well from this surgery as well, and was ready to go home after just another two weeks.

My last day in the hospital, I ordered Chinese food to feed all of my nurses and doctors on all three shifts of that day. My room was like a Chinese buffet with staff coming and going all day.

They were quite touched, but it was the least I could do to thank them for their special time and care. I know it's their job and they get paid to do it, but sometimes it's not a very nice job and people don't always treat them very well, so I thought this would be something kind and different.

Though I was going home, I still had to be flat on my back for three months before becoming upright. I had a hospital bed set up in the dining room so I could be in the middle of everything rather than being closed up in my bedroom. I always did like being the center of attention.

My mom stayed for a week after my return home and Norman continued as my caregiver. My father (Art) was also there for a short while longer, not much help. Soon everyone was gone and Norman and I found ourselves alone.

To my dismay, Norman was involved in another holistic health treatment, which involved rubbing his urine into his skin all over his body and drinking the rest. He said it was an old Indian culture ritual. Neither of us were old Indians, and I found it disgusting, but wasn't in a position to do anything about it.

His grandmother, the nurse, stopped over one day to visit us and had a fit when she heard about this. She lectured him about my open wounds, my susceptibility to infection, and the risk he was putting me at. He promised to stop.

I was too embarrassed to call my mom and ask her to come back, so I called Steve and told him what was going on. He told me he would return by the end of the week. True to his word, he was there by the following afternoon, at which point I asked Norman to be on his way. The following months were quite interesting to say the least.

Steve arrived sometime near the end of September to find me trying to deal with the pain. The first weeks after my return home from the hospital were primarily spent trying to be comfortable. I found every position imaginable for my legs with this lying-on-my-back thing.

While in the hospital, I received several pain shots a day in my thighs, and my legs were numb. I feared some nerve damage or paralysis from the stretching of my spine, but it was just from all the needles.

So, during all of September, even though I was taking pain pills I had a constant burning sensation in my legs and felt like somebody was holding a match to them. The pain pills offered no relief.

Art returned shortly after Steve came back with his wife Pat and their son, Artie, my half-brother, who was now 10 years old. They were supposedly there to help out, but truth be told, they usually went out in the evening leaving Artie in our care, and they slept most of the day, while he was in school.

Steve and I both slept in the dining room, leaving both bedrooms available to make them feel at home, but I believe they went a little overboard. It was really quite weird. The place belonged to me and Steve, but they often told us when we should go to bed and such.

Thankfully, sometime in October they decided to move to Tahoe and look for work. They asked us to keep Artie until they were settled. We got involved with his school, as now we were acting as parents, which we were both unprepared for. Parent-teacher conferences, school fundraisers, and homework were but a few things we were now participating in, and, to think, all of this from a gurney.

October found me in a little less pain, and I managed to wean myself from the pain medications. The burning sensation in my legs had subsided, only to be replaced with a constant itching. No matter how much I scratched, there was no relief from the itch. Supposedly it was all part of the healing process.

Steve and I had rented the gurney. He would transfer me to the gurney and wheel me out to my van and into the back as with an ambulance. We would often go to Artie's school functions, the lake, or even the swap meet.

Once at the swap meet we were piling clothes we purchased on top of me on the gurney. Steve parked me alongside a table full of clothing to look through it and my feet were facing the aisle. All of a sudden, I felt somebody grab my foot.

I screamed, as did the poor woman grabbing me. She thought I was a table of clothing and shoes for sale, never imagining they were attached to someone's feet. After initially giving each other a heart attack, we couldn't stop laughing.

Another time, we attended a show in Lake Tahoe. Jerry Lewis was performing an adult comedy routine. I was provided with a special section where my gurney would fit and I would be able to see. It was too perfect.

Everyone kept asking me why I was on the gurney and I replied, "I was trying to ski and there was no snow." This was funny because Lake Tahoe is known for skiing, but it wasn't ski season yet. I got a lot of strange looks. Steve and I had a good laugh.

The coolest gurney experience was at Halloween. Since I had so much of the hospital paraphernalia, I decided to go as a patient or an accident victim. I wore my hospital gown, wrapped my leg in newspaper and gauze to look like a cast, and used makeup to create bruises and gashes all over my body.

My head and arm were bandaged, I had a black eye, and I looked like I belonged in an emergency room. My friend who worked at a pharmacy got me an IV bottle. We hung it from a curtain rod mounted to the gurney and ran a tube down to my hand, where we taped it to look like it was actually going into my skin.

I also, had a bedpan by my feet holding our cigarettes and lighter and an emesis basin by my head for our keys and such. I really looked the part, if I do say so myself.

Steve, of course, was my doctor. He wore a pair of scrubs with a white overcoat. We stopped at the hospital where my friend Susan (the nurse from my surgery) worked to borrow her stethoscope. I waited in the car while Steve went in and he said he felt like a real doctor. It was funny.

Our night out included going to two bars that were having contests. We won $100 first prize at the first place for staying in character the whole evening. They didn't realize it was very real—at least parts were. I even managed to flirt with a few guys and got them to sign my cast with their phone numbers.

At the second place, we won first prize again, a weekend in Las Vegas. We couldn't believe we had won first place twice. We had such a great time. I guess you could say there was another benefit to my surgery. Another important lesson in my young life: even the worst situations can be made positive.

I think this is where the line came from, "When God gives you lemons, make lemonade." I had already been living my life with that guideline, but I came to recognize it at that time.

I finally got to sit up in late November. I was so very happy and so very dizzy. It was very strange; I was having a hard time balancing with these new inches added to my torso. I had grown from 5' to 5'3". As happy as I was about sitting up, there were some not-so-happy things that went along with it.

The first problem I had to deal with was that I could no longer bring my hands up to my face, which had a very serious consequence: I could no longer feed myself. At first we thought it might be due to the further distance my arms needed to go from the table to my mouth, but ultimately we figured it was the lack of use for three months because my hands were also much weaker.

Also ghastly, all of my hair broke off where the rubber band held it above my head. The cause was the combination of the anesthesia, lying down for three months, and not getting the appropriate circulation to the back of my head or my hair.

I was devastated. My hair was about an inch and a half long all over my head. Luckily, I had a dear friend who was a cosmetologist and he permed my stubble to make it look fuller, like more hair. I may have gained extra years on my life with better breathing, but the hair loss was difficult for me.

Within a few months, I tried my hand at making love again. I was scared the first time after the surgery, afraid I might break something. I am pleased to say I remained intact, nothing broke, but what I hadn't counted on was the change in my already limited physical ability. I didn't

Laurie Hoirup

know how lucky I had been until now.

Not only was I unable to raise my hands to my mouth to feed myself, I was unable to use my hands for pleasuring my partner. Secondly, my agility went right out the window. I could no longer lie on my stomach or bend sideways, nor could I lie on my side propped up on my elbow. I was limited to the missionary position and rear penetration with me on my side. I was anything, but pleased.

I couldn't feed myself, I had no hair, and my sexual ability had just been reduced to less than it already was. Here was that lemonade thing again, I just had to figure out where the sugar was. I was going to have to get creative and find a partner who was very understanding and really liked who I was.

One final issue I had after sitting up was my new brace, which I was going to have to wear for a year. It was completely flat in the front on the outside with the room for my breasts formed on the inside. Just like the time in high school before they cut down my brace, I was flat-chested all over again.

This time, however, I went to a women's lingerie shop, purchased some bra inserts, which looked like real breasts (sponge material with a nipple and pink in color) and glued them to the front of my brace. This way, I could go braless and look natural (very firm), or if I wore a bra, I didn't have to worry about stuffing.

I tried returning to school in January to begin my master's program in speech pathology, but it was too soon after the surgery and I couldn't keep up. I had my father (Art) take my brother back because I couldn't handle him either. Steve decided to move on with his life with a partner. So, with all of these changes, I asked my mom to come get me and bring me closer to home. One positive change was that I had regained the ability to feed myself.

In February (1980), Art and Pat picked up Artie and headed for San Diego, Steve moved somewhere in Sacramento, and mom picked me up. I went back to Arizona and stayed with my parents in their travel trailer in Globe, a small mining town where my dad was working.

Gosh I love them both so much, but the next few months were the worst months of my life. I had to go to bed at 9:00 when they did and up at the crack of dawn with them. I remember thinking if I ever got old and went to bed that early, I would shoot myself (I was only 23). Little did I know how quickly the day would come, and I am happy to say I am not considering shooting myself.

I had no friends my age and no way to go out or socialize beyond shopping with my mom. I was okay with all of this at first until I started getting my strength back, as well as my need for independence.

It didn't take long before I was contemplating moving and getting my own place again. I just wouldn't move quite so far away this time, so my mom and dad were within reach if I needed them. I chose San Diego as my next home and quickly visited there, putting my plan into action.

We drove to San Diego one morning and I went to the Community Service Center for the Disabled (CSCD), an independent living center providing information about accessible housing and names of caregivers. By end of day I had an apartment and a caregiver. His name was James and it looked like things would be fine.

About two weeks after moving in, my friend Susan (the nurse from my surgery) came down to visit me. We were sitting at the pool when we met a very nice gentleman named John. He lived right upstairs and across from me. We started hanging out together, going to the beach, out to eat, bowling, and the movies.

Soon, it was time for Susan to go home and back to work. I figured I wouldn't be seeing quite so much of John now, because I believed he was interested in her. However, after we took her to the airport, he asked me out on a date. Not long after, we were spending all our time together.

This however, provided too much free time for my caregiver, leading to other problems, and very shortly things started to go badly with James. He would come home late without calling, sometimes not showing up till morning. It wasn't an agreement between the two of us. He just did what he wanted to.

I know I was spending a lot of time with John, but it wasn't up to James to decide it was okay to not come home, figuring John would take care of me. Caregivers are a very delicate issue and not always easy to handle correctly.

Well, needless to say, I fired James, and John and I moved in together. This all happened within about two months after meeting him. I know, many would say that was pretty foolish, but young love is often pretty foolish.

I found someone who appeared to like me for me and was accepting of my limited sexual agility. He was comfortable with having to position me and even taught me a few things. I found that by placing his hand over mine while masturbating him (him doing the movement) enabled me to participate in pleasuring him.

A month later he proposed to me. I was so excited! All of my other close friends were already married with children and it was finally my turn. We had only dated about three months, but I was sure it was meant to be. I know, still pretty foolish.

I took a picture of my ring for all my friends to see because I knew it would probably be a long time before I got to see most of them. I wanted to have them close to share in my excitement, so I did anything I could to do so from afar.

Initially, I wanted to get married a year after our engagement, but John didn't want to wait that long. His urgency to get married should have given me a clue or a red flag that this was too good to be true, but as I've stated several times, I was young and foolish.

We were meeting one of my close friends in Las Vegas a few months later, so John suggested we get married while we were there. My parents agreed to join us, and Susan (my nurse from my surgery), who was going to be my maid of honor, agreed to meet us as well. Of course my friend Marian from Illinois, who we were meeting in the first place, would also be there.

I was getting married seven months after meeting John, which I know isn't very long, but we were together 24 hours a day, which in my mind doubled our time together. Besides, it wasn't the length of time together, it was how we felt about each other and the love we shared. Boy was I living in a fantasy world!

A few weeks before the wedding, Susan came down for a week and threw me a wedding shower. It was nice, with handmade decorations and a beautiful cake made by John. I got some very nice gifts. I also had a bachelorette party at the local bowling alley bar. I know, not the usual venue, but we had fun.

We left for Las Vegas on Friday, February 7, picked up the rings from the jeweler on the way (the engagement ring was being attached to the wedding band), and arrived around 10:00 p.m. to our really trashy motel with an hourly rate if you know what I mean. Not a good omen.

It was noisy, dirty, and in a bad part of town. I didn't know that when I made the reservation. Then when I got ready for bed, I found I had begun my period. Another bad omen, but my head was in the clouds and I didn't see anything negative. However, we did decide to change hotels the next morning.

We woke up bright and early on the morning of Saturday, February 8, 1981. My wedding day! We met my parents and friends for breakfast and picked up our marriage license. We chose the Circus Circus Hotel for the wedding (pretty appropriate considering the circumstances). We also got a room there.

We pulled up to the hotel and while my dad was putting me in my wheelchair, my jacket caught the joystick (driving controller of my wheelchair) pushing my wheelchair back out of the way. My dad was bent too far forward with my weight pulling him down and we went down together.

He tried to roll as we fell to avoid landing on top of me, but instead, he caught both my feet under him, spraining both my ankles and bruising my knees. Luckily, these were the only injuries; things could have been a whole lot worse. I know—this was the worst omen of all.

When we finally checked into our room, my mom and Susan and Marian got me dressed and did my makeup and hair. I had to take a pain pill in order to get my feet into my shoes, but I managed. We were married in "Chapel of the Fountain" in the late afternoon with four guests in attendance and a female minister.

We had a nice celebratory dinner overlooking the circus acts for our reception (maybe that should have been another omen) and by the time we returned to our room, John was feeling very ill and running a temperature. (How many omens does that make?) So much for our wedding night. I told you it was like a circus.

My mom and dad left Sunday morning and since John was sick, I spent the day with Susan and Marian, visiting and shopping. Susan left the following morning, leaving Monday for just me and Marian. She headed out on Tuesday.

Visiting with them was nice, but not at all what I expected for my honeymoon.

Since John and I weren't leaving until Wednesday morning and he was feeling well enough the night before, we finally made love as a married couple.

Along with making love, we also gambled a little together. We put a dollar on a keno ticket and won $240. Hopefully, my bad omens were turning around. I was embarking on a new journey, that of a wife. I was Mrs. John Anthony R——.

13. Matrimony, Motherhood, and a Master's Degree

As Mrs. John Anthony R—— I expected great things as a wife, and I couldn't wait to become a mother. The doctors advised me because of my disability, it would be better to get pregnant sooner than later. I would never be stronger than I was at that time. To my extreme surprise, I learned I was pregnant six weeks from my wedding day, which means I conceived the first night we made love as a married couple. I thought, how appropriate is that?

We first met Dr. Moyers in December of 1980 to discuss my disability as it related to pregnancy and to see if he would be willing to become our obstetrician. He was a perinatologist, an obstetrician who worked with women at risk of having a problem with their pregnancy.

I had gone to another obstetrician prior to him, who refused to take me as a patient. He felt I was being selfish to bring a child into this world knowing I could die before the child reached adulthood. But then, none of us has a guarantee we are going to be around to raise our children.

I also had a neurologist who told me I should not have children because of my disability and the risk of dying young. Ironically, he passed away the following year, leaving behind a 12-year-old son. That proves my point: no one is assured to live until his or her children are grown.

Luckily, Dr. Moyers was our second interview and he was wonderful. For those of you old enough to remember the TV show *Marcus Welby, M.D.*, Dr. Moyers had that same kind of bedside manner. He really was a great doctor.

After agreeing to be my physician, the first thing he suggested was I go off my pills that month to give my body a chance to get back to its normal state. He believed since I had been on the pill for several years, it might take some time for me to get pregnant.

He also let me know his primary concerns were my breathing capacity and circulation and if for any reason he thought there was a problem, he wouldn't hesitate to put me in the hospital or rehab for however long necessary.

He told me because of the scoliosis of my spine, the only way I could deliver a child would be through a C-section. Though my back had been straightened from a 145° curvature to 70°, there could be no alteration if the baby's head were to pass through the birth canal.

As it was, there was already very little space in a woman with a normal body to have a baby, and my curvature would definitely present a problem for childbirth. Therefore, a C-section it was going to be.

So, I went off the pill, continued to plan my wedding, and didn't think much more about it, other than using condoms because I was supposed to let my body return to its normal cycle. I can tell you, it wasn't pleasant at all.

It was very nice not having to use them once we were married. I would've never imagined I would get pregnant the first time having un-protected sex. I consider that an omen as well. This baby was just meant to be.

Rethinking what Dr. Moyers said about being on the pill for so long and having difficulty getting pregnant right away, I realized I was off the pill for 10 months before my back surgery because of blood clotting risk factors. So in reality, I had only been on the pill a year before trying to get pregnant. Good thing we used other protection the first few months or we would have been pregnant before marriage.

The first sign of my pregnancy was my breast enlargement. Even be-fore I had missed a period, my bra size increased from a "B" cup to a "C" cup and my breasts were extremely tender. Within another week or so, I missed my period and in my heart I knew, but I had to be sure. We de-cided to try one of those home pregnancy tests just for the heck of it.

John woke me early in the morning to get a urine sample to start the test. He put it in the little tube and then we were supposed to wait for two hours. If we saw a doughnut shape, we were positive for pregnancy and if not, we would have to keep trying (which wouldn't be so bad).

I managed to fall back to sleep while we were waiting for the results and soon, John was waking me with kisses! He picked me up, spinning me around the room, excitedly repeating, "We have a doughnut, we have a doughnut!" I couldn't believe we were going to have a baby. I was going to be a mother. I thought my wedding day was the happiest day of my life, but this day took the lead.

We quickly made an appointment with Dr. Moyers, as I did not want to tell anyone until we were sure (you can't always trust a home pregnancy test). We weren't able to get in for a month, which was making me crazy, but during that time, I started a pregnancy journal. If I was pregnant, I didn't want to miss a thing.

The day of my appointment eventually arrived. We were sitting in the waiting room for what seemed like forever, anxiously awaiting the confirmation of this pregnancy. I was reading through all of the pregnancy and parents' magazines getting more and more nervous with each passing moment.

We were finally called in and Dr. Moyers decided to do a sonogram versus a urine test to determine whether or not I was pregnant, as the results were more immediate as well as accurate. John got me on the table and prepared me for the exam.

Dr. Moyers came into the examining room and turned on the sonogram machine. He started moving the wand across my belly, and sure enough, there within my uterus was a beating heart, our baby's beating heart! My eyes welled up with tears of joy.

He said I would be seen every three weeks, more frequently as the pregnancy progressed and a sonogram would be done every six weeks to keep tabs on the baby. He prescribed prenatal vitamins and checked my weight and blood pressure, and I was on my way for another three weeks.

My initial weight was 112 pounds and my blood pressure 110/75. Good start for a pregnancy. I was approximately 10 weeks, or two and a half months, pregnant. I couldn't wait to start showing and letting the world know I was going to have a baby!

The first thing we did was call everyone and their brother. Of course, I called my mom and dad first. I know my mom had mixed feelings. She was excited about being a grandma, as this was something she never dreamt would happen for her, and on the other hand, she was fearful about how I would handle a pregnancy.

Was this going to be too much for me physically and how would John and I handle parenthood were but a few of her nagging concerns. She didn't say those things, but I knew she was thinking them. Well, anyway, they acted very excited.

I had a great time calling all of my friends and other family members too! John didn't have anyone to call because he hadn't been in touch with his family for years, but I let him tell our mutual friends so he could share the excitement.

John and I had my prescription filled and then we bought our first baby book, *A Child is Born*, which was just incredible. We were able to see exactly where we were, and would be able to follow every stage, every week. We also bought my first two maternity outfits. I know, not really necessary so soon, but we were so excited and I couldn't wait to start showing.

We started shopping early for nursery items and our first buy was from a thrift store. We purchased a chifferobe (a combination dresser and closet for hanging little clothes) that needed refinishing. We also went to a baby store in the mall and bought a beautiful crib on clearance.

A few days later at the swap meet, we got a changing table and bookcase. Both needed painting. Though we had six and a half months to go, these were neat little projects for us to work on. We spent most of our evenings doing just that.

John liked needlepoint and other arts and crafts. He started a needlepoint wall hanging for the baby's birth date, time and weight, which obviously couldn't be completed until after the baby was born, but he enjoyed getting a head start on it. He also did a teddy bear rug wall hanging and a teddy bear quilt wall hanging.

I put together a puzzle of all different kinds of toys and stuffed animals which we decoupaged and framed. The nursery was going to be adorable and made up of mostly handmade things, if not handmade, then refinished, painted or something personally done by us.

My morning sickness wasn't too horrible, though I did have bouts. Probably the most difficult thing about pregnancy for me was the need to pee more often. It was also difficult for John, as he was the one having to take me to the bathroom more frequently. Talk about sharing the pregnancy, we certainly did.

As time wore on, I gained weight, which John also experienced more than most expectant fathers. He was the one having to lift and carry me throughout the pregnancy for all of my regular care. Since he liked to sew, he even made me some maternity clothes to accommodate my changing figure.

Of course, there were the typical expectant father duties such as handling all of my unusual cravings at unusual times. He was wonderful about going to the store late at night for my cravings (pizza, cheesecake, and watermelon). He also had to adjust to my increased body temperature requiring the thermostat be set at 60°.

All of this sounds pretty wonderful, doesn't it? Things aren't always as they seem. Within a month after I became pregnant, John began lying to me, or at least that's when I became aware he was lying to me. One day he told me he had to run an errand, and I learned he had gone to meet someone. Shortly thereafter, I found out he had been untruthful from the first time we met.

You're probably wondering what he lied to me about. Sadly, it was in regards to his sexual orientation. John was gay. (His needlepoint and quilting had not been enough to tip me off.) I kept asking myself why he would have deceived me, and all I could come up with was that he must have believed if he married and had children, it would all go away—but it didn't.

I thought about having an abortion and leaving him, but in my young, foolish, inexperienced mind, I believed once he had a family and someone to really love him, he would be happy and content. Boy was I ever wrong. I wonder when you quit being young and foolish. I hadn't reached that point yet.

John began lying to me from the beginning. He told me he had been engaged and his fiancée had died. She had gone on a trip to see her family and was in a car accident on the way. How terrible is that? He felt guilty because she wanted him to go along, but he chose to stay home and work.

I felt so bad for him.

He had a big oil painting, which he told me she had painted. I wondered why he didn't have any other memorabilia from their time together. He said the reason he didn't have any other items was because it was just too painful. He was an expert liar and did such a good job.

First of all, there was no girlfriend, no engagement, no accident, and no death. Secondly, the painting which she had supposedly done, came from an art auction. How devious is that? How cold!

He also told me about his family. He was the baby of a family of 10 children, two sets of twins and one set of triplets. He had been molested by his older brother and no one believed him and that's why he left his family. I later found out he was the fourth child of six, no twins, no triplets and no molestation. I had been so gullible!

I began to suspect his honesty because on one occasion he referred to his younger sibling. When I asked him about it (since he had told me he was the baby), he explained he often called his sister younger because she was smaller. There was always a lie to cover another.

I also came to the conclusion John believed my sexual needs would not be as great due to my disability, and he could handle that as a gay man. As for himself, he could deny his own sexual needs, but soon realized it just wasn't a reality.

Regardless of my analysis, we had to find a way to make this work. We were about to become parents, and foolishly I believed that was more important than anything. Thankfully, I think John started to believe it himself.

From about my fourth month on, things between us started getting better. John stayed home more and we worked on our projects together planning for our future. Once in a while, we received a call from someone asking to talk with "Tony" (John's middle name), but they got to be fewer as time went by. I believed we were on our way to becoming a happy family.

We went to our next doctor visit three weeks after the last (three months, one week pregnant) and again, four weeks later (four months, one week pregnant). My blood pressure was consistent at both visits and I only gained about five pounds total over the seven weeks. I was doing really well.

However, there was a negative physical change; I was losing more strength in my arms and was unable to feed myself again, just like after my back surgery. I could only hope I would regain the function after the baby was born. In the meantime, I was provided with mobile arm supports, which allowed me to move my hands and arms from my tray table up to my mouth.

Our second sonogram occurred at the latter visit (17 weeks pregnant) and we saw little leg and arm buds with a lot of kicking and squirming about. I would be feeling the baby move very soon and I was anxiously awaiting the moment. I'd be about six months pregnant at our next sonogram, and able then to tell the sex of the baby. The question was whether we wanted to know.

To my surprise, Dr. Moyers said he could tell the sex of our baby already. He believed it was a boy. He explained sometimes a baby girl's genitals can be swollen and look like a boy, but in this case, this one was more than just a swelling. He was almost positive and because the baby was feet down, it was easy to see.

Time marched on and everything was going well. John and I were getting along, and my pregnancy was perfect. No problems with breathing or circulation. My morning sickness had ended right around three months, as it should have. Of course, there was still the frequent urination, which was a pain for both me and John, and I was starting to get a considerably bigger.

Since I have no stomach muscles, as my uterus began to expand, my belly just kind of pulled down and became very uncomfortable. We found a maternity corset, which helped a great deal. It supported my tummy while I was sitting up.

We took pictures quite frequently along the way and I kept up on my pregnancy journal. We continued to follow the stages in our book and I loved knowing what was happening inside me.

The first time I felt the baby move was just a few weeks after the doctor visit (I was 19 weeks, just shy of five months), while we were at the beach with my mom. She had come out to visit and we had taken a ride to the beach. I was sitting in the car watching the ocean and she and John were walking in the sand looking for sea shells.

The first little squiggle I experienced felt like gas, so I wasn't sure if it was the baby or not. A few minutes later it started again and by the time they got back to the car, I was sure what I was feeling was in fact, the baby.

It was the coolest thing, knowing I had this life growing inside me. I know, same old cliché that most pregnant women use, but it is so true! Over the next few months, what started out as a squiggle turned into strong kicks and somersaults.

We went to our five-month and six-month doctor visits and wanted to confirm the sex of our child. Dr. Moyers assured us we were having a boy. I told him he better be absolutely positive because I had bought a box of suckers that said "It's a Boy" instead of cigars, and if he was wrong, he would be paying me back and eating every one of them.

So when we did this sonogram, it was very apparent we were definitely having a boy. He was still in a feet down position making it really easy to see again. Soon we would have to prepare the nursery. Since sonograms aren't always one hundred percent accurate (even though Dr. Moyers usually is), we decided to go green and yellow, just in case.

The picture from this final sonogram was primarily a picture of his head, and he was sucking his thumb. He was already beautiful to me. My blood pressure was still good and my weight gain was up another couple of pounds, putting me at 122. Dr. Moyers decided to see me every two weeks instead of three, being cautious, though everything was going well.

We got a beautiful green quilt and pillow set with green bumpers for the crib. We painted the bookshelf and changing table yellow, and the dresser we stained in a darker brown to match the crib. His nursery was just about complete. We started buying diapers, so it didn't hit us all at once, and the same with baby clothes.

I was really big then. My tummy rested out on my lap, halfway to my knees. I also had my tray trimmed out in the middle every few weeks as my belly grew. I would have to get a new tray for holding and feeding the baby as a tiny infant, as well as a snuggly carrier to hold him against my chest without the use of my arms.

We had a special strap attached to my wheelchair from underneath the bottom seat, so when the baby became bigger he could sit in my lap. The strap came up between his legs, with my seatbelt going around both of us through a loop in the strap. He'd have to be around six months old before he could be carried that way, but I liked looking ahead. I kept calling the baby "him" because I trusted Dr. Moyers.

We continued to follow our book and to get more excited the closer the time came. We just kind of put the past behind us and didn't talk about it. I know, not the healthiest way to handle things, but for the time it worked.

We believed from our last doctor's visit that the baby still had time to flip over, which was going to feel just great in and of itself. I was always amazed to watch my belly when he did a somersault; it rolled like a big wave. However, this baby got too big, too fast and before long, he couldn't turn around like we had hoped.

So it looked as though he would remain feet down, head up. What made this difficult was that when he kicked, he kicked down, and I felt as though his foot was coming right out of my crotch. He had also gotten into the habit of throwing his head up, which hit me right in the rib. I actually had a bruise from the inside out on my rib because of his constant head butting.

I went back to the doctor at six and a half, seven, seven and a half, and eight months of pregnancy, and all was well. Blood pressure remained constant, weight gain was good, no circulation or breathing problems, and pregnancy was still fun. Dr. Moyers decided my visits were to be every week until delivery, which should be from four to six more visits. (I really hoped we were looking at four.)

During my pregnancy, I was given two baby showers. My friend Jeannie in Arizona had a shower for me, and it was absolutely beautiful. The cake had blue baby booties made out of sugar. (By then, we knew we were having a boy.) She invited her neighbors and they all gave me gifts, even though I didn't know many of them. We figured out what we were going to name our son at that shower.

Initially, I wanted to name him Cole William (William after my dad) and John wanted to name him Frederick (over my dead body). One of Jeannie's neighbors, who was a guest at the shower had a son named Chad, and both John and I really liked the name, so we decided on Chad William.

Laura, my upstairs neighbor, gave me my second shower with all my friends at home, and it was very nice as well. We got some really nice gifts from everyone. I really enjoyed all of the little baby things.

During the rest of my pregnancy we primarily focused on the baby coming and whatever that entailed. We completed the nursery and purchased a car seat, as you are not allowed to take the baby home without one. I was also diligent about keeping up with my pregnancy journal for Chad.

I put together my suitcase for the hospital several weeks before I was due. I was going to be there for about five days, so I packed a nursing nightgown, an outfit for Chad to wear home, change for the vending machine and the beautiful birth announcements we specially ordered and would complete once he was born.

We returned to the doctor every week for the last month. We met with the anesthesiologist during that time, so he was prepared with my special case for the C-section. My original due date was November 14, but Dr. Moyers didn't think I was going to make it that far. He felt if I went full term, Chad would be about a ten-pound baby, and it would be very hard on me to carry that big of a baby. I was becoming quite uncomfortable, both with breathing and the extra weight, and I was looking forward to having this whole thing come to an end.

My final visit with Dr. Moyers was on Friday, October 23. My mom came over to be with me, as we knew we were getting close. My dad was not able to come over, nor was he going to be able to be here for the delivery because of his work. That was the only sad thing about the whole event.

Dr. Moyers told me it was time to pick a day, either Monday or Tuesday, October 26 or 27. I asked him which was better for him and he said Tuesday, so October 27 it was going to be. I was to arrive at the hospital at 6:00 p.m. Monday evening and my C-section would be scheduled for 7:30 a.m. on Tuesday morning.

In just a few short days we would be parents! We went to lunch at a Chinese restaurant to celebrate. Then we went home and I took my nap. It was just a matter of waiting.

The next morning, John went to the van for something and the door was ajar. My heart sank, and sure enough, my hospital suitcase was gone. We were leaving it in the van in the event I needed to go to the hospital sooner than anticipated. I was devastated; the nightgown, baby clothes, and money could all be replaced, but the special birth announcements could not be replaced in such short notice.

There I was, pregnant as pregnant can be, emotional (we all know about emotional pregnant women), my dad couldn't be there, and now my suitcase was stolen. I cried for hours. Did I mention that I cried a lot during this pregnancy? Most of the time it was over stupid things, like the way John cut my sandwich or made the bed, but that time the tears were warranted.

I finally mustered the strength to go shopping. We spent the day running around buying a new nightgown, a new outfit and blanket for Chad's trip home, and a set of run-of-the-mill birth announcements. It wasn't one of my better days.

I woke the following morning to a knock on the door and it was one of the neighbor kids. They were playing in the field and came across my suitcase. They knew it was ours because of our name tag. The only thing missing was the spare change. A whole $2.50, I couldn't believe it, I was so excited!

Now I had my nightgown back and the clothes for Chad and more importantly, I had my birth announcements back. Shortly thereafter, there was another knock at the door and this time, it was my dad! Things were certainly looking up.

We spent the rest of the day running around returning the new nightgown and birth announcements. We kept the second outfit for Chad and managed to come up with another $2.50. We decided to keep the suitcase in the house until the next evening so I could have peace of mind, a restful sleep, and not worry about losing my birth announcements again.

Monday turned out to be a very nice day; we all went to the pier in Imperial Beach and watched the ocean and then went to an early dinner. I was supposed to be at the hospital by 6:00 p.m., so we left the house around 5:15 p.m. The hospital was about a 20-minute drive, but we allowed time for traffic.

John and I drove to the hospital in silence, both of us in our own little world about how dramatically our lives were about to change. I was terrified of being a mom. Would I make a good mom? Was Chad going to be okay? Were John and I ever going to work things out? So many questions with no answers at hand.

We arrived at Sharp Hospital right at 6:00 p.m. and went through the process of being admitted. I finally got to my room and into bed by around 9:00 p.m. John stayed with me for a while, but we both knew tomorrow was going to be a very big day and he needed his sleep if he was going to support me, and I needed my sleep, as well. He left around 10:30 p.m. and I did my very best to try to sleep.

I finally dozed around midnight, and of course, the anesthesiologist showed up around 12:30 a.m. to talk with me. We discussed what was going to happen in the morning, so I knew what to expect. He left around 1:00 a.m. and I managed to fall back to a fitful sleep for a few hours. Sometime after that, the nurses did my vitals and at 5:00 a.m. were back to prep me for my C-section.

John arrived around six o'clock that morning and they didn't take me up to delivery until 8:30 because the anesthesiologist was doing an emergency surgery during the time I was scheduled and he was running late. They started my IV and then set up my epidural block, which was supposed to numb me from the waist down.

The next thing I knew I was feeling a burning sensation every time they cut on my right side. It was the funniest thing because I would say "ooh, ooh, ooh" every time I felt the burning. The anesthesiologist wasn't sure why I wasn't numb, but decided to give me some Valium to knock me out until they got to the uterus, where there were no nerve endings, and then he would bring me back.

I guess it worked, because the next thing I knew, John was standing next to me holding Chad in his arms. Then they laid Chad across my chest and he reached his tiny little hand up to my face and I started to cry. Imagine that.

He was born at 9:00 a.m. on the dot, weighed 7 lbs. 4½ oz. and was 20 in. long. Having been born by C-section, he had a perfectly shaped head and was absolutely beautiful. Now it was real, I was a mom! There is too much to write about Chad, and like my mother and father, deserves a chapter of his own, which will follow.

Chad was about nine months old when I decided to go back to school and get my master's degree in Rehabilitative Counseling. It was a two-year program at San Diego State University (SDSU) and my goal was to become a rehabilitation counselor. I had four primary teachers, Dr. Fred McFarlane, Dr. Dick Jones, Ms. Patty Patton, and Ron Jacobs.

Ron began teaching in the program the same year my class started, so we made him an honorary member of the "Class of 84." He was young and we were able to relate to him quite well. He and Dr. McFarlane are still at SDSU and I saw them at my 30-year class reunion. Dr. Jones went into private practice, and sadly, Ms. Patton passed away.

My college career brought with it the reality I could no longer take my own notes. I knew I was losing my ability to write, but it didn't hit me until I had the need to write a lot, quickly and over and long period of time. Luckily, the Disabled Student Services provided me with a note taker and paid the fee. I hadn't dealt much with that office during my undergraduate years, but I am glad it existed.

Another physical change I was experiencing was the inability to operate my wheelchair when it was very cold or very hot. In the heat of the summer, it was as if I was weak and couldn't keep my hand on my control box. During the winter, my hands would get so cold I couldn't even move my fingers to drive my chair. The extreme temperatures resulted in complete loss of function of my limbs.

When I was young, my mom would hold my hands close to her tummy if they were cold. The sacrifices a mother will make for her child, a sure sign of unconditional love. She must have frozen doing that for me.

My first semester involved coursework and practicum. I hated paraphrasing as part of counseling, I just wasn't good at it, but I did well with the other courses. I didn't want to do basic counseling, but career planning instead. The last three semesters involved internships, starting out at eight hours a week during the second semester and increasing to 32 hours a week by the fourth semester.

My first internship was at an independent living center, the same one I went to find my first apartment and caregiver in San Diego. That was ironic. I didn't care for it, though, because it involved actual counseling, which I did not want to do.

They also made me feel more disabled than I ever felt in my life. Whenever I needed assistance, I was made to feel guilty, as though I should be finding a way to do it independently. Independence is great as long as it's possible.

My second and third internships were at the Department of Rehabilitation, which is where I really wanted to become employed. I had two different supervisors with two different styles, which was a good training experience. I also had an assistant who provided me with the help I needed in using the computer, answering the phone, filing, etc.

I had several exams and interviews to seek work from them, but I realized they weren't any better at hiring people with severe disabilities then the next guy. They hired a lot of blind individuals and people with mobility issues, as long as they were from the waist down, but not too many people with disabilities as severe as my own.

My experience with the Department of Rehab is both from a consumer viewpoint and now a counselor perspective, and they are very different. As a consumer, I highly respected the program, but as a counselor I saw many problems over all.

My other coursework had to do with disabilities, medical terminology, group therapy, cultural differences, and Department of Rehabilitation, most of which I enjoyed tremendously. Well, maybe not the group therapy.

Group therapy was a pain because there was one major project to be completed by the end of semester. We had to design a 12-week counseling program around alcoholism for any particular group we wanted (women, people with disabilities, teenagers, etc.) and we were supposed to make it cutesy. The project was to include all instructions, including materials needed to carry out the lesson, as well as research about the group the student decided to use.

I chose adults with disabilities, and my program was called "The Measure of Success." I used legal size paper and drew a ruler on the cover of each week, coloring in whatever inch we were up to and I gave each week a cutesy title.

The first week, I colored in the first inch and the title was "A New Beginning." It was an introductory week with several get-acquainted activities. The second week, I colored in the second inch and it was called "It Takes Two," all about communication. The following weeks' inches were colored in, and each had to do with problems someone with alcoholism might face.

The subsequent weeks were:

- Week three: "Three's Company," on working as a group,
- Week four: "Four Basic Food Groups," on healthy nutrition,
- Week five: "Give Me Five," on self-esteem,
- Week six: "Six to One, Half a Dozen to Another," on peer perception,
- Week seven: "7 Up," on changing attitudes,
- Week eight: "Eight Is Enough," on decision-making,
- Week nine: "9 to 5," on time management,
- Week ten: "The Ten Commandments," on following rules,
- Week eleven: "The 11th Hour," about how to deal with a crisis, and
- Week twelve: "Foot Loose and Fancy Free," about life after group.

I can't believe I was able to remember the whole thing after so much time.

I was quite successful with the whole graduate program. We had a choice of taking a comprehensive final or writing a thesis for our degree. We all decided to take the exam, which basically covered everything we had learned over the course of the last two years.

There wasn't really any studying to be done, because as I saw it, I either knew the stuff or I didn't, though I did review my medical terminology. I had a really good memory and it only took me about a week to go over all of the terms. John quizzed me until I had them down.

There were six sections to the exam, and if you failed any one of them, you could take those sections over again, up to three times. I took my exam in a separate room because I had to orally tell someone what to mark down, as I could no longer do my own writing.

I felt pretty good when I completed the exam, until I walked out of the room and realized I was the first one finished. Then I got really scared, thinking maybe I should have thought more about each question. Perhaps I had been too quick, too confident. Not that it mattered, as I already turned it in. It was going to be what it was going to be.

I am pleased to announce, I was one of three people who passed all six sections my first time through, as well as being the first one done. Not too shabby! Not only did I do well with the exam, I graduated with honors and I was chosen by my classmates as "Student of the Year." My name is on a plaque in the lobby of the Department of Rehabilitation at San Diego State University, along with others selected over the years with that honor. How cool is that!

Now that I was married, a mother, and a recipient of a Master of Science degree, my next challenge/goal was both to find a job and to try to save my marriage. Something told me neither was going to be an easy task. Where I had been successful in my past with most things I took on, I was fearful I might not be so lucky with these endeavors.

14. My Son: More Than I Expected

When Chad was placed across my chest and reached his little hand up to my face, I began to cry. He already knew who I was, and we would have a very special bond. He was such a beautiful baby, with a perfectly shaped head (due to the C-section) and beautiful coloring. He looked like he had a suntan because of an elevated bilirubin level.

My parents joined us outside the delivery room and the anesthesiologist was standing on one of the tables in order to get pictures. That day, my becoming-a-mom day, truly outdoes my proposal day, my wedding day and my finding-out-I-was-pregnant day. I was filled with a mixture of joy and fear. I would do my best to be a good mom, but you never know if it will be enough. I was about to embark on a journey of a lifetime.

Chad William was the name John and I compromised on, and I agreed to have him christened Catholic, as it was very important to John. He was baptized in Arizona because we could not find a priest in our area to do the ceremony, primarily because I wasn't Catholic, but also because John and I had gotten married outside of the church.

Most of Chad's infancy was a typical babyhood. He was colicky in the first few months, which was difficult for us as new parents. We often argued with each other over our helpless feelings. Once we got beyond those few months, things were better.

He was fairly average, with most of the milestones infants reach, though there were some he was ahead of. He rolled over, sat up unassisted, got his teeth, and crawled right on schedule. He walked about a month early, around 11 months, which was a great relief to me, as I was always concerned about whether he would have my disability.

He was very big for his age. He was in the 95th percentile for both height and weight. At six months, I was lucky to be able to hold him on my tray because he was such a large baby. It was a good thing he walked early, because one time while sitting in the stroller and because of his

145

size, someone asked me if he wasn't walking because he had what I had. I explained he was only nine months old and would walk soon enough, but that didn't help my anxiety.

The strap I had attached to the seat of my wheelchair worked out very well with him being a big baby. I had initially anticipated I would not be able to use it until he was about six months old, but because of his size, I was able to use it with him at about four months. Before that, I had a snuggly carrier that allowed me to carry him against my chest without using my arms.

I spent a great deal of time lying next to him in bed naked (per the pediatrician's suggestion) to have bonding time with him, since I was not the one dressing him, bathing him, changing him, or rocking him. I used my tray to hold him for feeding. It amazed me when others held him for feeding, as he would squirm all over, but when he was on my tray for me to feed him, he lay very still. It was as if he knew I couldn't hold onto him and if he squirmed too much, he could fall off my tray.

When he was nine months old, he would pull himself up on my foot pedals, holding onto my tray, pretty much standing on his toes, so I could carry him around. There were times when he refused to sit in his high chair and have John feed him, rather having me put the spoon in his mouth while he stood on tiptoe holding onto my tray. He could not have been very comfortable. These were but a few of the surprising things he did to have me care for him.

John and I continued with our problems, but I thought we were doing okay. He decided to take a nursing class to update his nursing license, which sounded good for our family. He wanted my parents to take me and Chad for a few days and he would join us in Arizona upon completion of his test. That made sense to me and didn't raise any red flags, until I tried calling him one evening and got no answer.

I called him every few hours throughout the entire night, until it became very obvious he wasn't home. When I finally got through to him the following morning he really didn't have an excuse. He just refused to talk about it. He came to Arizona to pick us up, and when we returned home, he let me know he'd met a guy and was moving to Florida. So much for my happy family and my foolish fantasy.

My mom came over to take care of us, but within a week, John was writing to me expressing his love for me and Chad and admitting what a mistake he had made. Stupid as it was, I took him back because I believed Chad needed a father and I believed John had seen the light.

When Chad was 15 months old, he attended nursery school on campus where I went to school. He got a cold that turned into an ear infection, and while he was on antibiotics to clear it up he caught a terrible intestinal bug. Anything we fed him went right through him and he was eventually hospitalized, off of all solids.

He was there for five days with an IV in his foot, tied to a five-pound weight. He was so strong they had to keep his hands tied as well. John couldn't go in to see him because Chad would get so upset, wanting John to pick him up. However, I could spend hours with him and not upset him because he knew I couldn't lift him.

When he was finally released, he was so weak he couldn't stand or walk. Once again, I was in fear, but the doctors assured me he would regain his strength and walk again very soon. It took him another week before he was walking like normal. I was very relieved. It was never good when he was ill, as nothing makes you feel more helpless.

Life went on and things were somewhat better. Chad was a joy, spending his second and third years exploring his world. We had a Tupperware cupboard just for him that he would routinely empty every night, leaving our kitchen floor wall-to-wall Tupperware. He was now in the 98th percentile for both height and weight and continued as such throughout his first few years, and he was a daredevil.

He developed an allergy to dairy, wheat, and soy, but with dietary changes and slow introductions, he eventually outgrew them. We found out about his allergy when my friend noticed he had dark circles under his eyes and explained to me that is often a sign of allergies in children. We took him to the doctor, and sure enough, she was right.

His second birthday was quite a challenge, since he couldn't have dairy, eggs, or wheat. We had to bake a special cake with egg substitute, and instead of ice cream, we made Jell-O molds in the shape of balloons.

None of the kids seemed to mind the cake or the Jell-O. Despite the challenges, he had a great birthday.

I had to learn to be creative with Chad, so I could be a mom and not always rely on John for everything. Chad seemed to want the same thing. Whenever he got hurt, he would come over to me, pick up my hand and move it up and down, patting wherever he was injured.

I usually sat with my legs crossed like an Indian, and whenever Chad wanted to kiss me, he would kiss my legs or my feet. He also used my wheelchair like a walker, pulling himself up into a standing position, and then I would slowly move backwards so he could take a few steps.

To take him outside by myself, I used a harness/leash that allowed me to do so without fear of him running off into a dangerous situation. I also had my tray strengthened with metal bars going right into the frame of my wheelchair, to support his weight while he sat on it. My tray was my lap for him and he sat up here until he was four years old, even as big as he was.

John and I had one more episode when Chad was a year and a half old. I caught him in another affair, but didn't have the will to leave him, not with a child so young. However, by the time Chad was three, I knew things were never going to work between me and John.

I also believed there weren't a whole lot of available guys who would be willing to accept a woman with a disability, let alone one with a child, so I made a decision. Before we split up, I was going to get one more child from him. Again, you're probably thinking, *how stupid is that? What was she thinking?*

Well, our family is small and I didn't want Chad to be alone if anything ever happened to me, so I set my mind to giving him a sibling. John had always wanted a daughter, so it didn't take much to convince him to try. The only problem was it took much longer to get pregnant the second time around.

I'm sure it had to do with my being on the pill for a much longer time. Chad was four and a half when I finally gave birth to his sister, Jillian. I will share more about her in the next chapter. I planned to stay with John until she turned five and Chad turned nine, at which point I could take care of them on my own.

Chad was three years old when we started trying for another baby. During that time John started to distance himself from Chad. He had been the perfect father during Chad's babyhood and early toddlerhood, but now, all he did was yell at him. I believe it is because Chad had developed his own personality and John could not direct his every move.

Chad attended daycare from the age of three for that very reason. He was there for the majority of the day because, truth be told, John couldn't handle him, I couldn't handle him alone, and I was back in school, so it was the best thing for him. Whatever the reason, it brought Chad and me even closer.

Attending daycare for two years had some advantages. Chad was a very bright child. By the time he began kindergarten he could write his own name and he knew how to spell probably 30 words, and he wasn't quite five years old. By the time he completed kindergarten, he could read.

He attended a private kindergarten, a follow-up to the daycare at the Lutheran Church. What they had started teaching him in preschool continued on into kindergarten. They gave him a great foundation for first grade in the public school.

His sister was born six months before Chad started kindergarten, and he took on the role of big brother. He was a wonderful big brother while she was a baby, but the remainder of their relationship put the term "sibling rivalry" to shame.

When Chad was four, he and I used to walk to Round Table pizza for lunch together on Saturdays. It was about a mile away. We would sing songs and play games as we strolled down the block. We had a park next to our apartment complex and the playground within our complex, and I was always the one to take him to play.

I tried to involve Chad in sports early on, but he couldn't pay attention or follow rules very easily. I was the Little League team mom, and Chad played third base. The problem was he was more interested in the grass and the bugs then the ball. That career ended fairly quickly.

Chad attended first grade at Wenzloff Elementary in Santee, California. The school was across the street from our apartment. This made it very convenient for me to walk Chad to school and volunteer in his classroom. Chad and I continued to be very close.

During the first grade he was diagnosed as having attention deficit disorder (ADD), which explained his difficulty with sports. The diagnosis came as a result of his always being in trouble at school for one thing or another. He really was a good boy, but he just couldn't control his impulsive behaviors.

He was the only first grader in the school to be placed on school suspension, twice. It broke my heart walking him to school, as he cried about having to spend the day in a room all by himself. The counselor watching him through a two-way mirror was concerned with his inability to stay focused and sit still. Upon her recommendation, we went to our pediatrician and he was diagnosed and put on medication.

I was very against putting him on medication, but after a great deal of research, decided it was better that than to have him hate school. Within a month, he received an award for "most improved" student of the month. His grades weren't affected by his having ADD, unlike many children. He had very good grades, and once he was on medication, his B's did turn into A's.

Chad continued to do well in school, didn't get in very much trouble, and kept good grades through sixth grade. Then he started to struggle. Before then, school work came to him very easily with no effort on his part. Sixth grade posed new problems for him because of unfamiliar information.

He actually had to open a book, read what was in the book, and do homework. He would excel in numerous subjects and lag behind in others. His teacher and I worked out a daily progress report so we could both help him stay on track. This was his final year in elementary school and I wanted to prepare him for what lay ahead of him in middle school.

Though Chad was doing well in school, he wasn't doing really great at home. His father and I split up while he was in the second grade. He didn't do very well with that and blamed me for his father's being gone. We had several caregivers, both male and female, who came and went through most of his remaining elementary school years and he had a great deal of difficulty with that as well.

The pastor from our church would come over and pick him up once a week for some male bonding time, but it wasn't enough. My dad and Chad were also very close, but my parents lived in Arizona, so their time was limited too. Even before John and I split up, he was never one to show physical love to Chad. Chad would hug him and John wouldn't put his arms back around him. It really was sad. I tried to make up for it, but there are some things you just can't make up for.

As mentioned earlier, Chad was a great "big brother" while his sister was a baby. However, once she was mobile, got into his things, and took up more of my attention and that of the caregivers, he didn't want to have anything to do with her. He looked upon her as nothing but a problem and wasn't very nice to her. It was apparent he was jealous of her, I believe because of the attention she received from his father.

John wanted a daughter so much, and when we had her, he really began to shut Chad out and worship her. No matter how hard I tried, I couldn't change the relationship between him and his father or him and his sister. I hoped once John was gone things would get better, but they never really did.

I met JR at the end of Chad's fourth grade year. We had moved out of the apartment into a house and JR was the new caregiver. Chad got pretty close to him, as they spent a lot of time with each other. JR attended all of Chad's important events

Chad was in Tiger Cubs, Cub Scouts, and eventually Boy Scouts. Initially, I was the one involved with all of the Scout activities. However, once JR came into our lives, he attended most of them. Chad earned the "Arrow of Light," which was a very prestigious award in Boy Scouts, and he chose to have JR there instead of his father. That tells you a lot.

JR became a steady part of our lives, especially as our relationship grew into a romantic one. He became permanent as we entered into marriage. JR was a wonderful dad to both Chad and Jillian. We became a family and did family things. My relationship with JR, like many parts of my story, deserves a chapter of its own. Since Jillian came first in my life, her chapter will precede his.

Chad was growing into a very good-looking young man and was very bright. Though he still didn't get along well with his sister, he did look out for her. We relocated from Santee to Ramona at the end of his elementary school years. Again, we moved into a house with a big yard in a somewhat rural area. It was great for the kids.

Chad got his first dog in our new place. She was a Black Labrador named Alexandra, Alex for short. At four months old, she was wonderful with the kids. Chad was responsible for taking care of her food and water, brushing her, and of course playing with her. Not long after, we adopted another Black Labrador. Shadow was big and lovable. Both dogs were great with both children.

Chad was still in Boy Scouts throughout middle school. He got quite involved with soccer and was very successful. He did much better than those earlier years in sports. His middle school experience was similar to that of sixth grade; he did well in several classes, while lagging in the others.

We would work really hard with him to bring up the lower grades and then the others would begin to drop. Needless to say, he was frustrated, as were we. However, the one class he always did well in was science. I think it had something to do with the animals.

Chad's science teacher had a classroom full of creatures—rats, snakes, birds, guinea pigs, lizards, spiders and any other number of things. Each summer the students would take one of the animals home to care for it. Well, there happened to be a Salvador Monitor (Monty), a huge, ugly, carnivorous lizard that only Chad was willing to handle.

Now mind you, you had to wear thick leather gloves to handle him because he wasn't exactly tame yet. The science teacher wanted someone to work with Monty on a regular basis to make him tame. He asked that Chad be allowed to bring him home. We foolishly agreed, and Monty became a guest for the summer.

He came in a very large aquarium with a heat lamp and a bag full of cans of cat food. Chad was to take him out every day and handle him and also put him in the tub once a day. I can tell you, I wasn't excited about any of this once I got a good look at him.

Monty was four feet long, including his tail, and he was green in color. He had spikes going down his back and a mouth full of sharp teeth. He was anything but a warm and fuzzy pet. The dogs didn't care for him either.

I was pleased that the teacher had enough faith in Chad to ask him to do this, but not particularly thrilled with Monty himself. Monty was worth about $300, which made him even more of a responsibility. I'm sure you're wondering why I'm telling you about Monty. Well it's quite a funny story.

One evening we were watching a scary movie called *Hsss* about killer snakes. Our house had bedrooms down the hall off the living room behind us. While we were watching TV, Alex got up, faced the dark hallway, and started barking like crazy.

Just as we turned around to see what she was barking at, Monty raced down the hall and went right under the entertainment center. I screamed and never moved so fast in my life. I was in the bedroom with the door closed before you could say boo! Thankfully, Jillian was already in her bed fast asleep.

It took JR and Chad about 45 minutes to get hold of Monty and put him back in his cage. They used a broomstick to push him out, and they stood on opposite sides of the room to corner him. He had pushed open the lid on his aquarium. From then on, we put a big rock on the top so he couldn't do that again.

However, several days later he went missing again. For days, we had no idea where he was in the house. The rock was still on top of the cage, but he pushed through a torn corner of the screen. Each night when I put Jillian to bed, we would check under her bed, in her closet, in her drawers, and in her toy box. It was like looking for monsters, which basically is what I was doing.

I didn't sleep very well for the days he was missing, and of course, this occurred two days before Monty was to be returned to school. Chad had to tell his teacher we were really busy and would bring Monty back as soon as we could.

About a day later, we returned from the store and there was Monty on top of his aquarium. I'm not sure if he was looking for heat or food, but whatever it was, he probably never moved so fast in his life as he did on his trip back to school. Chad did a great job at caring for him when he wasn't missing.

During spring break of Chad's eighth grade year, we took a family trip to Las Vegas. We were having a wonderful time, when we got the call that our male Labrador, Shadow, was very ill. We hurried home, but we were too late. Shadow passed away from gallbladder disease. We were all very saddened.

After the proper time of mourning, we acquired a Yellow Labrador named Buster. He was a doll, lovable, playful, and great with the kids and Alex too. Soon, Buster became Chad's, and Alex became Jillian's. It was like having four children.

I remember the day Chad graduated from middle school like it was yesterday. He looked so grown up in his black slacks and white dress shirt. He wore his hair like JR's, semi-long with a tail. I was very proud of him because I knew how he struggled and how hard he worked to reach this moment.

His father was supposed to be there, but didn't show up. It was either because my parents were there (he couldn't stand my parents) or because he couldn't claim the kids on his income tax (he was very mad about that). Whatever the reason, Chad never forgave him. He never received a call, a card, anything, and we were moving the very next day to the Palm Springs area, about three hours away.

I tried to give John our forwarding address, but he didn't want it. He didn't want to speak to me either. He got mad about the strangest things and most of the time I never knew why. It was like when we were together, and I was reminded why I divorced him in the first place.

We started our new life in our very own home in Desert Hot Springs. Chad was beginning high school and his pattern was pretty similar to middle school: successful with some classes, lagging with others, working harder on the others, only to have the successful ones start to fall behind as the others improved.

He continued with soccer, but was no longer involved with Boy Scouts. He was confirmed that year into the Lutheran Church. While we were involved with our church, Chad got to work on a float for the "Lutheran Hour" radio show for the Rose Bowl Parade. I've never even been to that parade, but Chad got to work on a float and go to the parade. That just wasn't fair!

He didn't get into too much trouble during high school, until the end of his junior year. During his sophomore year, we placed him in a school in a different district we considered to be better. He continued there through his junior year. He had a girlfriend who became his primary focus and often led him astray.

Since he was in a different school district, they did not have to allow him to stay there. So when he got in trouble, he was kicked out. He did not return to his original high school, but we were lucky enough to get him into continuation school, which is a school where students can work at their own pace. We thought that would be good for him, and he did quite well for a while.

JR started working out of town and we had a caregiver during the week. It was difficult managing Chad without JR there, but at times Chad would really surprise me by being so adult. One day the caregiver was out shopping and I had to go to the restroom very badly. Chad said, "Don't worry mom, Jillian and I can help you," and help me they did.

Chad lifted me onto my bed and Jillian took my bottoms down. She covered me with a towel and Chad put me onto my potty chair. When I was done, Jillian wiped me and Chad lifted me back into my wheelchair. I couldn't believe my 17-year-old son and my 12-year-old daughter assisted me in using the restroom. I was totally amazed.

Eventually, Chad got tired of continuation school. He wanted to work and make money, so with only four classes to go, he quit school. I was very upset, but he was 18 and there wasn't much we could do about it. However, we told him if he was old enough to be out of school, he was old enough to take care of himself. We explained he could live with us forever as long as he was in school trying to better himself, but if he was going to just work, then he could be out on his own.

He left home and moved in with a friend and his family, which was a good thing. But eventually he ended up hanging out with the wrong people. He got himself in trouble, really no fault of his own. He was set up by what he thought were his friends. JR and I stepped in and got him an attorney to get him out of trouble.

Once all of that got resolved, he moved to San Diego, got work in construction, and was doing well. He tried looking up his father to get some help, but all he managed to get was a pair of work boots and a free meal. Needless to say, Chad's opinion of his father never got any better. It really is John's loss. He could have had a relationship with his son.

Chad finally got his own apartment, which is where he met his wife, Jenn. She is a beautiful and bright young woman, a registered nurse. Chad brought her home for us to meet and we were quite impressed with his taste. He had chosen a great gal. She is exactly what he needed. We were so very pleased.

After living together for a few years, they got engaged and then married a few months later in December 2007, shortly before my becoming chief deputy director at my job. His life is on a good path. Most important, he is happy.

At the same time as their marriage, they announced they were going to be parents in about seven months, which meant we were going to be grandparents! I couldn't have been happier, and yet I couldn't have been any more in shock then I was right then. I was going to be a grandma, and life really does march on.

I want to say that Chad was my firstborn and as with any new parent, many things were by trial and error. I truly believe many of the problems Chad experienced were the result of things John and I did wrong. In any event, I can't begin to express, how much I love him and what a really good boy, good son, he is. I know he will make a wonderful father. *I love you, son!*

15. My Daughter: Just As I Imagined

Jillian Amber R—— was not as beautiful as Chad was when he was born. She had a head full of black hair, red-faced with splotches and squinty eyes. She looked similar to how my mom described me when I was born.

She was born March 6, 1986, at 2:04 p.m., weighed 8 lbs. 2 oz., and was 21 inches long. She was considerably larger than her older brother. Her birth was certainly planned, but the plan was probably not the healthiest of ideas. I had her with every intention of leaving her father when she turned five years old.

John and I tried all the tricks the books suggested for having a female child. Now whether or not any of them resulted in Jillian or it was just God's will, I will never know, but I got my daughter, which is all that mattered. Chad would now have a sibling no matter what. That somehow provided me comfort. As John would be out of the picture, if anything ever happened to me, Chad would not be alone.

My pregnancy with Jillian went as well as with Chad. I didn't have any major complications, I only gained 21 pounds, and of course I had her by C-section. Dr. Moyers was again my obstetrician and I had the same anesthesiologist.

The routine was for the most part the same. I went in every three weeks having a sonogram every six weeks. Time between my visits shortened to every two weeks during my seventh month and then every week during my eighth month.

Probably one of the biggest differences was how long it took me to get pregnant. I had gallbladder surgery during the summer and Dr. Moyers wanted my incision to completely heal before having the stress of a growing belly. So we waited until November 1984 to begin trying. I conceived Jillian on the Fourth of July, 1985. There were definitely fireworks going on inside my uterus.

I started this pregnancy much heavier than I had the first time around. I was 127 pounds versus the 112 pounds with Chad. Luckily, the first four months I wasn't much into eating and I lost four pounds. Though I had morning sickness with Chad, I had actual vomiting with Jillian. The only craving I had with her was ice water, but it didn't stop my belly from growing.

I got big very fast and started using my pregnancy corset almost immediately. My blood pressure was identical to that of my first pregnancy: 110/75 and for the most part, remained at that reading for the rest of my pregnancy. My breasts went from a "C" to a "D" cup and I felt as though I was all boob, especially considering how small I am. I really did look funny.

I felt her move much sooner than I did Chad, probably because I knew what to expect. I knew what it felt like. Sometime near Thanksgiving I was thinking how much I had to be thankful for. The second sonogram showed her arm and leg buds and everything was perfect. Things went along like clockwork and I got bigger and bigger, day by day.

By the third sonogram, Dr. Moyers was able to determine her gender. Again, he was absolutely positive we were having a girl. Once again, I warned him I was doing the nursery for a little girl and I was buying the suckers that said "It's a Girl," so he better get it right or he was going to pay to redo the nursery and eat every one of those suckers.

Since he was correct with Chad, we went ahead and decorated the nursery in rainbows. It was adorable, with quilt, bumpers, and curtains to match, as well as a wall hanging and dresser skirt. Of course, all of this was handmade by John.

The wallpaper was done in rainbows and we covered two walls, painting the other two a light yellow. It was a nursery made for a princess. John also did her birth announcement in needlepoint just like Chad, but couldn't complete it until after her birth. The design was a dollhouse with the information in each room.

Jillian wasn't due until March 27, but by mid February I was pleading to get her out of there. Dr. Moyers agreed to take her a few weeks early, as long as the sonogram showed she was large enough. She proved to be plenty big, so our C-section was scheduled for March 6 at noon.

My last visit to the doctor was the week before my scheduled C-section. By then, I weighed 143 pounds, the heaviest I've ever been in my life. I prayed I would be able to take off the weight as easily as I did with Chad. I also prayed everything would go as smoothly as it did with his delivery.

Luckily, we were prepared since the doctor agreed to take her early. The nursery was complete. Of course, we didn't have to get so many things this time around because we had everything left over from Chad: crib, dresser, bookcase, highchair, diaper bag, snuggly carrier. What we didn't have, we received as gifts for my baby shower.

One of my friends, Carla, recently had a baby herself and we often babysat. We were friends with her and her husband, and we did real couple things. For a short time, I started to believe that maybe this baby would bring John and me together and that our marriage might make it.

Carla threw me a baby shower in February, and it was very nice. I got a lot of little-girl clothing, which was good, since none of Chad's clothes were appropriate. We also got diapers, bottles, baby toys, and bedding. The only things we still had to purchase were a car seat and a stroller, as Chad's weren't in very good shape by the time he outgrew them. All we needed now was the baby.

Due to the problems with my epidural when I gave birth to Chad, the anesthesiologist decided it would be best to do a total spinal block this time. He didn't want me feeling any pain like I did before. He also wanted to be sure my back had not fused together, so he took an x-ray to take a look. He assured me the pregnancy was far enough along that an x-ray wouldn't hurt the baby.

After taking my x-ray, I got to see and it was amazing. There she was, my Jillian lying across me sideways with her perfect little skeleton inside my bigger skeleton. The x-ray was so much more detailed than the sonograms. It was incredible, making things much more real!

I arrived at the hospital around six o'clock in the morning and I was too tired to think about things as philosophically as I had on the way to the hospital for Chad's birth. I had gotten up at 3:00 in the morning to begin my newest journey.

I was also scheduled to have my uterus removed, as we didn't want to have any more children and I was going to be 30 the next week. Since I was having a C-section anyway, there was no greater risk for me. The computer, however, refused to register me for both childbirth and a hysterectomy. The baby was manually given a number. I sure hoped they wouldn't lose her!

The nurse came in around 9:00 a.m. to start my prepping. No complete tummy shave this time around, we had this one worked out. I was also hooked up to a monitor for my contractions. I was told we had picked a good day for the delivery because I was actually in labor as my contractions were about 10 minutes apart.

As the contractions grew stronger and closer together, I requested to have someone from labor and delivery come and teach me how to breathe through them because I had never prepared for this. A nurse was soon at my side guiding me through the process. It was very exciting even though it hurt, since I hadn't experienced labor having Chad.

My mom was staying with us to help with Chad, and after dropping him at preschool, she came to the hospital to be there with me. She watched the monitor and would tell me "here comes another one," and, thankfully, the nurse was there to help me with the breathing. I believe mom was as excited as I was. John was feeling helpless and nervous.

By the time they came to get me at 11:30 a.m., my contractions were four minutes apart. The anesthesiologist had also come in to numb my nasal passages for intubation in the event the spinal block didn't work. Oh boy, I was going to be a mom again. John was pretty quiet through most of this, probably because my mom was there.

In the delivery room, we had some difficulty once again. They tried four different holes and about 15 different angles trying to get into my spinal cord for the block. They were never able to get in, so they had to give me a general anesthetic.

They had almost as much difficulty with my intubation. It took three doctors to get the breathing tube down my throat. One of them held my head at different angles, the second maneuvered the tube, and the third monitored my vitals. Though Jillian was scheduled for delivery at noon, by the time they got me anesthetized and performed the C-section, she wasn't born until 2:04 p.m.

I was back in my room when they brought her to us. No delivery room pictures this time, nor did I get to experience her lying across my chest. She was all bundled up and sleeping at first. When she woke up she was fussy, but all I had to do was talk to her and she quieted down immediately. She obviously recognized my voice. She knew who her mom was.

I didn't try to nurse her because of the difficulty I had with Chad. It was much more positive just holding her and feeding her with a bottle. No pain, no fever, just a wonderful bonding experience. As I looked down on her in my arms, I was once again completely in awe of what I had created.

My mom brought Chad to see us later in the day and he looked so cute in his child size scrubs. He wasn't very interested in Jillian though, but rather all of the cool equipment surrounding him. We had tried to prepare him for her birth by giving him his own baby to take care of (a Cabbage Patch doll). We showed him how we fed her and changed her just like he did with his baby.

Jillian quickly turned into a beautiful baby. Her hair started turning lighter in just a few weeks and her coloring became a golden brown, just like Chad. She was a very good baby, not colicky at all. She would entertain herself for hours with her surroundings, often talking to the flowers on her baby seat.

She reached all of her milestones at the appropriate times. The only thing she took her time with was walking. She wasn't a daredevil like Chad, but was really quite the opposite. She was not going to let go of the table and walk on her own until she was absolutely sure she wasn't going to fall. She didn't walk until she was 13 months old, two months later than her brother.

When she was 10 weeks old we had a hospital stay with her. Chad had brought home a cold from preschool and she caught it. She was having a great deal of difficulty breathing and with a 103° fever they decided to hospitalize her for a few days to receive breathing treatments. She was so good, IV and all. She would lie in my arms and just snuggle. I was so relieved when we finally brought her home.

I lost all of my pregnancy weight by the time she was three months old. I actually returned to less than my pre-pregnancy weight. I started pregnancy at 127, lost 4 pounds during the first couple months to 123, and delivered at 143. I was down to 117 pounds. How cool is that?

When she was two months old, I had her ears pierced and she looked adorable. However, they kept getting infected and by the time she was 18 months, I decided to let them close up. We would pierce them again when it was her decision.

She was four years old when she decided she wanted them done again. She never gave me a hard time about cleaning them this time around, and we never had another infection.

Jillian was baptized Catholic just like Chad, though I'm not really sure why, since John never went to church. Nonetheless, it was something he wanted, so I went along. She was three months old and was so good during the ceremony. My friends Carole and Gene from Illinois were her Godparents.

They came for her christening, and as Carole is such an incredible seamstress she made Jillian her christening gown. (She was the friend who made my prom dress.) It was absolutely beautiful, all lacy and white with a matching bonnet.

I was worried about Jillian having a Christian name for her baptism, but I learned Jillian is the feminine of William, which was acceptable. She was named after her grandfather, like Chad, and I didn't even know it.

Chad was really good with her until she started walking. He would hold her, sing to her, tell her stories and play with her, and she adored him. However, when she became mobile, she followed him everywhere and was constantly into his things. He considered her a pest and didn't have the patience for her at all.

Of course, this might have had something to do with the fact that John was distancing himself from Chad, while at the same time smothering Jillian. Naturally, the more Chad ignored her, the more she would do for his attention. If she couldn't get it through positive ways, she would get it any way that worked.

Ironically, when John knew he would be leaving, he also began to shut Jillian out. At a year and a half old, she didn't understand how this man who had worshiped her no longer wanted much to do with her. He still fed, bathed, dressed, and changed her along with all of the other necessary things, but he wasn't there emotionally, and I know she sensed that.

He was still living with us at her second birthday and went all out for her party. He made her a wonderful cake with all the fixings, but I believe that was more for his ego and all the compliments he was going to receive than for her.

When he left, I already had everything in place for who would come in for the morning and all through the day. My friend Shirley came in the morning and got her up, keeping her until my caregiver came in and got me up.

I would get Chad up and walk him to school and volunteer for the morning. Jillian would go to my friend Cheryl's house until lunchtime. I would come home and she would bring Jillian to me for her afternoon nap. She was available to me in the afternoon if something came up and I needed help.

A teenage girl, Joy, from upstairs, came in for the afternoons and evenings. She would help me get dinner ready, do laundry if there was any, get the kids fed, and Jillian bathed and into bed.

I spent most of the late afternoon and early evening playing with Jillian to give her some of my time, since we didn't have much during the day. Once she was in bed, I would spend the rest of the evening playing with Chad and helping him with his homework, and then put him to bed.

When both kids were down for the night, my friend Cheryl would come and visit with me until my caregiver arrived at my bedtime. I had a baby monitor set up at Cheryl's house, in the event of an emergency through the night. It worked like that for several months.

Then I hired a full-time live-in caregiver, to whom Jillian became very attached. Sadly, he only worked out for about four months. Cheryl took over and tried being my caregiver for a while, but it was too much for her with my kids and hers. Besides, she threw out her back and couldn't do any lifting. So after another four months, we were looking for someone again.

At that point, we met Robb, who became my caregiver for almost two years. Jillian also became very attached to him. When he left, my friend Charlene stepped in for a few months and Jillian became attached to her. Eventually, JR came into the picture, but was back and forth for a while with different people in place when he was gone. Of course, she became attached to him, as well as the others.

Through all of this, Jillian started having terrible temper tantrums. I tried everything; she was in counseling, taking medications, most of which were trial and error, and I spent a great deal of time with her. She was experiencing separation anxiety in the worst way. Everyone in her life with whom she formed an attachment ended up leaving, and she was too young to understand why.

As with Chad, I took Jillian to the park and for walks. We played Barbie, I read to her all the time, we played games, and we were close. I tried hard to make up for the people who came into her life and walked away. I know she loved me very much, but it didn't make up for her loss.

Another problem was when John finally decided to take them for a visit. After just one weekend, he couldn't handle both of them together. At seven years old, Chad was easy to manage, but at three years old, Jillian had to be watched all the time and John didn't have the patience. His solution was to take Chad the first weekend and Jillian the third weekend, not much of a break for me.

Conveniently, every time it was Jillian's weekend, something would come up and he wouldn't be able to take her. After two months, I got wise and put an end to it. They were his children and he was either going to take them both or not at all.

Some of my friends said I wasn't being fair to Chad, but I wasn't concerned about fairness, but rather the message being given to Jillian. She had enough problems with people walking away from her in her life.

Jillian attended preschool for two years as part of the Head Start program. She did well; like Chad, she was very bright. I was chairperson of the Parent Advisory Council and very involved with the program. I knew her teachers well and participated as often as I could. She could spell a lot of words and write her own name, and knew how to read before entering kindergarten.

Jillian was very active. She loved to swim; both she and Chad had swimming lessons at the age of three. She was in gymnastics at age two and amazingly did two hundred cartwheels in a contest to raise money for the YMCA. Jillian was my award winner. She had more awards than any child I have ever seen.

While she was in kindergarten, I had a new caregiver. He molested my baby girl. Fortunately, there was no penetration, but the trauma resulted in many tantrums, nightmares, and counseling for her. None of this helped her separation anxiety in any way, shape, or form. My little girl had been through more than I would have wished upon my worst enemy. JR was an important factor in helping her heal.

She was great in school, an overachiever I would say, and was disappointed with herself if she got anything less than an A. First grade was a good year for her; she excelled in math, reading, and spelling. By second grade, we had moved into a house with JR as a family, but she was having trouble in the new school.

She hadn't been in counseling for some time, nor was she taking any medication. I decided to have her assessed once again, and sure enough, she was diagnosed with attention deficit disorder (ADD) like her brother. The differences between them though, were quite extreme.

Chad was impulsive, with no thought to consequence, but he was basically happy. Jillian on the other hand, experienced terrible mood swings. She could get so angry, so fast. She was put on new medication, which seemed to help; not perfect, but better.

In third grade, she continued to excel in academics and was placed in the GATE program for gifted children. She came in third place in the spelling bee and was learning to finger spell in American Sign Language. She started having migraines, but even with all of her problems, school was a breeze for her.

Fourth grade found her in another new school. We had moved to

Desert Hot Springs and bought our new house. Experience showed Jillian did not do well with change, but she held her own academically and was again put in the GATE program.

She, like her brother, got involved with soccer. Unlike her brother, she did quite well and stuck with it for four years. She loved sports, all kinds of sports; soccer, gymnastics, swimming, anything involving physical activity was right up her alley.

Middle school still found her doing well in academics. She went to the district spelling bee, making the top 20. Her interests expanded to include playing the flute, earning her a position on the marching band throughout high school. She tried her hand at tennis, volleyball, golf, softball, and water polo, doing best at golf and water polo.

As the star water polo goalie for several years, she was one of the few goalies to score a goal from the other end of the pool. Again, she received many awards for just about every sport she played, but water polo was her love.

Awana, a nondenominational Christian youth group, and Rainbow, a young ladies group of the Masons, were two of her other activities. As with all else, she excelled in both, earning numerous awards. She learned proper etiquette and was selected with very few others to attend summer camp several years in a row.

She was chosen to attend a youth group in Washington, DC, to learn about government, which was quite an honor. The trip also included time in New York City. I was quite concerned about sending her off on her own at such a young age, but it was a chance in a lifetime.

She worked to raise her own money within our community in order to attend, and was quite successful. Everyone was supportive; our friends and neighbors came through for her. We were very proud of her accomplishments. She continually gave it her all.

In her last two years of high school, she participated as a peer mentor for incoming freshmen, all the while taking honors and advanced placement (AP) courses, which were college-level. Even with all of her extracurricular activities, her grades were good. She graduated with honors, a 3.85 GPA. I told you she was bright.

At 14, Jillian started having problems with ovarian cysts. She got used to them and dealt with the pain when they occurred. Once she went to college, her health really began to decline, with no diagnosis as to why.

Accepted to San Diego State University (my alma mater), her initial plan was to major in forensic pathology and play water polo. However, after becoming very ill her first months there and during water polo tryouts, she didn't make the team.

Disappointed and ill so much of the time, she became depressed and started having problems with her classes. This brought her home to us for a while to get her health under control. She attended the local community college.

Before leaving for San Diego, she was dating a young man whom I consider to be her first true love. Their long-distance relationship didn't help her school situation. Being back at home did not improve her health situation either. She wound up in the hospital with no diagnosis other than a kidney infection.

During her recuperation, she and her boyfriend broke up, leaving her more depressed than ever. A month later we found out about my job in Sacramento and invited her to come along. Wanting a new start, she took us up on our offer. Sacramento was a go.

We moved to a good-sized house that a had bedroom and bath with a separate entrance. She decided to rent from us. She got employed at an In-N-Out Burger, as she had worked at one when we lived in the desert and also in Riverside. She had a job and a place to live; now she needed to make friends.

About seven months after we moved to Sacramento, Jillian met Josh. Josh was quiet and a really nice guy. Before long, they were living to-gether. Josh was planning on a career with In-N-Out Burger, and Jillian was going to school, not quite sure about her future career path.

While we were in Riverside, she took a sign language class and real-ly liked it. She continued with that course of study in Sacramento at the community college. Soon she decided that was going to be her career path. She also found out that the community college in Fremont was a better school for Deaf Studies.

So, in January of 2007, she and Josh got their own place in Fremont, as she worked on her Deaf Studies program and he on his career with the In-N-Out Burger franchise. He was able to transfer from Sacramento to Fremont and she was easily accepted into the program there, as well. They were on their way.

I didn't like the fact they moved so far away. It was two hours from me and I didn't get to see her very often, but she was doing well in school and had a good job. I supported her decision, and I was impressed with them for venturing out on their own.

Before moving, she discovered she had a kidney stone and had it removed, believing maybe it was the cause of her health problems. However, once in Fremont, her pain continued and she was diagnosed with endometriosis, which was taken care of.

The problem was that her pain kept coming back and the doctors kept guessing. It was just like in Riverside. They tried every test under the sun, yet no one could identify her problem.

I had a strong feeling, call it mother's intuition, that Jillian and Josh would eventually get married, and I hoped the doctors would figure out her medical problem. She had so much going for her and I didn't want ill health to get in the way of her career or her relationship.

Jillian and I have a very special relationship. We are more than mother and daughter, we are best friends. She knows she can come to me with anything and I feel comfortable going to her when I need to talk. Our relationship is similar to what I had with my mom, for which I am thankful.

Another true sign of our relationship is that she would put my ice-cold hands on her warm tummy when I had difficulty driving my wheelchair due to numb fingers. Even when she was little she did her best to assist me. She would push my head up if it fell back, put food in my mouth when I was hungry, massage my feet, and early on did my makeup.

At three years old, she even helped me with coughing. She was in no way strong enough to push in on my abdomen, but if I was lying down she could straddle me and bounce as her way of providing pressure. It was a very unique way of conducting the Heimlich maneuver.

Chad and I were close while he was growing up, but he was never very comfortable doing personal things for me, like feeding or massaging. He also drifted away once he moved. Of course, now that he's married, his wife and future child have become his life, as they should be.

Jillian and I have remained close, even with her living elsewhere. I believe if she gets married and has babies, we will still always remain close. At least, that is my hope. *I love you, baby girl!*

16. Marital Mayhem

I discussed part of my marriage to John in what should have been Chad's and Jillian's chapters, but it was almost impossible not to do so and still give a clear picture of Chad and Jillian's lives.

My marriage to John was like a roller coaster. I really was in a constant state of mayhem. The first few months, which I thought were wonderful, turned out to be one big lie—about his parents, his brothers and sisters, his make-believe girlfriend, and the list goes on.

Once I learned the truth, I tried to convince myself love would cure all, but that was just my fantasy, my defense mechanism. For the most part, I was in a constant state of skepticism and doubt. Our relationship was dictated by mistrust, rather than love, which is really sad for anyone to deal with as a steady diet.

Once the initial lies were behind us, I thought we could move forward and build our family, but again, that was foolishness on my part. During the latter part of my pregnancy with Chad, right up until the week before I went to the hospital, John was having an affair with a man.

We had gone to the independent living center in San Diego to check into some services and saw a gentleman working behind a glass window. Shortly after returning home, John carried on about knowing the person. A few days later, he made contact with the guy. As I should have expected, he didn't know him, but amazingly, they struck up a friendship.

Supposedly, the man was married and John had plans for the four of us to get together. I agreed because we certainly needed new friends in our life, as we didn't have any who were a couple. John wanted to get to know him better before getting us all together, so they met on several occasions for lunch and such.

After weeks of this, I finally grew impatient and demanded we all meet. Not surprisingly, after what turned out to be their last meeting, John came home upset and angry. He told me the guy had made a pass at him and he couldn't believe the one friend he made turned out to be gay.

Now mind you, this sounded pretty fishy to me. I decided to do my own investigation and eventually talked with the guy. His story was completely different from John's. He said John was the one who made the pass. He had no wife and there was never any talk of meeting me.

Here I was, only a few days from giving birth to our son, in total shock that he could do this to me. I was in no position to confront him or leave him.

The birth of Chad was an incredible experience. I truly believed this would be the deciding factor for John, and for about six months he seemed to be really happy. However, around the same time, he came up with the nursing school scenario.

Supposedly, before we met he was a nurse, but had let his license expire. I never really saw anything indicating he had been a nurse, but when he suggested taking a class and renewing his license, I thought maybe he hadn't lied.

It was pretty much as I described before; I went to my parents' place in Arizona with Chad so that John could study for the class and take the test. Had I not tried to reach him late at night, the whole night through, I would have never known he was out all night with someone.

My already having that knowledge allowed him an easy way out for his trip to Florida. He went with Mike, our neighbor's caregiver, whom he had obviously been involved with for God knows how long.

He was only gone a week when the letters and phone calls started coming in. He pleaded with me to forgive him and accept him back. He said all he wanted in his life was me and Chad. I wanted so badly to believe him and for Chad to have a father, so once again, foolish me, I took him back into our lives.

Things went along fairly smoothly for about a year or so, until we had a visit from my old friend Steve and his partner, Tony. I had known Steve since high school and he and his partner had been together for about eight years. Tony was a really nice guy too. I was excited to have him back in my life.

Sometime after that visit, John wrote Tony a letter indicating he really loved me, but he was extremely attracted to him. John asked if he could write him on a regular basis. Unbeknownst to me, John had a secret post office box, and though Tony never responded to him, I wondered how many other secret pen pals he had and how many were limited to only letters.

I didn't actually find out about this until years later after John and I had split up, because Steve didn't want to be the cause of our marriage breaking up. Not that it mattered, as this was just one more of John's many deceitful activities.

So, John and I continued to live a lie. I filled my life with Chad, and John busied himself with housekeeping, crafts, cooking, and more lies. He often went to the bank, not getting back for hours, blaming it on the traffic or the lines at the bank. I never believed him, but it wasn't important enough for me to concern myself with.

During this time, I was pretty much convinced we were not going to be able to work things out. I thought, why not get a sibling for Chad? Once they were old enough for me to care for them by myself, I could leave him. As you can tell, I was in my own fantasy world.

You need to understand the other aspects of my life with John were hell! He had terrible mood swings and would be angry with me for days, not speaking to me at all. Most of the time I had no idea why he was upset. Since he wouldn't talk to me, all I really had was Chad and my life was very lonely.

When he'd finally get over his mood, I was so thankful to have him speaking to me again, that I didn't dare press the issue. Even in his moods though, he took care of my personal needs: dressing, bathing, feeding, and such, but I hated having him do anything for me when he was like this. I'm sure this was because he didn't want to feel guilty or be accused of neglecting me.

He had also started pulling back from Chad, both physically and emotionally, once he turned two years old. This was probably because of his independence beginning to develop. The older Chad got, the less John had to do with him.

Once when Chad was only a few months old and very colicky, John got very angry with him. He put him in this room and closed the door on him. I was outraged and tried to push the door open with my wheelchair. It was latched tight and my foot pedal put a hole in the door. It was an accident, but John became so angry, he grabbed me, raising his hand to slap me across the face. He stopped in time to lessen the force of the slap. It didn't hurt, but was a slap nonetheless.

On another occasion John almost hit me. Chad was four years old and was whining about being hungry and wanting a snack before bed. John told him no, and when Chad continued to whine, John pushed him down on the floor and started throwing the plastic snack containers at him.

The protective mother in me snapped and I ran into John from behind, yelling at him to stop. He spun around with his hand raised, but he didn't slap me. I looked at him and said, "go ahead and hit me, but it better be good, because my dad will kill you!" He pushed me back and stomped off to our room.

We obviously didn't have much of a sex life for quite some time (which was fine with me) until I convinced him we should have another child, hopefully a daughter. We began trying when Chad was three and I prayed every time I would succeed with my goal.

Many of our angry episodes occurred even while we were trying, but all I cared about was having another baby, a sibling for Chad. When I finally conceived, our sex life returned to nil. This was good because I didn't enjoy it anymore and I was fearful he would give me something besides a baby (a disease).

Jillian was born when Chad was four and a half years old and in preschool every day, all day. That sounds very sad, but it was best for him to be in a place where people were good to him and liked him. Not that I didn't love him dearly, but John made it clear he didn't really care and I just could not manage with Chad all on my own.

John, of course, was the perfect father for Jillian. He made everything in her nursery, as we did for Chad, but included her curtains, her quilt, and her bumpers this time. He wallpapered her room, made her baby clothes, and doted every minute he had available on her.

Soon she was crawling and he worshiped the ground she crawled upon, but our relationship was deteriorating quickly. I wasn't sure how much longer I could stay with him. My original plan was to stay together until Jillian was five years old, but I was more depressed day by day.

I also stayed with John because he said no judge in the world would give me custody of my kids with me being in the wheelchair. He also threatened to take them where I would never see them again. Occasionally, he would play on my sympathy, saying he would kill himself if I ever left him. I'm not sure which of these reasons had a bigger hold on me, but I'm sure they all played a part.

John never liked my mom, nor did she like him. There was no love lost on either side, but in the beginning it was killing me. I loved them both dearly and it hurt to hear each of them talk so badly about the other. Of course, as time went on, my love for John slowly died off and I was more and more in my mom's court.

My mom was visiting when Jillian was 15 months old and Chad was almost six years old. John decided to pull one of his mad moods. I was fed up with him and here was an opportunity to call it quits. My mom helped me pack some bags for the kids and myself. While he was at the laundry room doing the laundry, we took off. I know, that sounds really cold-hearted, but I just couldn't take it anymore.

I was relieved to finally be away from him, but what lay in store for me was not much better. My parents are wonderful people and I love them both very much, but moving into their home returned me to my teenage years, and my children became my mother's. Since it was her home, it was her way.

Before I had even decided what I was going to do permanently. Mom had an addition put on the house for the kids' rooms. I admit shortly after we got to her place, John attempted suicide, so I rented a truck and with a friend, wiped out the apartment, taking just about everything. I know, I was cold-hearted again, but I had to take care of the kids. I can see how she thought we were moving in for good.

He had taken a bunch of pills and then called the paramedics himself, so he must not have wanted to die too much. It was a dramatic play on his part to get everyone to sympathize with him. I didn't fall for it. I even took my old van from him, but left him a car so he wasn't without transportation.

I quickly learned that my parents did not have a lot of patience with the kids either. I also had to conform to their bedtime, their TV shows, their foods, and so on. Once John left the hospital, he began calling and writing, begging me to come home. I didn't want to get back together with him, but I had a new plan. I was going to return home, reclaim my apartment, and kick him out.

My parents were not pleased with my decision. They were so displeased they refused to help me get my furniture back home. John was willing to come and get us, but not at my parents' house, nor was he willing to move the furniture back. I arranged to have my friend pick us up and drive us to meet John at the park.

He left his car with my friend to return to my parents and drove the kids and me back in the van. I also arranged for my friends to pick my furniture and bring it back to California, along with my other van. So, with the help of friends and none from John or my parents, I was able to complete my move back. They say, "You can't pick your family, but you can pick your friends." I picked some incredible friends.

Of course, my life back home wasn't great either. Matter-of-fact, John would not allow my parents into our home, so in order for them to see the kids I had to make other arrangements. He also informed me it was going to take a long time before we slept together again (like this was a punishment), which worked fine for me. We still didn't talk much and he was still very depression-prone, but I wanted my apartment back, and ideally, I wanted my kids to have a dad.

I wanted to give my marriage one more try and suggested marriage counseling. John was willing at first, but as soon as the counselor addressed accountability with each of us, he was done. We were given communication exercises as homework between our sessions, but he wasn't willing to do them either. He said it was dumb. I continued with the counseling for my own sanity.

Our counselor was also my pastor from church and was my friend, as well. John never attended church with the kids and me, for no reason other than he didn't want to. It wasn't long before my pastor was counseling me to end my marriage. As he saw it, I had three options: stay with John hoping things get better (he pointed out I had pretty much run that one into the ground); stay with him and just live in misery; or leave him and move on with my life. I chose the latter.

When I told John I wanted a divorce, he talked about how he had supported me through school, how he had given up his life for me and the kids and now had no backup plan for taking care of himself. I agreed to let him stay while he finished a word processing course and got a job and a vehicle.

It took him four months to complete school and find a job. He bought a new truck, and a month after Jillian turned two and Chad was six, he moved out. I immediately filed for divorce. He had a new partner by then and moved in with him. Imagine that.

A little over a year later my divorce was finalized, June 14, 1989, to be exact—not that it was a memorable date for me, just the beginning of a whole new life of sanity and serenity, at least to a large degree.

Shortly after my divorce was final, I also decided to change my last name. I didn't like having my name different from the kids, but it was necessary to protect my credit, and I just didn't want to be Laurie R—— any longer.

Changing my name was part of the divorce decree and was the perfect opportunity for me to finally take my stepdad's name as my own. As a child, there were too many medical records and too much cost to change my name. Now however, I was Laurie Nelson and very proud to carry the name.

With the support of my friends, neighbors, and several new caregivers, I somehow managed to keep my family together and raise my children without John or my parents. The first year was difficult because caregivers came and went, but then I found Robb, who was an answer from God.

Robb was wonderful with both me and the kids and stayed with us for about two years. He had health problems though, which forced him to eventually leave us, but the time we had together was great. We became best friends and my children adored him. He was so good to us and treated us like family.

One year he threw me a birthday party and hired a stripper for me. All of my single girlfriends and gay friends really enjoyed that. We went on vacation together to Illinois to see my friends and family, stopping in Oklahoma on the way home to see his family and friends.

We rented a house together to get out of the apartment complex, and though he was only my caregiver, he used part of his income to enable us to live in the house. He was my lifeline keeping me afloat while I got my head on straight, got out of my ugly depression and realized there was a lot of life ahead of me, for both myself and my children.

From the time the kids were two and six until they were five and nine, many of my friends had willingly stepped in as my caregiver. There were a total of eight: Shirley, Ruthie, Joy, Cheryl, Steve, Gina, Charlene, and Robb.

Before John and I were even separated, Cheryl and I were best friends. She watched Jillian while John was going to school, and did my care for several months after he moved. We did everything together and were inseparable.

It was her attorney who did my divorce. I was her maid of honor, and along with her husband, also her childbirth coach. She was one of the few who put my frigid hands on their tummy, a true sign of friendship. We are best friends to this day, though she lives in Denver and I miss her greatly.

I had another birthday party at a restaurant called Bobby McGee's, and sitting there with everyone I was close to, I realized I had showered with everyone around the table. Talk about a close group of friends . . .

Since Robb could no longer do my care, it was time to find someone new. I hadn't interviewed for a caregiver in a very long time and it seemed kind of strange now that I was. There weren't too many people out there willing to be a caregiver for someone with a disability *and* for the person's two children.

My girlfriend Charlene took care of us during the process of looking for a live-in caregiver. It was kind of funny, as she couldn't even lift me because of her bad back. My best friend Cheryl was eight months pregnant and couldn't lift me either, so we had to get creative.

Robb's father lived in the neighborhood, having moved to California to help take care of him. He was kind enough to make himself available every morning to lift me out of bed. Charlene would get me dressed and he would put me in my chair.

For evening time, my cousin, who also lived in the neighborhood came each night to lift me into bed, and Charlene would undress me. Twice a week, while the kids were in school, Robb came over to put me in and out of the shower. It was quite the extravaganza, but it worked until we could find someone new to live in.

As you can see, my life was anything but simple. Trying to juggle everyone's schedule to ensure my care and still keep the kids lives as normal as possible was certainly a challenge. God must've been watching over me, because when I was beginning to think I couldn't do this anymore, there was JR Hoirup.

We weren't having much luck finding a caregiver. I was advertising in the paper, through church, and by word of mouth. Then one day I received a phone call from a gentleman asking if I was still looking for a caregiver. He'd seen my ad at the independent living center (ILC). I wasn't even aware there was an ad at the ILC.

Ironically, the ad was about two years old, from when John and I first split up. I didn't know they still had the ad, let alone that someone was actually responding. I couldn't be more thrilled and thankful. God really does act in mysterious ways.

I set up an interview for the next day. JR showed up right on time (a very good sign), was neat and clean (another very good sign), and had several references about his history as a caregiver (an excellent sign and totally unfathomable). I was sure he was sent down from heaven!

I was so excited things might finally work out! I told him about the kids, and he was good about the whole thing. He appeared to be completely comfortable with my situation. I asked him to come back one more time to meet the kids before making a final decision (yeah right). Charlene and I wondered, "Is he gay?"

17. My Miracle Man

L ittle did I know, the man who answered my ad, who was my life-saver, who enabled me to manage my situation, would someday become my husband. I am not an overly religious person, but as I said before, I have to say, sometimes God acts in mysterious ways. JR was definitely one of those mysterious ways. You might say that he was a miracle.

My first contact with JR was in February 1991 when he called me about the job. I had my initial interview with him and was quite impressed. Because of my experience with John, and because Robb and Steve, my closest friends, were gay, it's only natural I suspected JR might be. Not to stereotype, but it just goes with the job. I will say though, he had no mannerisms or anything else indicating he might be gay, it was just his profession.

He came back to meet the kids a few days later and Jillian immediately crawled up into his lap. She even asked him to read her a story and put her to bed. Chad showed him his room and a bunch of his things and it seemed to be a natural fit.

About a week later though, JR called, turning down the job because he wanted to have his weekends off. I was willing to do whatever was necessary to get him to come to work for me, so I guaranteed him he would have them.

I worked out a plan where Charlene and her husband would come every other weekend and John would take the kids on the other two weekends, so Robb could come and do my care. He wasn't healthy enough to handle all of us.

So, it was a go. JR would move in on March 1, 1991, with his weekends free. One of the reasons he was interested in this job was because I had a garage and he wanted to work on cars on the weekends and sell them for extra money. So my situation worked for him.

He agreed to help cover the rent until I was able to get back into my subsidized apartment. Since he would only commit for six months, I figured I would be moved by then and he could be on his way.

My friends gave me a hard time about how I was going to feel having a straight man give me a shower. I just laughed and said it wasn't going to be any big deal. I never admitted I was nervous and embarrassed about having this new guy doing my care, knowing he wasn't gay and wondering how he felt about this.

I knew he had taken care of other women, but their physical conditions were much more severe than mine and they never got out of bed. His care for them was more medical than mine. I just kept my nervousness under wrap and waited with anxiety and anticipation.

He started by showing up at 7:00 in the morning, so Robb's father wouldn't have to come over to put me in my wheelchair. I knew I just had to have him begin immediately with my care, no matter how embarrassed I might be.

So, when he showed up first thing in the morning, I was in bed naked. He first took me to the restroom and then I showed him how to put on my brace. It was like he had been doing this his whole life. He immediately put me at ease with his sense of humor; I very quickly felt comfortable.

Sadly, he only got the first two weekends off. Charlene did the first one and John took the kids the following weekend, so Robb could do my care. However, the next weekend Charlene got very ill and JR had to cover. The weekend after that John's house flooded and he couldn't take the kids, thus Robb couldn't do my care and once again, JR covered.

The following weekends seemed doomed; JR basically got no more weekends off. So much for our deal. He was a really good sport about it, but I know he wasn't thrilled.

My birthday was two weeks after he started, and he took me out to dinner and a play. It was the most enjoyable time I had experienced in a very long time. We also began what I would call very subtle flirting with a lot of sexual innuendos, which was a lot of fun too.

His birthday was two weeks after mine, and I took him out to dinner. It was very nice to be in such pleasant company. Not only did he have a great sense of humor, he was witty and very intelligent. I found myself very attracted to him, though I knew I was walking down an extremely dangerous path.

During the third week of March, my old apartment complex called; there would be an apartment available for me on April 1st. I *really* didn't want it to be this soon, but I knew I had to take it. I actually cried because here I was, finally in a situation where I felt safe with someone to lean on and I knew JR would be leaving me much sooner than my anticipated six-month window. I was very sad.

My mom and I made up after not talking for several months. She came over to help us pack and move, and to meet JR. On April 1st, she moved in to the apartment with the kids, so they could go to school in the mornings. JR and I remained at the house to do some final cleaning. Well that was the story we were using and sticking to.

We both knew we had some underlying plans. The temperature was getting quite warm and I was having a lot of itching in my genital area, so he offered to shave me to make me more comfortable (likely story). The whole thought was quite erotic.

We had a bottle of wine to make me more relaxed and he set up my room with leg props, so he could reach me easily. We tried to act as though this was purely clinical, but the candles and the music would indicate otherwise. Needless to say, by the time the process was over I was as aroused as I had ever been, and I do mean ever.

He was very good to me and didn't let me suffer. He easily brought me to orgasm over and over again just using his hands. Things didn't go any further that night. We didn't do anything to take care of him, but oh how I wanted to! It was strange, no kissing or affection, just masturbation. I never did anything like this before; it was exciting, yet very unnerving.

The new apartment was only a two-bedroom, until a three-bedroom became available. Jillian had her own room, Chad and JR shared a room, and I slept on the couch. As small as the place was, JR and I continued our foreplay on a regular basis, and after about two weeks, he was letting me use my hands on him, as well.

I couldn't get enough of him. We were pleasuring one another every chance we got. Of course, never when the kids were around, and we never let on to anyone. Over the course of another few weeks, our foreplay grew to include oral sex. He was even better at that than with his hands. He turned me into a monster.

We went to Las Vegas together for a weekend and rarely left the room. I bought a blue silk robe with matching panties and we basically spent the whole time pleasuring one another with a little bit of gambling thrown in for good measure. As amazing as it was, we still didn't kiss and he refused to sleep in the same bed with me.

I guess in his mind kissing and sleeping together signaled commitment and held more intimacy than he was willing to give at that time. He said the way he would propose to a woman was by making love to her because he wasn't going to do that again until he was sure he was in love. I made a conscious choice to take things on his terms. I thought I could handle a casual relationship with him.

Don't get me wrong, our relationship was more than just sex, he was good to me in so many other ways. He always did nice things for me, often surprising me with special plans for an evening out or a gift for no reason, and he was one of those special few to place my cold hands under his shirt upon his belly.

He surprised me on Mother's Day with tickets to see Steve Winwood. After a wonderful family picnic with friends, he arranged for child care so he could take me to the concert. He also got me a gift from each of the kids—perfume and earrings—so very thoughtful. Their father didn't do anything for me at all. Of course the evening ended with the perfect sexual release.

Things weren't always wonderful. We had an episode of Jillian getting lice from the lady who drove her to preschool. Since she always stood on the back of my wheelchair, I was quick to get them from her. Luckily, JR and Chad never got them, but oh what an ordeal to make sure we were rid of them in the house.

Since I slept on the couch, all of my linens were put back in the cupboard each day, leaving everything contaminated. The shampoo, spray for the carpet and drapes along with the cost of washing everything in the house, cost us a very pretty penny. It was a very unpleasant and expensive experience.

JR was wonderful about the whole thing. To alleviate my stress, he once again arranged for child care, he got us a good bottle of wine and took me to the drive-in. He always had a way of making things so much better.

My three-bedroom apartment became available in May and I found another live-in caregiver to start on June 1st. I was devastated at the thought of JR leaving, but he had always been upfront with me about his plans. He helped me move in to my bigger apartment and got me all settled in, very nice of him.

He bought me my favorite perfume (Adolfo) as a goodbye gift and he actually kissed me goodbye. I had wanted him to kiss me for so long and now here it was, happening for the worst possible reason.

The kiss was everything I imagined it would be: soft, sweet, tender, erotic. I thought we kissed exactly alike, but anything he did would have been perfect in my book. The reason he kissed me made it bittersweet.

He moved in with a friend who had a house about 15 minutes away and we continued to be close. We really enjoyed one another's company. We went to football games, camping, swap meet, movies, and it didn't matter what we did, we always had fun together.

In less than a month, my new caregiver (I'll call him "Louis") became deathly ill with pancreatitis, and JR came to my rescue. Louis returned home to his family for care for several months. Chad went to his grandparents, while Jillian and I stayed with JR for about a month. We all moved back into my apartment in August waiting for Louis to return in September.

After he returned, JR started looking for another job. However, before he left, he agreed to take me to see my sick Aunt in Illinois, until we learned of the most shocking and terrible news about Louis.

My aunt was very ill and not expected to live long. JR and I planned to pick up my mom in Colorado on the way to Illinois for a visit. Louis would care for the kids for two weeks, since most of the time they'd be in school. My girlfriend was available whenever Louis needed a break and to do the personal stuff for Jillian.

The night we were supposed to leave, Jillian shared with me the worst news any mother can ever hear. She told me in her very childlike words (she was only five) that Louis had molested her. I was horrified, but tried to remain calm for her sake.

Of course, I didn't want to believe what I was hearing; I wanted her to be making it up to keep me from going on the trip, but in my heart, I knew she was telling me the truth. There was too much detail for her to have made something like that up. I laid there in my own little nightmare waiting for her to doze off.

Once she was asleep, JR came into get me up and I hysterically told him what had happened. He just held me while we figured out what to do next. Initially, I was going to go to my friend's house, while JR fired him, but then JR talked some sense into me. We couldn't just let this guy walk away.

I went to my friend's house and called the police. They immediately sent over two plainclothes detectives. In the morning, after we took Jillian to school, they had me bring her to Children's Hospital to be examined and interviewed. It was a horrible experience watching my baby talk about things she should never have known about and to be examined in such a personal way.

Luckily, there had been no penetration, and Louis was arrested that morning and sent to prison for two years. He actually confessed, which meant Jillian was not forced to testify. All of this happened in October of 1991, probably the worst month of my life.

Again, JR came to our rescue. He knew how much I was suffering emotionally and decided to stick around through the holidays. Jillian was having a terrible time as well, so we let her stay with grandma for a few weeks to be removed from the situation. JR was strong and at some point talked some more sense into me, making me realize I couldn't fall apart, as he couldn't do this by himself.

So together, we moved forward and the holidays were wonderful. His friend Ross visited us, making Christmas and New Year's especially nice. I enjoyed meeting someone from JR's past. I wanted to learn as much as I could about him. Jillian was in counseling and doing better, and I began to let go of some of the guilt I was feeling.

I got sick right after Christmas and was very upset because we had tickets for the Holiday Bowl. JR and Ross went ahead to the game, while I stayed at home with a friend, wallowing in my sickness and depression over having to miss the game.

A few days later, the three of us went to Laughlin for New Year's Eve. Though I thought I was better, the trip proved to be too much for me and I had a relapse. I spent New Year's Eve in the hospital having breathing treatments, while JR ran back and forth checking on me and Ross.

We decided to stay an extra night so I could get some sleep and do a little bit of gambling. My parents had Jillian at their place for the week after Christmas and brought her back to us in Laughlin, figuring we were heading right home.

Instead, everyone took turns staying with her in the room, ensuring each of us got time to gamble. She felt like a princess with all of the attention. I won $100, which made the trip worthwhile, even if I had gotten sick.

Sometime in late January, 1992, I once again hired a new caregiver. His name was Gus. Jillian let him know up front, what was done to her and she wouldn't hesitate to tell the world if it happened again. I believe this was a good thing.

We drove JR to Poway to a McDonald's and dropped him off near the freeway. He was going to hitchhike, taking a trip north to visit his friend Ross. He kissed me goodbye again, and it was as incredible as before, but I was tired of kissing him through tears. I longed for the time he just kissed me because he wanted to.

JR was gone for several weeks, but sent me a card for Valentine's Day, not a mushy card, but nonetheless a card. He also called me on a fairly regular basis. He returned sometime around my birthday, and what a birthday present it was.

He came back because while he was hitchhiking, he was stopped by a police officer who ran a check on him and found he was wanted in

Washington State for larceny. He had no idea what larceny was or what he had done, but luckily for him, Washington didn't extradite from California.

He really didn't want to know, but just wanted to get back to work. He stayed with me for a couple of weeks and looked for work. He got a job taking care of Jeff, a man with a disability, who at least was close. Visiting often, we continued with our sexual activities, still limited to hands and oral, with no kissing.

I enjoyed doing fun things for him. I put together an Easter basket for him and left it on his doorstep late at night. I also pulled a terrible April Fools' joke on him; I called and told him the police had shown up at my house looking for him, which totally freaked him out. When I told him I was joking, he wasn't at all amused.

Ross came down to visit him again and they took me to my first horse race. That was a lot of fun. Ross had come down several times while JR was my caregiver and several times while he was caring for Jeff. He was a nice guy with a really good sense of humor.

He had Cerebral Palsy (CP) and JR had been his caregiver for a six-month period of time during 1990. We all went to Las Vegas together a couple of times and had a lot of fun. The kids enjoyed Ross as well, but especially Jillian, who had no problem understanding him.

During the month of May 1992, we started arguing a lot. I think mostly because I was beginning to fall in love with this man and he wanted nothing more than a casual relationship. It wasn't his fault; he had always been straight with me. I knew I couldn't keep doing this casual thing.

I also knew the only way I was going to get over him was to stop seeing him for a while. I explained this to him and he accepted it without a problem. I was hoping for a different outcome.

I started dating a month later, figuring that, as I was seeing someone else, I could be friends with JR. We started hanging out together again, doing the things we liked to do minus the sex stuff. So here I was, dating a guy I hoped would help me get over JR and at the same time, spending hours with JR having the time of my life.

Not too much later, the other guy and I quit dating and JR and I slipped into our old habits. I told him someday he was going to realize he loved me too, and he just laughed. I was going to have the last laugh.

By midsummer, Gus was no longer my caregiver. Joy had taken over the job. She was the young lady who did afternoons the first year John and I split up. She was out of high school now and looking for work, so we did each other a favor.

While doing my care, JR, Ross, she, and I took a trip to Las Vegas and had a really good time. It was difficult for JR and me to get time alone, but we always seemed to manage. You know what they say, if there's a will, there's a way.

In September, I hired Stacy, and by October Joy replaced her, working for me again. Stacy was into drugs and slept a great deal of time. I was thankful I had Joy to fall back on because JR wasn't available to help me out this time. He was switching jobs (his six months with Jeff were almost done) taking care of a woman with MS (multiple sclerosis) and he was busy with his move.

We all decided to take one more trip to Las Vegas before the holidays: JR, myself, Jeff, Joy, Ross, and his caregiver from San Francisco. JR and I got into a big fight because Joy and Jeff were having a fling and JR believed I should talk with her about the inappropriateness of her behavior. I disagreed and refused.

The flight home was a long one and the ride to his house where we dropped them off was even longer. We basically wrote each other off and said we were never going to see each other or have anything to do with one another again.

He moved on to his new job, and eventually Joy and Jeff quit seeing one another on their own. Then out of the blue I got a call from JR. He told me he was going to Las Vegas to make a new start, but before leaving he wanted me to know I was right; he had in fact fallen in love with me, but didn't believe we could make it as a couple because we were so very different.

I felt like I got kicked in the gut. I asked why he bothered to tell me, because it was like finding out you just won the million dollar lotto and then right behind came the IRS agent taking away $999,000. I told him he couldn't just spring that on me over the phone, he at least owed me a face-to-face meeting. He agreed to get together a few days later.

My friends drove me to his place for a barbecue. We played in the pool together for the afternoon. Our friends had a bit too much to drink and went to bed in the only bedroom there was, leaving JR and me to sleep in the living room. When we were finally alone, we had a very long, serious talk. He told me he did love me, but he just didn't think it would ever work for us because of our differences.

He also explained that he wanted to go to Las Vegas and work for a while, to figure things out, and maybe we would get together. He assured me he would keep in touch and we would always be friends.

As he was saying those words, he got undressed, undressed me, took me into the pool, and we kissed for a very long time before finally making love. It was beautiful, everything I wanted it to be, but I was confused. Was this the marriage proposal he had spoken of a while ago, or just a sweet way of saying goodbye?

The following morning, my friends and I were in the car ready to head home and he gave me a long, lingering kiss goodbye. All the kissing and making love completely . . . I still wasn't sure about anything.

I always worried about how making love was going to physically work for us because he was such a big guy and I was so small, but again, when there's a will, there's a way. There was no problem with him knowing how to position me or what my capabilities were, since he had been with me so long already.

I contacted my mom later in the day to let her know JR was leaving. She knew I was devastated, and in her own motherly way came up with a plan. She said that she and my dad were building a garage and that my dad needed some help. She hoped JR would come there before going to Vegas and help out.

She offered him free room and board and also some pay. I believe it was her way of keeping him close to me. He would be at their place through month of December, and the kids and I were going there for Christmas, so we would get to spend more time together before he officially left for Las Vegas. She certainly was a smart lady. He even drove one of my vans back to them.

Over the next few weeks, mom called me often and I called her, giving ample opportunity to talk with JR. I missed him so badly and was counting the days 'til Christmas. The time finally arrived and again, my friends drove us to my parents' place in Arizona. He looked so good to me, I could hardly contain myself.

18. A Rare Relationship

Seeing JR made me realize just how much I missed him and how much I loved him. I knew I had to step back and let him live his life as he chose, without any pressure from me. I would tell him when the moment was right and enjoy the next two weeks to the fullest extent possible, making more fabulous memories.

Things were a bit crowded, but cozy. We slept in the living room on the floor with Jillian in the guest bedroom and Chad on the couch. That didn't leave much room for romance, but what did happen took me by complete surprise. He let me know he had every intention of coming back to me.

We were doing some last-minute Christmas shopping and finally alone. I told him I loved him very much, but wanted him to be happy and if it meant letting him go, then so be it. He said he loved me too and thought it was funny after years of pursuit, I was willing to let go, now when he finally recognized what we had. I couldn't receive a better Christmas present!

He explained he just wanted the opportunity to save some money, get his life on track, and buy a car. I think he was really hoping if we were apart long enough, things would fizzle out. News Flash: They weren't going to fizzle away for me!

After the holiday and before his departure, we took a few days and went to Laughlin, leaving the kids with my parents. Once again, it was bittersweet. We had a marvelous couple of days with some incredible lovemaking and yet, I knew in a few days he was moving to Las Vegas and I wasn't really sure he would ever be coming back.

On January 3, 1993, my friends came for me and the kids, returning us to California from our fantastic Christmas holiday. JR was heading out for Las Vegas the same day. He helped my parents complete their garage and was now ready to continue with his plan.

We kissed goodbye and I cried almost the entire way home. He on the other hand, hopped on a bus going in the opposite direction and though he appeared sad, I don't believe he cried. I know, men don't cry.

We talked on the phone as often as when he was at my parents' house. He found a job a few days after arriving in Las Vegas, taking care of an elderly gentleman who lived with his family. He was trying to save money, but most was going towards our long-distance phone calls. Imagine that . . .

After a few short weeks of being apart, JR wanted me to come and join him for Super Bowl weekend. The family he was living with said it was perfectly fine for me to visit. He got me an airline ticket and I was so excited, I couldn't stand it.

My friend Chrissy kept the kids for the weekend and I embarked on this very exciting journey. JR met me at the plane and carried me off. We rode the bus to his new place, where I got to meet the family he was living with and the gentleman he was taking care of, and of course, I got to see his room.

I had given him a portrait of myself for Christmas and it was on his dresser (at least while I was there). The family was very kind, and since JR only had a twin bed, they set up a queen bed in the dining room, which closed off and made a separate bedroom for us.

I loved sleeping in his arms again, but I knew it would be short-lived. I would have to leave him again, making the whole weekend bittersweet. If you haven't noticed, there were a lot of bittersweet experiences the first few years of our relationship. He did tell me he loved me and talked about us being together again; I was ecstatic!

I thanked God every day for answering my prayers. Of course, saying goodbye and getting back on the airplane without him made Monday very difficult. I knew I had to be patient and things would work out.

I was on the telephone most of the next month. For what we spent on the phone bill we could have traveled back and forth many times over. Valentine's Day brought me a beautiful love letter, flower seeds (instead of flowers), and an airline ticket to come to Las Vegas again. This time, he got us a hotel room to stay in, instead of with the family he worked for. Much better, I might add!

As before, he met me at the plane, we took a shuttle to the hotel and we spent all of our time in the room. We were holding on to every minute we had and didn't want to share it with anyone. Most of our meals we ate in the room and spent our time talking, making love or sleeping when necessary. It was an incredible couple of days, which also had to come to an end.

The shuttle took us back to the airport, he loaded me onto the plane, and again I cried all the way home. I spent an awful lot of time crying in this relationship, and yet, believe it or not, I was amazingly happy. Maybe it's true, absence does make the heart grow fonder. All I know is my love grew stronger every day and I'm not sure how that is even possible.

We decided we had to save some money, so though both of our birthdays were in March, we didn't travel to see one another, just shared a lot of time on the phone. He sent me a beautiful pair of aquamarine earrings for my birthday present.

I had another new caregiver, Lily. She did a good job, but she was very controlling. I was looking forward to the day I wouldn't need to be the only boss. Once JR and I were together, caregivers would behave as they were supposed to. and I would welcome that time.

In April 1993, JR came to California. We spent a few days doing things as a family. The kids missed him as much as I did. Then we took a few days and went off by ourselves for our alone time.

We had a nice room at the Red Lion and I don't have to tell you how things went, though I will say we used the hot tub at night, which was heavenly. There was the usual goodbye I always dreaded, but I was getting more and more confident in our relationship and I believed we would be together fulltime very soon.

However, it seemed like an eternity waiting for the days to pass until we would see each other again, and yet, time also marched by with all the day-to-day stuff having to be done in taking care of the kids. Thank heavens for school and sports.

Then, the day finally came. It was early May, and JR called saying he was done with Las Vegas and wanted to come home to be with me and the kids where he belonged. I couldn't believe what I was hearing, it was really happening!

My mom was visiting when the call came and she graciously offered to drive me to Vegas to him to bring him home. We were on the road in less than two hours from the time he called. We arrived at his place around 11 p.m., at which point, he took over the driving. We got home early the next morning. As I lay next to him, watching him sleep, I knew everything was right and good.

The following morning, we were making love on the rim of my waterbed, which has a wooden frame. I had a pillow under my hips, but it slipped out, allowing my tailbone to ride down the hard wooden edge. I was sure I broke it (my tailbone, not the bed). JR took me to the emergency room, and luckily, I was only badly bruised. What an inauspicious start to our new beginning!

I wasn't sure how I would explain this to my mom or anyone else for that matter, but I was quick to come up with a plausible explanation. When JR takes me out of the car, he often uses my bottom to push the door closed. I told people we caught the door with my tailbone instead of my bottom. Everyone believed my tale. What can I say, it hurt so good.

Within a few days we decided we were going to move out of that apartment complex and find a house to live in. JR was going to be my caregiver for a while until we found other ways to bring in an income. He still wanted to work on cars and resell them and I wanted to return to school to get my teaching credential.

We were excited about our future! We quickly found a house in Ramona with a big yard, hot tub, and fireplace. We gave our 30-day notice and gave Lily two week's notice, and our new life together was on its way! It took us less than a month.

We got the keys to our new place in mid June, and he and I just walked around the place somewhat in disbelief. We were in our own place and it wasn't an apartment. We moved in when the kids finished school and had a great summer.

We got our first dog, a Black Labrador puppy. She was about four months old and her name was Alex. She was wonderful with me. She listened to me without my having to raise my voice, was gentle, knew not to step on me, and responded to the wheelchair immediately. She was the perfect dog for someone with a disability.

The kids got a slip-and-slide, which fit perfectly in our new big yard, and Alex loved to run up and down barking as the kids slid by. She was a great dog for kids too. The yard was perfect for kids and dogs. We also lived up the hill from a nice park and close to school. Ramona was a small town, and the kids made friends easily.

We started camping a lot and doing other family things. Soccer, Boy Scouts, and Girl Scouts consumed a great deal of our time. I volunteered at both kids' schools, and of course, there were the endless parent meetings for everything.

I went back to school to get my teaching credential at National University. I had five classes to take before starting my student teaching in the spring. I completed all of them with straight A's. I really enjoyed what I learned and it was wonderful.

JR took Jillian to the father/daughter dinner dance and I believe they were equally happy. Jillian had begun calling JR "Daddy" basically since we moved in together, though Chad wasn't quite ready. JR went to every game they had and he and Chad grew closer.

For our first family Christmas, we had a family portrait taken. The picture shows our happiness. We also got a family Christmas tree ornament: a fireplace with stockings, dated with each of our names. The year 1993 proved to be a very good year!

The new year of 1994 also began well. JR started a new job, working with developmentally disabled adults as an employment coach, and we hired a new caregiver for part of the time. Her name was Dahlia. JR couldn't work and take care of me, the kids, the house, and my running around, so that worked out nicely.

Dahlia's English was limited, but we worked well together, she tutored me in Spanish while I tutored her in English. She was very nice and we remained in contact for many years. I was student teaching while JR was working, so Dahlia got me ready for work and helped with household chores. It was a good system.

Our second Labrador Retriever, Shadow, kept Alex company. Being a male, he was much larger than our Alexandra, but he was just as lovable, and solid black like her. Our family was complete, or so I thought at the time.

My student teaching was fantastic. I started at a school in Ramona teaching fifth grade. I began with the responsibility of one subject and by the end of the first nine weeks I was teaching all subjects. I enjoyed my students very much and I believe they learned a lot from me above and beyond academics.

My second nine weeks was spent teaching a second/third combination class in Santee at the school my children had attended. I knew the school and the teachers well. I was in a very comfortable situation and I had a great class.

I completed the program with a Clear Professional Teaching Credential in Elementary Education and a Cross Cultural Language and Academic Development Certificate (CLAD). I was sure I would get a job with no problem. Boy was I wrong.

During my first assignment, I developed a lesson on Disability Awareness. As a matter of fact, it was the first lesson I did for observation with my supervisor, and it was a hit. Chad's seventh grade art class drew posters for several disability groups and I created color-coded booklets with reading material for each group.

One group used cotton balls in their ears so they couldn't hear the directions, which were given very softly by the instructor while facing away from the students; they were simulating being deaf.

A second group wore dark glasses with lenses covered, some completely and others with tiny holes so they could not read very well, or not at all. That simulated blindness or a visual impairment. The old sunglasses purchased from a thrift store were covered and modified by my daughter, who was in third grade.

A third group had reading material with the words all mixed up, and though the words were common words most of us would know, they made no sense as used, simulating a learning disability.

The fourth group had to sit on their hands and figure out a way to open up their book using only their mouth or upper body, simulating a physical disability. None of them ever thought to just ask for help.

The last group were given reading material in German, so they could experience being linguistically different. Even those children who were bilingual, speaking Spanish and English, could participate.

The lesson included conversation about feelings and what would make their lives easier. I had them write a paper about how their lives would be different if they had a disability, but they were not to write a totally negative essay.

For homework, the students were to look in their community for modifications made to assist someone with a disability. My students thoroughly enjoyed the lesson, and at the same time learned a lot. My supervisor was very impressed.

During that semester, JR and I decided to take Chad to Hollywood for spring break. The day before we were supposed to leave, JR drove Jillian to grandma and grandpa's place in Arizona as I had an important meeting to attend for school. What began as a great day, ended in disaster.

When I got home with my friend, I had no key to the house. The rain was pouring down and the Paratransit bus had already taken off. I huddled under the porch, while she ran next door to call a locksmith. Almost 45 minutes later we were finally in the house, soaking wet and freezing.

As if that wasn't bad enough, we went to let the dogs in from the garage, Shadow raced by me, catching the toe of my boot, and snapped my leg backwards. I felt it crack and knew immediately that it was broken. Luckily, my boots were cold and wet, which kept the swelling down for a while.

JR finally arrived home expecting we were going to go to bed and get up early to begin our vacation, and instead, learned we were going to the emergency room, probably for the remainder of the night. Well, at least we were going somewhere.

It was just as I predicted, I had a clean break of both bones. Once I was x-rayed, they had to pull my boot off (which about killed me), to cast me. They put me in a temporary cast to allow for swelling, gave me something for the pain, and sent me on my way almost seven hours later. I was miserable and our trip was ruined.

We got home around two o'clock in the morning and realized JR's wallet was missing with all of our money for the trip ($500). Talk about a bad day. I couldn't see how things could get much worse. Throughout all of it, JR was wonderful—angry, but wonderful.

The following morning, while in the backyard with the dogs, Chad started finding wet and muddy $20 bills. Then he found JR's wallet with all of the contents pulled out and teeth marks on everything. He hadn't lost his wallet, nor was it stolen by anyone but the dogs. Believe it or not, we found all the money.

Not only did we get all the money back, but after three days of bed rest, my podiatrist put me in a hard cast, eliminating all of my pain. Since my leg was now immobilized, we were able to go on our mini-vacation. Hallelujah!

We had a great time visiting the Hollywood Wax Museum, Universal Studios, Grauman's Chinese Theater with all of the stars' handprints and footprints, and of course, Ripley's Believe It or Not museum. We stayed at the Roosevelt Hotel, a Hollywood historical place in and of itself. We had a very touristy time.

That summer, with school complete, we took the kids to Las Vegas to celebrate. We were having such a good time, but then we got a call our Shadow was very sick, so we rushed home. We were too late. He passed away from gallbladder disease while we were on the road. We were all very sad, but it was hardest on JR, as Shadow was really his dog.

After a few weeks of mourning, we realized how hard this was on Alex as well. She was like a lost soul without Shadow and we knew we had to get another dog. JR found a male Yellow Labrador needing a home. He was about a year and a half old, same as Alex. So Buster joined our family.

Did I mention he was insecure and liked to chew? It took several months before we had him trained and gained his trust. He was also very different from Alex in that he didn't have a clue about my disability. He didn't listen to me, wasn't gentle (he was a natural klutz), and was oblivious to my wheelchair.

However, I once again, figured our family was complete, but it became very apparent the Labs were perfect for Chad, but Jillian needed something smaller she could hold on to and cuddle. She needed a kitten.

Cheryl's mother raised Himalayan Seal Point cats for a living and had a mix she couldn't sell. She trained the kitten to be held all the time, and we gave her to Jillian for Christmas. She was quite beautiful, all black with very long hair tipped in silver. Jillian named her Mistletoe for Christmas.

For the most part we called Mistletoe "Missy." How odd, after being Missy myself for so many years, I now had a kitten by that name. I had to be sure not to answer when she was called. Now the family was complete. Everybody had someone to take care of, to call their own, and we were good.

The year 1995 found me substitute teaching at several schools for several different grade levels. I always began each new class with my disability-awareness lesson; it was a great icebreaker. I loved teaching!

JR was a stay-at-home dad because the other job was too far away and he just wasn't making enough to cover travel costs. Besides, things were better this way, as he was available when I needed him and he was there for the kids, as well.

We established contact with my ex husband that year and encouraged him to connect with the kids. One of the weekends John took them, JR turned on the romance and surprised me.

First he took me to lunch at a beautiful restaurant on the Bay and when we got home, he set up our mattress on the floor in front of the fireplace. We picked up dinner and had a picnic on the floor in the living room with a beautiful fire blazing. After a beautiful lovemaking session, he gave me a gorgeous diamond necklace. He really knew how to make me feel special. I love him so much.

Chad was graduating the day before Father's Day and we had been renting our house for two years. In March we decided the time was right to start looking to buy. I was still on SSI, with JR paid as my caregiver, and though my credit was good we would never qualify to buy a home. So, mom and dad came to our rescue again. They agreed to purchase the house and let us make payments, and when we could afford it, they would sell it to us.

We looked long and hard in several areas and finally found a place up in the desert. It was a 1400-square-foot, three-bedroom, two-bath ranch house with a nice backyard. Our purchase price was $55,000, simply unheard of in California.

We closed in late May, visiting on weekends to paint and clean. My mom stayed there until we could move in, which was going to be in June on Father's Day, the day after Chad's graduation. What a nice Father's Day gift for JR.

Chad had a very nice graduation. We had a small, simple party and went to dinner; he got some really nice gifts and it was a perfect ending to our first family experience. We left early the next morning for our new home and our second journey as a family. Not only had my dream come true about JR, but now I was a homeowner. If only I could get a job.

Our first summer was hot! We purchased an above-ground pool, and soon, it was too hot to swim in. Plus the desert winds made it almost impossible to keep clean. Then we started looking for someplace else to spend our summers.

During Christmas of 1995 JR finally proposed to me. We were out shopping for Christmas gifts and I happened to stop at the jeweler to show him ring I wanted. We often talked about how he wanted to propose to me, but never seemed to be in a financial position allowing him to be as creative or exotic as he wanted. I didn't care about the proposal. I just wanted to be his wife. Since we found the perfect ring, he bought it and would propose in his own way.

A few days later, he called me into our room, as my parents were visiting and were in the other room with the kids. He got down on one knee, took my hand, told me how very much he loved me, felt I could do better and he didn't deserve me, but would be honored if I would be his wife.

What a silly question. Of course, I said yes! We chose April 1996 as our marriage month and the 27th as the date. He wanted a small private ceremony, to which I agreed and we were going to have a small reception of close friends and family to follow. What a year 1995 turned out to be!

January through April 1996 was pretty much consumed with wedding planning. JR took care of another gentleman several days a week to give us some time apart and to make a little extra money. We hired a lady to stay with me and do household chores while JR was away, and she cost less than what he was making, so we were coming out ahead.

I was so very happy with my life. JR was finally going to be mine in every sense of the word. He had committed to me in a way I never thought he would. I always knew what it was like to feel for someone who didn't return the feelings or have someone care about me who I didn't feel the same about, but here I was about to marry the man of my dreams.

This wasn't hurried up or rushed. We had been together for more than five years and experienced some pretty tough times. I was completely confident in what we had and what our future would be together. The most important thing for me was I had complete trust in JR, as he really was my best friend. I could share anything with him and we always had fun together, no matter what we were doing. *Thank you for coming into my life, honey. I love you!*

19. My Marriage Marvel

*T*hank you for coming into my life, JR. As I previously indicated, JR proposed to me in December 1995 and we selected April 27, 1996, as our wedding date. The reason for that particular date is a funny one.

My best friend Cheryl (who was going to be my matron of honor) was married on April 28. Her husband's birthday is March 28, and they got married a month later to be sure he would always remember their anniversary.

JR's birthday is March 29, so I thought it would be neat to get married on April 29 for the same reason. However, April 29, 1996, landed on a Monday, which wasn't going to work for a wedding. April 28 fell on a Sunday, which wasn't going to work either. So by default, we chose April 27, two days shy of a month after JR's birthday. Close enough that he'd better remember.

We chose a morning ceremony (not our first choice) because the church was already booked for the afternoon. So our official wedding was on Saturday, April 27, 1996, at 11:00 a.m. at Our Savior's Community Church (a Lutheran Church, as we are both Lutheran) in Palm Springs, California. A reception followed at 1:00 p.m. at the Hilton Hotel, also in Palm Springs.

I basically had four months to plan the wedding, and for the most part, everything went well. JR wanted a small, private ceremony, so only a few people were in attendance. Cheryl (my matron of honor), Ross (JR's best man), and of course both of the kids made up the wedding party.

Cheryl's husband, Leroy, was our photographer, and Pam, a member of our congregation, was there to sing several songs during the ceremony. My parents and Ross's caregiver were in the audience. And of course, there was the pastor.

My wedding dress was made by a friend of Cheryl's, who was also making her dress. She did a beautiful job on my dress and veil. I had them weeks before the wedding and they fit perfectly.

My dress had a round, off-the-shoulder neckline, with a lace bodice and chiffon semi full skirt. The bodice was a soft, stretchy type of material, so it would easily fit over my body brace and be comfortable for the very long day. The veil was scrunched at the top right behind the white satin beaded headband.

I also planned to wear my white pearl necklace, which was originally my grandmother's, and a pair of matching white pearl earrings. The pearls were my something old, I had a lot of something new, I borrowed a hanky from Cheryl, and my garter was something blue. Tradition is a good thing.

Jillian wore a knee-length white chiffon dress with white patent leather shoes, white lace anklets, and short white gloves. Her hair was done in long ringlet curls that bounced as she walked. She looked like a little princess.

Her dress was very reasonably priced because we were in confirmation season, so instead of buying her dress at a bridal shop, I was able to purchase it at a regular department store. My mom wore a long peach-colored gown, which went very nicely with the teal colors of the wedding.

JR, Ross, and Chad wore black tuxedos with teal accents. JR wore a vest with a high button collar, no tie, whereas the others wore cummerbunds and bow ties. They all looked very sharp. My dad wore a regular suit and looked very sharp as well.

Then there was Cheryl. The day before the wedding, she and her husband were supposed to come up early so the guys could go out for a bachelor party, and she and I were going out together too. It would be our last girls' night out for a long time and would give us a chance to catch up on everything since I moved away.

Late in the afternoon, she called me in tears because the friend who was making her dress wasn't able to complete it. She was devastated, as was I. It was too late to go out and buy something, and she had been working on losing weight and only had one dress that fit her. It wasn't even a formal dress—it was black, red, and grey plaid.

She lived about two hours away. I told her it didn't matter what she wore, just as long as she was there. The ceremony was going to be small and we weren't having professional pictures taken, so it wasn't a big deal.

They arrived in time for Leroy to join the bachelor party and Cheryl and I decided to stay home and visit. We hadn't had much chance to spend quality time with one another in the last few years, so we were happier staying in rather than going out to someplace that was crowded and noisy.

JR and Ross stayed at a motel, so we weren't together the night before our wedding. I slept with Cheryl and of course, my parents and the kids were there as well. We got up bright and early, around 6:00 a.m., so Cheryl could get me dressed before my hairdresser arrived.

My regular hairdresser was so kind, she came to my house to do my hair so I wouldn't have to drive many places with it all done up. I was actually a pretty bride, prettier than I expected.

To my dismay, when my dad got back with the bouquets, the bridal bouquet was too big for me to carry on my tray. It completely covered me. Cheryl and I decided to trade bouquets. Although it was unusual for the matron of honor to have the bigger bouquet, who was going to notice?

Jillian's bouquet was the perfect size for her. My mom wore a corsage and the center of the bridal bouquet was also a corsage for me to wear at the reception, which Cheryl would have to give up. There were boutonnieres for JR, Ross, Chad, and my dad. The flowers were beautiful.

While planning the wedding, one of the first things I did was order our invitations and announcements. On the front was an open Bible with candles and the verse read, "This Day I Will Marry My Friend, The One I Laugh With, Live For, Dream With and Love." The inside contained our names and wedding specifics. I absolutely loved them.

We all arrived at the church around 10:00 a.m. and since both Ross and I use a wheelchair, we decided to have a sit-down wedding. JR, Cheryl, the kids and even the pastor were going to be seated—different, but appropriate. I wanted my wedding to be unique and this was better and easier than getting married underwater or on a roller coaster.

Cheryl touched up my makeup in the bathroom, while she and I joked how I had won. I finally got my man after many, many years of pursuit.

The moment finally arrived and the wedding march began to play. The kids walked out first together, Cheryl next, and then my dad walked me up the aisle to the altar (we provided the ramp to get me and Ross up to the altar).

The pastor asked "Who gives this woman to this man?" and of course, my dad said, "I do." There really was no one to object, as it was a private ceremony, which I guess provides some advantage. At that point, we all sat down or should I say, everyone else sat down. Then the pastor recited a beautiful prayer.

It was probably a good thing we were sitting down, because I found out the guys had been up drinking most of the night. They didn't get to bed until 7:30 a.m., showing up at church around 10:00. I truly believe JR was still drunk. He often uses that excuse, saying he didn't know what he was doing and can't be held accountable. He is such a charmer.

I could see the perspiration running down his face and his voice was almost gone. None of this was because of being nervous, but rather from too much drinking, too much smoking, and no sleep. He was lucky he made it on time. He was smart enough to know he had better manage through the day, or else.

The remainder of the ceremony was really beautiful. Pastor Coppersmith put together a beautiful piece of scripture especially for us. Pam sang "This Is a Day the Lord Has Made," in her beautiful voice. Before exchanging our vows, Pastor told a beautiful story about our wedding rings.

He talked of how on this day, our rings were shiny and new, but the day will come when they are tarnished and worn, and that wear will be symbolic of how long we had been together and what we have gone through.

After reciting our vows, exchanging rings, and making promises of a lifetime to one another, we were pronounced husband and wife. We kissed and were introduced as Mr. and Mrs. JR Hoirup.

I couldn't believe this was really happening. I had waited so long for this day. Second to the birth of my children, this was the happiest day of my life. I was Mrs. JR Hoirup, I really was! I needed someone to pinch me to be sure I was awake and everything was for real.

Of course, part of having a disability also means living on benefits, such as SSI (Supplemental Security Income) and IHSS (In-Home Supportive Services), both of which mean survival. The first was how I paid for my everyday expenses, and the second was how I paid for my caregiver.

JR had been my caregiver for many years, and by the time we got married, he was working away from home a lot and I was using the caregiver money to pay someone else. Nonetheless, there was no way we could give up my benefits and still survive without my working. Anyone with a disability knows this story.

My benefits were important for my survival, but it was also important to me for everyone to believe we were married because of my children. They were an age where they understood right from wrong. I didn't want them to believe I was just living with JR, especially since we were active in our church. So, truth be told, we went through all of this with no marriage license.

Our pastor understood and agreed to do this for us and no one knew the truth except for my parents. In my heart and in the eyes of God, we were married, but in the eyes of the state, he was my fiancé living out of town.

I wanted to make our marriage legal, but I was going to have to wait until I could work and we could both contribute financially to this marriage. I knew it would happen in time. This was very common for seniors, as well as people with disabilities, and it is a shame we have to go to such lengths. You can't even live with the person you love because it isn't allowed in terms of benefits.

Well, legal or not, we were husband and wife. Our reception at the Hilton Hotel was underway. The room was elegant with a mirrored ceiling and beautiful chandeliers. Our head table was in front of six round tables. There were mints on each one, along with the napkins and matches. A disposable camera was placed at each table so the guests could take pictures as well.

Recorded music played throughout the afternoon and there was dancing after dinner. Dinner was chicken or beef, and both were delicious, I had the chicken and JR had the beef, so I was able to try both.

The wedding cake was part of the hotel wedding package, and was surprisingly delicious. There were three layers, chocolate bottom with mousse filling, white cake middle with raspberry filling, and the top was the same as the bottom, but that layer we took home for our first anniversary.

Our cake topper was a heart surrounded by white lace with wedding rings in the center. The cake was trimmed with teal colored icing over white whipped cream frosting. The cake was as beautiful as it was good.

We did the usual first dance, JR kneeling on my foot pedal, so we were close in height, arms around each other and we just rocked to the music. He also danced with Cheryl, my mother, and of course Jillian. My dad is not a dancer, so we didn't go there, but Chad danced with grandma, Jillian, and Cheryl as well.

Jillian helped me to throw my bouquet and JR did the garter toss. I had two garters, one to throw and one for a keepsake. I wore them both, so he could take one off to toss and the other I kept on for my keepsake. Instead of a money dance, we had a money tree, because of the difficulty I would have dancing with everyone. We also took the time to open our gifts while the guests were there to see the wonderful things we received.

The afternoon ended around 4:00 with some of our closest friends coming back to our room. We were staying at the hotel for our wedding night, as the room was also part of the wedding package. It was a beautiful suite right off the pool.

We didn't have any honeymoon plans, although we were thinking about taking the tram up the mountain the following day, as we had never done that before. My mom and dad took the kids home for our wedding night and said we didn't have to be back until late Sunday night.

The party broke up in our room around 7:00. Cheryl stuck around to help me change, while Leroy took JR to the bar. I changed into a sexy white negligee, leaving my white nylons on with my hair still up. I looked like an angel, pretty darn good, even if I do say so myself. She left, sending JR back to the room, and they took off for their own anniversary trip.

JR came back and told me how very beautiful I was and how much he loved me. He wasn't feeling very well though (too much drinking again, or should I say still), so we ordered room service for dinner. After eating, we made love and it was beautiful. We tried something we had never done before to make things new and different and it was. No need for detail, just know he made it memorable.

However, through the night he became very ill, burning up with fever. We bought a thermometer in the morning and his temperature was 103°. I assumed alcohol poisoning was the culprit. We ate breakfast, but by the time we finished, he was still feeling awful and we decided to head for home, so he could die (either from the sickness or because I was going to kill him).

On Monday morning, we mailed our announcements and everyone went on their way, leaving me as JR's wife. I couldn't be happier (well maybe a little if he weren't so sick). He remained sick for several more days, so maybe the alcohol wasn't to blame. He must have picked up a bug somewhere along the line. Life eventually returned to normal and all was good.

We began our life as a family, not that we weren't before, because truth be told, we have been a family since 1993, but something about marriage makes it official. For the first time, I could look to our future knowing JR was truly committed to us and we had our whole future together.

A few months after the wedding, the kids were out of school and we decided to get out of the heat of the desert. We headed up to Big Bear to camp for the entire summer. The cost of the campground per month was about equal to what we would spend if we were running our air conditioner for the month, and the trip provided us with quality family time.

We had the system down. JR and I used a tent camper for our room and storage of dry food products. The kids had their own tents and dog to sleep with them—Buster with Chad and Alex with Jillian.

We would try to do something different every day as a family—fishing, hiking, miniature golf, going to the zoo, canoeing, and going to the library.

By late afternoon the temperature was usually pretty warm, so we would generally rest and read. After dinner, we would play games around the campfire, do some night fishing, or play cards by lantern light. Whatever we did, we did as a family and always had a great time.

One canoe trip really stands out in my mind. It was a three-hour tour of one of the bays. Jillian sat in the front of the canoe paddling to get us to our destination. JR sat in the rear, controlling the rudder, giving us direction, and I sat on the floor in the middle between JR's legs to support me sitting up with the role of Captain.

By the time we finally made it back to shore, everything about me was in pain. My knees were sore from pressing into the sides of the canoe, as I was sitting Indian style. My bottom was killing me, my arms and shoulders hurt from hanging down, my neck was aching, and I longed to be back in my wheelchair. This would probably be my last canoe trip. I don't remember having those problems on the other canoe trips I took at summer camp, but that was many years ago.

Another standout activity was a two-and-a-half-mile hike we took with Jillian, one of her friends, and the two dogs. JR was pushing me in my "stroller," and before long the trail became very steep and rocky. We had to keep a close eye on the girls and both the dogs were off their leash. Every time a hiker came by we had to stop, hang onto the dogs, and keep the girls from wandering further ahead.

After about an hour, JR was really struggling with my chair. He changed from pushing to pulling, and yet it didn't get any easier. Then he realized both of my tires were flat. Since we had no idea how far we'd come, we saw no point in turning back. We continued to trudge on with the hope we were nearing the end.

When we finally reached the car, I thought JR was going to have a heart attack. He was completely out of breath, grimacing, but still managed to swear under his breath. Needless to say, as with canoeing, we were done with hiking.

Our time allowed in one park was only two weeks and then we had to be out for two weeks before we could return for another two weeks, for a total of 30 days in one park. We did exactly that. We spent our first two weeks on one side of the lake and when our time was up we would fold our things without really packing up, transport all to the park on the other side of the lake, and spend two more weeks.

We would do that two more times, allowing us to spend two months camping in the mountains. We were generally there from the middle of June until the middle of August. The timing was great, because we needed to be back by then to get ready for school and such.

We did that for four years, and then in the fifth year we were only able to get away for a week because of JR's job. The next few years we rented a cabin for a week because we were both working and that was all the time we could get away, and the kids were older. In fact, Chad had already moved out.

I often ask the kids what their best memory is of their childhood, and they both say camping at Big Bear! We of course, had a lot of other good times, but nothing compared to those summers. Probably the second best times for all of us were the holidays. All of the holidays were a big deal, but especially Christmas and Halloween.

We both loved to decorate, and JR went along for trick-or-treating while I passed out candy at the door. I usually dressed up with the kids for their Halloween festivals at school. The gifts from Santa Claus were wrapped in paper different from the gifts from each of us. JR made boot prints on the carpeting from the fireplace to the tree and nibbled on the carrot for the reindeer. He was a wonderful father, though there were some things he backed off from participating in.

He didn't particularly like all of the school activities, and he often left them to me. But he was always there for the important ones like graduation, musical recitals, sporting events, marching band, and award ceremonies. He left the science fair, school meetings, and classroom volunteering to me.

He, on the other hand, was there behind the scenes to make sure the kids had whatever they needed. Even when he worked away from home, he was sure to always be where he needed to be for the kids.

Speaking of JR working away from home, one funny story I have is about taking my showers outside. I had long since quit using a lawn chair, because we had a roll-in shower in Riverside, using my potty/shower chair on wheels. We didn't have a roll-in shower in our new house, so we purchased a plastic shower chair.

JR had no problem carrying me, lifting me in or out of the tub, but my female caregivers did. While he worked out of town, we had various caregivers who were unable to carry me from the bedroom to the shower. So we found a great chair on wheels that would transfer on the base into the tub.

While trying to get that shower chair, I had no choice but to shower outdoors. I would wrap up in a towel, wheel out to the back patio, and use the hose, which always had warm water. One positive thing about the very hot summers was my ability to shower outside.

I was still on Medi-Cal at that time and having a lot of difficulty getting approval for this unique shower chair because it was quite costly. I eventually managed to get the phone number for the field office, and when I called and explained my showers situation, I was approved in less than a day. I'm guessing they didn't want it to get out that I was bathing outdoors. It wouldn't look good for the state.

Not only was JR great with the kids, but also a fantastic cook, a knowledgeable mechanic, good with any type of home project— remodeling, plumbing, electrical, and overall repair. And did I mention he's an extraordinary lover and best friend?

He really is a jack of all trades, but he does have one major flaw: he doesn't do hair and makeup. I tried to convince him to go to cosmetology school, but he would have no part of it. So much for getting my hair styled and my makeup done daily, but I guess you can't have everything. All in all, he is pretty close to being my everything.

Probably the most important thing about JR is that he always made me feel normal. He always let me know he was proud of me and never ashamed. In addition, I must say his intelligence, wit, and sense of humor kept us so strong. Those drew me to him and kept me always wanting to be there.

Now I don't want you to think we never had problems. Like any other couple, we had our issues. We argued, sometimes over silly things, but that's what people do. We are two different individuals and are not always going to agree.

We even had a brief separation during our wonderful relationship, but we were both quick to recognize we were miserable without one another and vowed to always work on our relationship to keep it strong.

During the first few years of our marriage, I started providing disability awareness at schools for money. From 1997 through 2001, I was hired by several schools to conduct the lesson and generally earned $250 a day. But I couldn't get enough commitments to actually make a living.

As I mentioned before, I developed the lesson while I was in my student teaching and it went over so well that I tried to make it my career. With not enough schools, not enough money, and not enough marketing, I never got there.

I also started speaking at conferences about my disability and my life story. I wasn't paid for this, but our room and meals were covered. At one conference I was asked to speak about my sexuality. That workshop was so well attended that people were backed up out the door.

JR hid in our room because he knew our sex life was the topic of discussion and was embarrassed to show his face. I don't understand why. He was a great lover and I sang his praises. Everyone there must consider him a "stud"!

During the same conference, I decided to head down to the bar to visit with the other presenters and coordinators while JR went to the room to go to bed. I had not ridden in an elevator alone, since that ill-fated Friday afternoon when I almost got stranded on the floor under construction, and did get stranded in the elevator for 45 minutes.

I decided I was being ridiculous, so I got in the elevator, he pushed the down button, and he walked away. The elevator did not move, and I realized he had pushed the wrong button. The elevator was all glass, so I thought someone was bound to see me. Of course, it was 11 o'clock at night and not a lot of people were moving around. I could only hope.

I saw someone across the hall and tried wiggling my head and moving my mouth, as I couldn't move my hands or arms. They obviously thought I was being friendly, because they waved back to me. Now I was getting nervous. I knew even if someone called for the elevator, the chance of it being the one I was in was 50-50. After a half-hour, I began to panic. I might be here all night.

Fifteen minutes went by, and finally my elevator began to move. Someone had checked into the hotel late, and luckily my elevator responded when she pushed the button. I was in tears by that time. The poor woman personally escorted me to my room and knocked on the door.

JR somewhat groggily answered the door to find me very upset and crying. He felt really bad, though it wasn't his fault, and I reaffirmed my pledge never to get on an elevator alone again!

I continued to speak at conferences for several years, and finally in 1999 I began to substitute teach again. Like before, I used my Disability Awareness lesson for the icebreaker with each new class. I loved teaching and strongly believed this would become my career.

I hadn't been teaching since we left Ramona in 1995, and I really did miss it. Now I taught in two school districts, grades second through fifth. I had teachers who would call me back on a regular basis. I had my favorite schools and classes.

Soon I realized I wasn't going to be hired full time. After about a year, I decided it was time to fight for myself, so I hired a discrimination attorney and sued one of the school districts.

They were hiring teachers with emergency credentials (no student teaching experience) and teachers from out of state because they were so desperate for teachers. I couldn't believe they wouldn't give me a chance. They had no problem using me as a substitute teacher, which in my opinion is a lot tougher than having your own class, but they refused to put me under contract.

Litigation is one of the most difficult things I have ever done. It was a long hard battle, resulting in tears every time I left the attorney, but I was determined to stand up for myself. After many meetings, arbitration, and appeals, the school district and I settled outside of court. I only received a year's worth of salary after paying the attorney, but it was enough to end my SSI benefits.

No longer receiving SSI meant JR and I could get married legally, because there were no more benefits to worry about. I was still able to receive SSA because it isn't affected by your spouse's income, and JR was still able to be paid by IHSS as my caregiver, but I longed for the day when I would have a real job and could walk away from all of the benefits. I hated the control they had over my life.

Right in the middle of all of this, March 2001, I learned I had several cavities in my top molars way in the back of my mouth. The only way to reach them was to put me in the hospital under general anesthesia and break my jaw for access to be able to fill the cavities.

It only made sense while they were in there to check all of my fillings and do a deep cleaning. I survived the anesthesia well and the fillings turned out to be no big deal, but the broken jaw was horrible. All of that for a simple filling.

They wanted me to do stretching exercises to keep my mouth from contracting, in the event I needed work done in the future, but all that the stretching exercises did was irritate my wound. I formed an abscess. I had bone rubbing against bone when I opened my mouth wide, which wasn't good. With the increased swelling and high temperature, they decided to leave my jaw alone and let it heal, which it did in no time once the injury was no longer aggravated.

One of the hardest parts about having a disability is when something as simple as getting a filling, which takes most people about 15 minutes, has to become a major life-threatening surgery. I have often been asked, "If I could change something, what would it be?" Many believe I would say, "to walk again." However, it would be to not have to go through things like this.

Perhaps being able to take care of myself would be another. Even though JR has taken wonderful care of me, I would prefer to be independent. I hate having to rely on others and I would love to do for myself. I guess that is my nature.

I received my settlement in early April and was notified my SSI would be terminated on May 1, 2001. We decided to get married on the same wedding day we had before so there would be no confusion.

Laurie Hoirup

We went to our pastor and asked if he would marry us in a private ceremony in his office. He agreed, and on April 27 we took him our marriage license and he performed our second ceremony. This time when we said "I do," we *did*.

We arranged for the kids to spend the weekend with friends, and after the ceremony we drove to Long Beach. We hopped on the Catalina Express and headed for Catalina Island for the weekend. We had a room right on the beach and the weather was beautiful.

We went to dinner at a comedy club, which included a great show. Afterwards, we bought a bottle of wine and a bunch of candles. We went back to our room and consummated our marriage once again. This time we were a legally married couple. The candlelight and the sound of the ocean made this wedding night as special as the first one, and JR wasn't sick.

The rest of the weekend we hiked around the island (paved pathways and power wheelchair), visited the Botanical Gardens, relaxed, and enjoyed one another. This time was more like a honeymoon because we actually went somewhere romantic and spent time alone.

I guess you could say the first time we had the wedding and reception and the second time, we had a honeymoon. Just like our relationship, things weren't very traditional, but we are far from being a traditional couple.

Other than having two weddings and not being like most couples in many ways, our lives were typical of most families and marriages in other ways. We had our ups and downs, but weathered the storm. Our love was strong enough to keep us together and the kids turned out pretty good.

I look around at our friends and other marriages and I must say, I believe we have one of the best. *I love you, JR, and I am glad you are my husband, my partner, my best friend, my lover, my life.*

20. Eventually Employed

Now I was legally Mrs. JR Hoirup and it was time to get employed one way or another. While I was substituting on a fairly regular basis at one school, a principal asked me to do reading recovery three days a week, which I gladly agreed to. Instead of running all over, I taught my own students in my own little classroom, was part of the regular faculty, and always knew my lesson plans. It was nice.

I did this for a year from fall 2000 through the end of the summer. I was still on substitute pay with no contract and no benefits or promises. Sure enough, the principal who hired me retired and her replacement wasn't thrilled with the program. He cut it back to two half-days per week and my little classroom was taken back for storage.

I was discouraged and certainly did not want to sue another school district. I just wanted to work. Substituting was difficult, and I longed to have a regular full-time job at the same place, working with the same people as part of a team.

In November, I received a call from the local Independent Living Center inquiring about my interest in working full-time. Of course, I was interested. I met with the program manager the same day. He was leaving the state and had no luck with the people they interviewed. He remembered me from my participation on their community advisory group and suggested I apply.

As soon as I said yes, he went into training mode. What I expected to be an hour meeting to talk about the position turned into six hours of training. He introduced me to staff (five of them), showed me all of the files, and talked about everything they did and then some. I took an application and the exam home for the weekend.

I headed home somewhat dazed. This all happened so quickly, and I wasn't sure I was going to get the job. I did my best on the exam and e-mailed it to the director. On Monday, I attended a workshop on accessible transportation with the program manager and met many members of the community who worked with individuals with disabilities.

I was asked in on Tuesday to meet with the executive director, Lucille W——, and to attend a staff meeting. I met with Lucille first and she offered me the job starting at $32,000 a year! I couldn't believe this was happening.

Five days ago I was unemployed with no prospects in sight. Now, I was the Program Manager for the Indio branch office of Community Access Center (CAC), the independent living center serving Riverside County. I was ecstatic and at the same time terrified!

She wanted me to begin immediately, but I had a few things to tie up and would begin on Monday, December 1, 2001. At the staff meeting, I was introduced as the new Program Manager. Everyone congratulated me welcoming me aboard. I learned Mike was leaving the next day, so when I came in on Monday I would be on my own, supervising five others. Unbelievable!

Monday morning taught me a lot. Luckily, JR agreed to come with me for however long was necessary while I figured out my office needs and what assistive technology I needed. I quickly learned that I needed first and foremost a voice-activated computer, and second, a telephone I could use independently.

Getting the computer system was no problem, but the telephone certainly was. It took a lot of research to find a phone system to work for me. In the meantime, I brought a headset from home so I at least could talk on the phone. After weeks of continued research, I still could not find a way to answer the phone by myself.

JR stayed with me for about two months, when I finally had a handle on things. I operated my computer by myself using Dragon Dictate Naturally Speaking and I eventually found a phone system that worked for me with our office system.

Originally called Ariel, the phone system company changed over to Saje under new ownership. This program allowed me to dial and answer from my computer and had a headset with a switch enabling me to change to dictation. It was an absolutely incredible find for me.

I immediately purchased one for my home as well. I utilized my staff

216

to learn everything else about the office. I hired a support services person to drive me to meetings and to feed me. I usually carpooled in order to have my van at work, and things settled into a nice routine.

The office was in complete disarray when I first arrived, with resources stored in boxes completely disorganized, and the case files were also mixed up. I'm not sure how anyone found anything to do their job. It took about six months, but I finally had everything filed in an orderly fashion.

We now had a resource cabinet, a supply cabinet, alphabetized case-file cabinets, one for open cases and another for closed cases, and the computer program could now produce the reports we needed for our funding. I credit my wonderful and talented staff, as we were a team and work was fun.

I can't talk about this position without acknowledging my office manager, Velma. She taught me everything I needed to know about this office. Not only did she do an incredible job as an office manager, she also traveled with me as my support staff and she was a great friend. She made my first real working experience a wonderful experience! *Thank you, Ms. Velma.*

March brought the spring and our annual employee reports. Though I had only been there for three months, I received a raise and was now making $33,000 a year. How cool was that? By July, she bumped me up to $34,000 for no apparent reason other than I was doing a good job, I guess.

The following September, while sitting in a management meeting, the director informed us she would be leaving for another job and was recommending me as the acting director if I was willing to take the position. I couldn't believe how fast things were moving again. Of course, I would take it.

Lucille spent the following month training me on everything there was to learn, unlike when I first started with no training at all. I officially took over as the acting executive director on November 1, 2002, only 11 months after starting my first full-time job. I was now earning $52,000. Not too shabby for someone who was unemployed a year before!

The drawback of this position was that it was in Riverside, an hour's drive from my home. Jillian was in her junior year in high school and we refused to pull her out at this time of her life, so the only option was to make the long drive. It meant my getting up at 5:30 each morning, earlier on shower days, and hitting the road by 6:30 to make it to work by 8:00.

We bought a second vehicle, a small Ford truck, so JR could drive me to work and leave my van with me. He would drive our little truck back home and head back to get me around 3:30, arriving by 5:00. Then, we would leave our truck overnight at the office, drive home in my van, falling in around 6:30.

It made for a very long day. I had just enough time to eat some dinner before crashing into bed at 8:00 and passing out, just to begin another day. JR spent a minimum of five hours on the road, so it was certainly no picnic for him either.

The two round-trips' cost in gas alone was outrageous, primarily because I had a full-size gasoline hog van. Luckily, when I agreed to take the position, my increased salary helped to cover the extra cost. The $52,000 sounded like so much, but I wasn't seeing a lot of it.

In January 2003, the Board of Directors did a search for the director position. I applied and I got it! I competed with one of the other Program Managers who had actually been there about six years, so I was surprised at my selection.

One of the other managers, who didn't care for me, filed a complaint about my having to be fed and taken to the restroom. The complaint was so personal it even included information about changing my tampon. I found that part quite amusing because I hadn't menstruated since Jillian was born, 18 years before.

It was however, embarrassing because the complaint went to OSHA and had to be publicly displayed for all staff to see. So for several weeks, it hung in the break room. Most of the staff ignored it, trying to spare my dignity, and the complaint was eventually dismissed.

It didn't make my interview any easier though, looming over me like that. It obviously didn't make any difference to my Board of Directors either because I got the job. When I received the call with the confirmation, everyone in the office cheered. We had a celebratory dinner and the majority of my staff were there.

When I was appointed as the official executive director, no longer acting, I was offered another raise and my salary went up to $53,000. I was somewhat in a state of shock, and very happy. At this point we decided to hire a driver for the evening trip home, both to keep JR sane and our marriage intact.

Now JR would drive me to work in the morning in my van and drive our little truck home. Our driver would take me home in the evening in my van and drive our little truck back to the office, where their vehicle was located. Between the cost of the driver and the gasoline, you wouldn't have known I was making any more money at all.

It didn't take us long to realize we needed a minivan. This was the first time I was able to buy a new vehicle on my own, and it felt good. We ordered the van online from a vendor we met at the Abilities Unlimited Exposition. My new van was a 2003 Silver Dodge Grand Caravan, modified in a really neat way.

The hatchback when open had a foldout ramp and a dropped floor. I was able to drive right up into the middle with a seat on either side of me. There were no hydraulics to break down and it was easy to use. With a sliding door on either side, tying me down was easier too. The van was delivered in August, and what a difference it made in our gas consumption.

We also purchased our home from my parents, another first for me. I was able to qualify to buy a home and a car. We refinanced the house to do some major repairs, as we were planning to sell as soon as Jillian graduated in June 2004. Our plan was to move to Riverside and see where that took us. We would save on gas and sleep when it actually happened.

It is important that I also recognize my incredible staff in my new office. I had two support staff who helped to make my job easy, Jonathan and Noe. They were both in college, and I knew by their character they would become very successful.

They were always there to help no matter what the project was—moving furniture, driving, feeding me—and I can't say enough good things about them. Jonathan recently graduated from law school and Noe is a social worker doing counseling in a state hospital. I still see them on occasion when I'm in the area.

I also had two amazing executive assistants at the new office. Mary was older and had been with the agency for some time. She was completely supportive and I could not have done the job without her. When she decided to leave, I was devastated, but then I met Mary #2.

Mary #2 was much younger, with no experience as an executive assistant, but I knew the minute I met her she would be perfect, and she was. She was a quick learner, warm and kind to everyone, and always happy. She was a joy to have around and to work with. As with Velma, Mary and I became great friends.

It's kind of amazing that the three women who helped me to run the office were all so similar in their personalities. I grew to love them all. *Again, thank you, Velma, and thank you, Mary and Mary! I couldn't have done it without you.*

Of course, there were other staff who made working at CAC wonderful. My system change advocate, Mary Jo, my financial officer, Faye, my special program manager, Kim, and a host of others. Each played a special role in my employment history. I take this opportunity to thank the staff of Community Access Center from December 2001 through 2005. They know who they are.

The year proceeded somewhat uneventfully. I worked, ate and slept during the week, and on the weekends we played and did fun things. Finally, 2004 arrived and I was anxiously awaiting our move.

We spent a great deal of time house-hunting, and decided the most we could afford was about $60,000. That didn't leave us many choices, but since we did not plan to live in Riverside for very long, we figured a mobile home would suffice.

We found a very nice double-wide in a nice park only a few miles from my job. It was a 1985 three-bedroom, two bath, 1275 square foot model. We liked the basic layout, but there was much work to be done, as things were old and dingy.

We gutted the kitchen and living room, remodeling to what we wanted, an open floor plan with new cabinets and hardwood flooring. We had a roll-in shower put in, painted all of the rooms, and put new carpeting throughout. When we were done, it looked like a house. JR did most of the work, which saved us a bundle. He is so talented and I am so lucky.

Living so close to work was like having a whole new life. I could sleep until 7:00 and be to work by 8:00 with no problem. I was generally home by 5:30 with the whole evening ahead of me for dinner, movies, or whatever activity I wanted to do. I was very happy with the new arrangement. JR and I were thoroughly enjoying ourselves and life was good.

In April 2004 we took a cruise for our anniversary. This small vacation occurred before we moved to Riverside. We left on Monday morning, April 26, and we docked in Catalina the following day, April 27, which was our actual anniversary. The ship was beautiful and our room was completely accessible.

Unbeknownst to me, JR planned a third marriage ceremony for us. He arranged for both sets of our parents to be on Catalina Island that morning and he hired a minister to conduct the ceremony on the beach with the ship in the background. Sounds absolutely romantic, doesn't it? Well some of the best laid plans go awry.

We were told by our friends we should gamble the first night out to sea because that's when you usually win. Sure enough, we won big—$600 worth of big! We couldn't believe it. What a perfect way to begin our journey.

The next morning, JR got up first and left to get coffee, as he usually does when we travel. I awoke to him mumbling under his breath how screwed we were. After hearing this several times over, I started thinking he gambled our winnings away, but realized we were in port and gambling was only permitted at sea.

My second thought was, "Oh, my God, we are sinking!" I finally just said to him, "What is your problem?" He came and sat down beside me and began telling me about his plan and how it was ruined. He was almost in tears and I was in tears by the time he'd finished his story.

When he got topside as he was going for coffee, he looked out the window and realized we were several miles from shore. He asked the purser how to get to the island and was informed you have to take a ten-der.

JR was irate! Prior to sailing and making the plans, he had contacted the cruise line, explained our situation, and specifically asked whether or not I could go ashore. They assured him there would be no problem. Well, I can assure you, we had a problem.

There was no way my wheelchair and I were going to be carried down the skinny flight of stairs, together or separately, and there was no way the wheelchair was going to fit on the tender. After cursing out the purser (although none of this was his fault), JR returned to our room fum-ing.

What really set him off was the purser's suggesting that he must not have clearly explained our situation to corporate headquarters. Give me a break! After 15 years together, I think he knew how to explain about me pretty accurately.

When he arrived back in our room and I woke up, he told me the whole story. I couldn't believe he made these incredible arrangements and I was going to miss out. He even bought me a diamond necklace since I already had a wedding ring, and he wrote vows too. I could do nothing else but cry.

After taking some time to calm down, we decided not to let this ruin the rest of our trip, as we still had several more days to go. We called the parents and told them to enjoy themselves and to let the minister know what was going on.

We went out for a late brunch, and as I stared across the water at the island, I thought about the wedding I was supposed to be having on the beach, but then I made myself think about the other fun things we were going to be doing and promised myself not to cry again.

Shortly thereafter, we were approached by the purser. He had talked with the captain and they decided to bring our wedding party on board to make it up to us. We couldn't believe it. I was going to have my special wedding after all!

They took a private tender out to the pier, met our parents and minis-ter, and brought them aboard. They set up the library with a red carpet, two white pillars topped with flowers, and seats for our family. The door was guarded to prevent others from coming in, and we had a beautiful ceremony.

Our family was allowed to stay for the afternoon until we set sail at 4:30. They took the minister back early at her request and the rest of us just toured the ship and relaxed by the pool. Our family was treated to lunch and we were given a bottle of champagne, all compliments of the cruise line.

They also gave us a leather photo album and a voucher for 10 free eight by ten inch photographs to remember our trip. They really did go above and beyond to make up for their error. Not that I'm complaining. Did I mention anywhere throughout this story about how romantic JR can be when he sets his mind to it. He continues to outdo himself.

The rest of our vacation was really nice. We visited Ensenada, Mexico, via accessible van. We loved all the shops and had lunch in an outdoor café. On the ship, we went to a few shows, played some games, relaxed on the deck, and overall, had an absolutely wonderful time. I wonder what the record is for getting married or renewing one's vows. I think we have a pretty good start.

Jillian graduated in June 2004, and we moved into our place in Riverside sometime in July. She remained in the house in Desert Hot Springs until she left for college in August. Shortly thereafter we were able to sell the place.

The profit enabled us to pay off all of our bills, take a trip to Hawaii, and put money down on a piece of property in Big Bear. The Hawaiian trip and the property purchase happened in early 2005.

The new year of 2005 found JR and me living in Riverside, Jillian going to college in San Diego at SDSU (my alma mater), and Chad also living and working in San Diego. It's funny, they were both drawn back to the area where they were raised.

We had purchased a ticket to Hawaii for Jillian for Christmas, but she was waiting until February to go to the Big Island to stay with one of her friends. At the same time, we were going to Oahu with JR's sister, brother-in-law, and two nephews.

Hawaii was beautiful! We waited until February because the weather was usually perfect. We couldn't have asked for any better. Our hotel was only a few blocks from the beach and every morning we ate breakfast on the beach with fresh pineapple as our appetizer.

There were so many things to do. We hiked to a waterfall, watched surfing on the North Shore, visited a pineapple farm/packaging plant, and went on a whale-watching tour. I also got to see where JR lived during his youthful, promiscuous days, and of course we attended a luau.

We did a lot of sightseeing along with all the activities. Since JR once lived here, we had our own personal tour guide. Our evenings were usually spent at an open-air bar overlooking the ocean with Tiki torches glistening off of the waves, or just strolling along the beach, as the evening weather was always warm and balmy.

One night at the bar, JR reached across to pick up a few coasters between some people who were sitting there. As he stepped back, a woman next to him turned and slapped him across the face. He was shocked and came to us in disbelief.

Before he could say a word to tell us about what happened, the woman came rushing over apologizing to him. She was pinched on the bottom and thought he was the culprit until the gentleman on the other side of her confessed to having done it. We all thought it was very funny. I can't take him anywhere. I wished I had the camera.

The luau included roast pig in the ground, dancing, and plenty of activities—making leis out of orchids, weaving palm tree leaves into crowns, and games to participate in.

One of the games was throwing a spear at a target. I can proudly say my husband was one of few who succeeded in hitting the target, not only once, but three times. He not only had his personal cheering section, but most of the other guests were cheering him on as well. We had a really fun time, laughing, eating, and playing. The evening ended with a show of hula dancers and fire dancers.

On our second night, Jillian was returning home from her two-week vacation. We met her at the airport on her layover between coming from the Big Island and waiting to fly out to the mainland. What was supposed to be only an hour turned into several hours, as her flight was delayed. It was nice, because we were able to pick her up and take her to Waikiki for dinner with all of us.

Like any vacation, it was beautiful, but it was also nice to get home. Sometime in early March our property in Big Bear closed, and what a nice birthday present it was. Our plan was to eventually build a cabin for both summer and winter vacations. As I said before though, some of the best laid plans go awry.

Having just gone to Hawaii, we kept birthdays and our anniversary pretty simple. But I was traveling a lot for work. In May, I was on one such trip to Sacramento for a Respectability Conference and Capital Action Day seeing lots of my friends.

I was venting to one of them about helping me find another job. I wasn't serious, because I loved my job, but about a week or so earlier I was put in a position of having to fire one of my staff for sexual harassment. I hated having to do it and even worse, this staff person knew better. So I was going on and on to my friend, unaware there was another acquaintance hearing me. Always be careful for what you ask for, because sometimes you may get it.

A group of us were having dinner and the acquaintance joined us. He asked me about the seriousness of my wanting other employment. I explained I really wasn't looking for another job, but rather I was just letting off steam. He told me about a job opening with the State, a deputy director position, with the State Council on Developmental Disabilities (SCDD), with a $75,000 a year salary.

Now, mind you, I had received another raise at CAC and was up to $54,000 a year, but this new position certainly sounded intriguing. He said I should send him my résumé and he would review it. I took my time, but eventually mailed it.

To my surprise, he called me to let me know he had received my résumé and had sent it up the ladder to the appropriate parties. I was shocked, because I hadn't even submitted an application at this point. He told me I should really think about it because I had a very good chance of getting the job.

Just a few weeks later, while at a different conference in Sacramento, I got a call from a friend who was very well connected with the Governor's Office. She told me she received a phone call inquiring about me and if I had any inkling that I might want the job, then I should get my application in quickly. She also said she would write me a letter of recommendation. What could I say? Everything was pushing me to do this. What did I have to lose?

So as soon as I got home, I submitted my application and three letters of reference, one from my well-connected friend with the Governor's Office, the second from my board chairperson, and the third from one of our city council members with whom I had been working closely. I believed if it was meant to be, then so be it.

By end of June I had submitted everything, and early in July I received a phone call from the Governor's Office, more specifically, the Assistant to the Secretary of Health and Human Services.

They conducted an interview right there over the phone. I didn't have time to be nervous, nor did I have much time to plan. They wanted to know how soon I could come to Sacramento for an in-person interview. We planned for later in July. Now I had plenty of time to be nervous.

I continued doing my job and I conducted my disability awareness lesson throughout the community. We received a grant around community education and I donated my lesson to my agency for the purpose of this grant.

Since I was the one who knew how to present the lesson, I was the one who carried it out. I did it with both children and adults and it was very well received. I usually brought staff with me, though, so they could be trained on how to conduct this lesson.

I was also trying to establish a Mayor's Commission on Disability. Riverside had five other commissions, and though the Commission on Aging handled needs similar to those of the disability community, many needs were not addressed.

Only 11 other cities in the state of California had such a Commission. I began working with several city council members to make this happen. The effort involved a lot of meetings, including meetings with the mayor and city attorney, but was finally coming together and looked as though it might really happen.

I interviewed in Sacramento with the Assistant Appointments Secretary and her assistant. They took me into the center of the Governor's horseshoe suite and I saw the infamous smoking tent in the courtyard. After talking to me for about an hour, they suggested I go over to the State Council office and meet the director. I hadn't planned on that interview, but I went forward full speed ahead.

A half hour later, I was meeting with the executive director and the deputy director of communication. I thought both interviews went well. Now, they had to check out my background and put my name before the Council for confirmation, and the Governor had to make the appointment. I had no idea how long that might take, so I carried on with business as usual.

In October, I had a conference in Hawaii. I know, rough work, but somebody has to do it. As the trip was for work, we got to stay in a hotel right on the beach. The conference was for rural independent living centers, which included members from Guam, the Philippines, and other states serving rural communities. Part of the area we served was very rural and that is why we were involved.

Since work was paying for my transportation, my caregiver, hotel room, and my per diem, we decided to purchase a ticket for my mom for her birthday. She had always wanted to go to Hawaii, whereas my dad had no interest. His loss, her gain; happy birthday, Mom!

The night we arrived in Hawaii, it took longer than usual to bring my wheelchair to us. We are used to being the last ones off the plane, but usually no more than 20 minutes once everyone else is gone. After an hour, they asked us to exit the plane using a manual chair, so the flight crew could go home. They are required to remain on the plane as long as one person is still on board.

As I said, normally it's about a 20-minute wait and during the day, usually no big deal. However, this flight didn't arrive in Honolulu until 10:00 p.m. Adding the hour wait, it was already 11 o'clock. So, it was becoming a big deal.

The only way I could balance in the manual chair was to be propped up against the wall. I wasn't very comfortable, to say the least. Finally, my chair arrived, pushed by one person and followed by a supervisor carrying a roll of duct tape. There was my control box, hanging by a wire, completely snapped off its mount.

Between being exhausted, sore, and frustrated, the thought of my wheelchair being nonoperational was more than I could handle. I started to cry. Of course, I should've remembered I had JR.

He was able to tape everything up so I could at least drive my chair. We left the airport with authorization and directions in hand to give to the wheelchair repair shop the following day. Not a very auspicious start to our beautiful trip.

By the time we caught the shuttle to the rental car company, picked up our rental car, found our hotel and checked in, we were all at the end of our ropes. We quickly found our room, crawled into bed, and passed out. Unpacking was going to wait until morning.

We stayed at the Waikiki Marriott, right across the street from the beach. Our room was huge, with two double beds on one side of the room and two twin size beds on the other, separated by a living room suite. There were two bathrooms as well, one of which was accessible. We could have shared with at least three more people. Had I known, I might have raffled tickets as a fundraiser for CAC.

The following morning we were able to really check out our room, and it was gorgeous. The lobby was tropical and we were sad we had to spend our first morning downtown at the wheelchair place. Because my control box was so old, they did not have a replacement and couldn't find one to order, so they used JB Weld as a temporary fix, but it was going to take hours for it to set.

So now we had several hours to waste, and with no wheelchair. We had no choice but to drive around and sightsee. Once again, thankfully, we had JR to drive us to places without having to get out of the car. We spent several hours taking in the sights. Finally, by early afternoon, my wheelchair was ready for use. At least we didn't waste any more time.

While I attended the conference, JR acted as a tour guide for my mom. It worked out quite nicely. The evenings and late afternoons were ours. Though we arrived a few days before the conference to have some playtime, a part of those days were spent at the wheelchair repair center instead.

The rest of the vacation was similar to when we were there in February. We ate breakfasts on the beach, went to the zoo, attended a luau, watched the North Shore surfers, and shopped. My mom had a really good time and it will be a birthday she will always remember.

I got the call about my appointment on November 7, 2005, at 4:30 p.m. I was at a Health and Disability Advisory Council meeting in Sacramento. I was just leaving the meeting, so I found a private office where I could talk freely. They let me know my appointment was finally signed, but wouldn't be made public until the press release came out.

Again, I had no idea how long this was going to take, but at least we had progress, even if we did have to wait to let everyone know, as it was considered confidential. I was beginning to think it was never going to happen and JR was telling me to walk away. I was offered $74,000, not exactly what I requested, but it was $20,000 more than what I was making now. Of course, I accepted the position.

If nothing else, I was learning patience and getting a clear picture of how the state operated. I was very excited, very scared and continued to feel as though I were in the middle of a whirlwind romance. Everything kept happening so quickly. Here I go again . . .

21. Employment Extravaganza

I anxiously awaited the announcement of my appointment so I could share my news with family and friends. Though it seemed to take forever, it was only a few days later. I got the call from the governor's Office telling me everything was confirmed and public. I was the new deputy director and my employment extravaganza was about to begin. How cool is that?

The press release came out a few days after the initial call offering me the position. The date was November 11th to be exact, the same day JR first told me he loved me. November 11th proved to be a very special day for me, as well as a national holiday.

Later in the month, I attended a State Council meeting and was introduced to the members as the new deputy director of area board operations. A few weeks after that I attended a meeting with all of the area board directors (branch offices across the state) for my introduction to them.

I began to wonder if I shouldn't have my head examined. This position was supervisory to the directors with no real authority to do so, and theoretically I had two bosses: the Governor, who appointed me and could get rid of me just as quickly, and the executive director of the State Council, whom I worked with on a daily basis. What was I thinking?

I would be starting on January 9, 2006. Jillian moved back home during the summer of 2005 and was attending Riverside Community College during the fall of 2005. She and her boyfriend had broken up and she was more than ready to make a new start, so she decided to come to Sacramento with us.

I gave notice to CAC and my final workday would be December 31, 2005. Our scheduled move to Sacramento was January 1, 2006, a new life in a new year. We previously made two trips to Sacramento to find a place to live, and on the last hour of the last day there, we found a place. I was getting nervous.

There were a lot of tears at my office and many of my staff were horrified I was leaving. Rather than conducting another search, the board of directors decided to hire the program manager who had initially competed against me, since he was their second choice.

My final act as executive director of CAC was announcing to the public at a City Council meeting that the "Commission on Disability" was finalized and permanent for the city of Riverside. At the same time, the Mayor announced I was resigning from my post due to an appointment by the Governor. I was very honored by the community reaction and support.

My staff threw me a wonderful going-away party and many of the community came to offer their congratulations and say their goodbyes. They presented me with a beautiful framed portrait of all of us and a notebook filled with personal messages from each of them. I was very sad to be leaving them all and yet, very excited about the journey that lay ahead.

The home we found was the home of the mayor of Sacramento from the 1960s. It was beautiful, 3000 square feet, marble floors, living room, family room, formal dining room, great room, butler's pantry, bar, three bedrooms and bathrooms, and a coy pond with a waterfall in the backyard. It was incredible and completely accessible.

Even more amazing, the rent was only $1500 a month. Jillian had her own room and bathroom on the opposite side of the house, which I believe was originally the maid's quarters. She would pay rent and do her own thing.

We spent New Year's Eve with JR's uncle, as our house was empty. We also attended a New Year's Eve party, which probably wasn't the smartest thing to do, since none of us got much sleep. JR left a few hours before us to get things set up before we arrived, and we did some final odds and ends before heading out.

Jillian and I drove through pouring rain, but we finally made it in around dinner time. We were tired, but couldn't wait to start unpacking. One of JR's other uncles also came along to drive our third vehicle (Jillian's car) and help with the unpacking. The next few days were very busy while we made this our home.

I began work not knowing what to expect. To my surprise and relief, my assistive technology was there for my computer and my phone system, but it wouldn't work with the existing phone system in the office. However, I had a new phone line within a few days and everything worked fine. I started interviewing people right away for a support service assistant and hired someone to start March 1.

I quickly learned my job and in no time at all developed a good relationship with all of the area board directors. I traveled about every two weeks, going to an area board office or meeting so I could have a feel for their environment and the people they worked with. I was very busy that first year.

I was the liaison between the area board offices and headquarters. I made sure their reports were in, their needs were met, their timesheets completed, and anything else handled that was associated with their providing services to the local communities.

I held monthly meetings with them, spoke on their behalf, represented them to the Council, and assisted them with their personnel and complaints from their consumers (clients of the system). I also represented the Council at many other disability-related meetings with other state and community agencies. I had my fingers in everything involving disability.

Jillian got a job right away and met Josh, the man of her dreams, in the summer of 2006. JR's grandmother came to live with us in November 2006, adding to our family, and Chad got engaged during the fall. Life was moving on for all of us.

In January 2007, Jillian and Josh moved to Fremont, California, leaving just JR, Grandma, and me. She was going to junior college majoring in sign language interpreting, and found out about a school in Fremont that was supposed to be one of the best in this field. I was sad to see her go, but she was only two and a half hours away. I was probably going to see her more now than when she lived with us.

In May 2007 I was offered the chief deputy director position, but I declined because I didn't feel I had enough state experience for the job. Another woman was hired and I learned a lot from her. We also acquired a policy and planning deputy director and were finally running with a full boat.

Sometime near the end of the year, the new chief deputy decided to move on. The deputy director of communication moved over to the Office of Emergency Services to ensure that our special population was covered in the event of a disaster. So much for a full boat. Now we were down by two.

My life was never dull—always something happening either at work or in my personal life. In November, I decided I was ready for another pet. We adopted a Lhasa Apso puppy from a private party. He is adorable and his name is Bear.

We thought he was only one year old, but he turned out to be a few months shy of three years old. He is very well behaved, does wonderfully with my wheelchair, and is small enough for me to hold on my tray, even when I move around.

The first week of December was my son's wedding in San Diego. It was absolutely beautiful, as was my daughter-in-law, Jenn. We also got the shock of a lifetime when they announced we were going to be grand-parents sometime the following summer. We were so very happy for them and for us.

Upon my return back to the office, the executive director approached me again about becoming chief deputy director. I still didn't feel I was qualified, but I knew I was a quick learner and decided to give it a shot.

Interestingly, over two years I received merit raises, cost-of-living raises, and finally a raise that moved me up two levels to be comparable to the other state agencies. That final raise placed me at $94,000. The new position would put me at $98,800 upon official appointment.

After I agreed to this offer, my office was moved up front next to the director. It was much roomier and I really liked it. The lower half of the walls were done in wainscoting and the upper part I had painted in a light shade of lavender. My office was feminine and very tastefully done.

Not only did I change offices, but we also bought a house. JR built a deck and ramp to the front door and put new flooring in the family room, kitchen, laundry room, and one of the bedrooms and bath. It closed on

December 18, 2007, and we officially moved in December 28, 2007.

The New Year began with some major life events, and we handled them all like a breeze, probably because we had each other and everything was going in the right direction. We were finally settled in Sacramento— new job, new dog, new house, new daughter-in-law, new grandchild on the way and we were very happy. Life was good.

The Council couldn't begin to look for a new deputy director of area board operations until my appointment was complete, leaving a vacancy. So until then, I was going to be doing two jobs for the price of one, which happened to be the lower priced one. I was a bit overwhelmed doing both jobs, but I was managing.

My new position entailed administrative oversight of the entire agency. I was doing very little program stuff because the other took up so much of my time. Since I enjoyed being out in the community and keeping a handle on the disability information, I continued attending various meetings.

My job duties included facilitation of the administrative and executive committee meetings, liaison to the Governor's Office for appointments to our Council (I put together the packages of the candidates), and supervision of the office managers and deputies. I also supervised the Clerk of the Council and intervened whenever there was a problem. I learned a great deal about state operations and I liked my other position better.

My voice-activated computer, my computer-operated telephone, my support staff, and my executive assistant (EA) enabled me to carry out my workload. The first two allowed me to work independently. The third provided me with the personal care and driving I needed, while my EA took care of the busywork, allowing me to focus on the more serious stuff.

During my first month of doing both jobs, I took a week off for dental surgery. One of my upper molars had broken several years before, after biting down on a carrot. I knew access to that tooth was going to involve general anesthesia and breaking my jaw like in 2001. Along with the broken molar, I also had a lot of bone loss and tissue breakdown in the front of my mouth for all of the incisors.

The plan was to pull the front teeth in the dentist's office in enough time to heal prior to surgery, which we did. My broken jaw would allow my mouth to open enough to pull the molar and get impressions for a bridge. I thought I had everything worked out with the hospital dentist, the oral surgeon and the anesthesiologist, but again, best laid plans often go awry.

While I was under anesthesia, the oral surgeon determined he could remove my broken molar without breaking my jaw. That was wonderful except he left before the hospital dentist had a chance to explain he couldn't get in there to make the impression for the bridge without the extra space. So I went under general anesthesia and put my life at risk for no reason.

Here I was with no front teeth or impressions to make them. I was devastated. The only good thing I can say is I handled the anesthesia really well and got to go home the same day. Having said that, I was so upset about the other piece, I wanted to shoot the oral surgeon. How could he have done this to me?

I contacted my regular dentist, Dr. Hanefield, in tears over my situation, and he had me come to his office because he had an idea. He had some very pliable material he thought he could use to make an impression and we could have a partial plate made. To my absolute amazement, it worked.

We began with the top plate, letting me get used to it. After several weeks, it was like a part of me, similar to my body brace. We then did the bottom plate and it worked just as well. The man is a genius! He is also one of the kindest men I know. *Thank you, Dr. Hanefield! Thank you, thank you.*

This might be a good place to address a few of the other changes that have occurred in me physically over the years. Remember, when I first became sexually active, I had a great deal of agility and a fair amount of strength. Later on, my spinal surgery put quite a damper on both. My first pregnancy also resulted in even more loss of arm strength.

Luckily, my first husband and JR accepted me with all of my limitations. I believe my ex was thankful for those limitations, hoping our sex life would be minimal, and JR accepted me because of his love for me. JR was always one to make the best of everything and I'm sure he saw these limitations as a means of just having to be more creative.

As my limitations increased with age (stiff joints, tight muscles, etc.), the removal of all of my front teeth enabled me to do for him that which I had never been able to do for anyone else. It was only fitting. I was always bothered by what I couldn't do and most other women could, and this was good for my self-esteem. Here was another example of the "lemonade out of lemons" thing.

While on the subject of doing for one another, I have to tell this really funny story; I'm not sure if I ever mentioned I have always had a thing for firemen, as do many women, but I acted out my fantasy with JR's help.

One of my friends was a friend of a firefighter, and at my request, he borrowed a firefighter's uniform and loaned it to me for a few days. I was going to give it to JR as a birthday present, but realized it was more of a present for me.

I told him I had received a gift at work from the Director's Office, which I would bring home to open. He suggested I open it with my employees at work, but I explained none of them were available.

I brought the gift home from work and he wanted me to wait for morning to open it, which was my actual birthday, but I refused. He gave in and helped me and as soon as he felt the helmet, he knew I was up to something.

The uniform was the real thing, belonging to a captain, with his name on it, and it even smelled of smoke. I assured my friend JR would not wear it in public. I had no plans for being out in public. A new T-shirt was even included for JR to keep.

He was a really good sport about wearing it for me, even modeling for pictures. However, my real birthday present was the following morning when I awoke to my own personal firefighter standing over me, clad in nothing, but a jacket and helmet ready to put my fire out.

While my surgery was going on, things were moving forward in the

Governor's Office. I got my new teeth and my new appointment at around the same time. On March 10, 2008, I was appointed Chief Deputy Director of the State Council on Developmental Disabilities.

I was in a new office making a new salary of almost $100,000 a year, and to think, only seven years before I was unemployed and living on SSI and Medi-Cal. I am not implying those are bad things, but I am evidence that someone with a severe disability can go to work, be successful and give back to society if given the opportunity to do so.

Laurie's Legacy

Life has continued since I completed the preceding chapters in March of 2010, and some subsequent events deserve mention.

First, and most remarkable, was the birth of my absolutely fantastic, gorgeous, amazing grandson, Michael Damian R——. Not that I am a proud grandmother, he is just the perfect grandchild. He came into this world on July 24, 2008, and completely overshadowed his own mother's birthday, which happened to be the same day. As I write this, he is now 19 months old and a real charmer.

Did I mention how smart he is? I look at him in utter disbelief. I was supposed to die at a very young age, certainly wasn't supposed to have children, and by no means was I expected to be around to see them grow up and have families of their own. Michael is my true legacy. *Grandma loves you so much, Michael.*

Another really huge affair was the marriage of my baby girl. I don't know what she was thinking, but she went and grew up on me without even asking if it was okay. Her wedding was utterly beautiful, second to her, of course. I get to take credit for both, considering I brought her into this world and I coordinated and organized most of her wedding.

She was married on May 30, 2009, and is now Mrs. Joshua W——. I can take comfort in knowing if I ever lose my job, I have another whole career I can enter: wedding planner.

Jillian not only got married, but she graduated with an Associate of Arts degree in Deaf Studies, was accepted into the American Sign Language certification program at the local college and she and her husband purchased a new home about 20 minutes from us.

I love having her close by again. We have a mother-daughter day once a month where we go and have our nails done and have lunch together. I am so very proud of her. *I love you, baby girl, my Jillybean, my daughter, my friend.*

Josh continues to climb the corporate ladder at his place of employment. He is a store manager, soon to have his own store, eventually planning to become a regional manager. I like knowing he is going to be able to take good care of my baby girl. I am proud of him too. They work well together and have a bright future ahead. Now, I just have to wait patiently until they are ready to make me a grandma as well.

The construction business has really been at a standstill for the past year or so, leaving my son with very little opportunity to work, though he has done some well-paying side jobs. However, when he isn't working, he is a stay-at-home dad with that beautiful grandson of mine, while Michael's mommy, Jenn, is out working hard as a nurse. She is a good provider for the family and both she and Chad make a great team. I am very proud of them both.

On a sad note, we lost JR's grandmother and Tom, my dad's brother, in January 2009. The passing of JR's grandmother wasn't such a shock, as she was 96 years old and had been living with Alzheimer's for the two years prior.

Tom's passing, on the other hand, was a complete jolt. He took a spill in February 2008, just prior to my beginning to work on my book, and was diagnosed with a brain tumor. The cancer was very aggressive, and even after two brain surgeries and an experimental treatment series, he lost his battle in less than a year. I guess we somewhat expected that, but we were all in denial.

Tom was my first big brother, my friend, my uncle, and even now, it's hard to accept he is gone. He left behind his wife Ellen, three grown children, two of whom are married, and a brand-new granddaughter whom he was able to meet before his passing. *I miss you and love you, Tom, but I know you are in a better place and can watch over all of us without pain.*

Moving on to a brighter part of my life, JR and I are doing wonderfully. I love him more every day, which is really hard for me to imagine, considering how much I loved him 19 years ago.

We are about to celebrate our 14th anniversary (at the time I am writing this), and to think, this with the man who wanted to keep things casual, having no ties or commitments. I like to remind him every now and then that I once told him he was going to realize he loved me. What can I say? That was a good lesson for him, that he should listen to me more often.

We took another trip to Hawaii in February 2009. That time we went to Maui, which is as beautiful as Oahu. JR spent a great deal of the time snorkeling with the turtles early each morning. I spent a majority of my time watching the whales go by as I sat on my lanai (balcony) sipping on margaritas each afternoon.

We saw the lava trails, visited the aquarium, went on a whale-watching and scuba-diving tour, did a fair amount of sightseeing, and traveled around part of the island on an unpaved one-lane highway to hell, but we had fun. We also attended an outdoor Jimmy Buffett concert, having dinner at his restaurant, "Cheeseburger in Paradise." How tropical is that?

I think we have really begun to appreciate and understand what we have together. I'm sure this happens to many couples as they grow old together and I am thankful we were together long enough to discover that appreciation and understanding. You reach a point where you can't imagine life without your partner and I have definitely reached that point.

I am pleased to say we don't take each other for granted and most of the time we put each other first. We have fun together, we laugh a lot, we still have a great sex life, and JR continues to be very romantic. I am one very lucky lady.

As for myself, I learned about an experimental drug being used to slow down the progression of my disease. Being the risk taker I am, I decided to give it a try. I really didn't have anything to lose, but much to gain.

There were three potential negative side effects, but each was reversible if identified early enough: increased white blood count, increase in a liver enzyme, and a deadly skin rash. I was somewhat concerned about the deadly part, but they assured me at the first sign of redness I was to discontinue the medication and I would be fine. I had my blood tested every three months for the first year and then once a year thereafter.

Though I am a risk taker, I am not foolish, so I chose to have my blood tested every six weeks during the first few months and every three months thereafter, just to be sure I was being closely monitored.

I began using the medication in September 2008 and by May 2009 I was actually getting weaker rather than remaining the same or improving. I brought this to the attention of the doctors and they chose to monitor me for a few more months before discontinuing the drug.

By August 2009, I was doing some research of my own and learned I was supposed to be taking the experimental medication with a second medication to prevent the loss of function of the muscles. I was horrified by this information.

I quickly brought this to the attention of the doctors and sure enough, after testing my carnitine level they discovered mine was considerably depleted. They immediately added carnitine to my medication regime and within a few months, I had full return of my muscle function to what it was before beginning the experimental drug. It's a good thing I'm my own advocate.

However, as I was getting full function back sometime in November 2009, I started noticing I was really having problems with language, both with remembering words and using the wrong words. This was happening several times a day and gravely concerned me.

The drug I was using affected the central nervous system. I quickly brought this to the attention of my doctors, as well. Though there were no previous indications with other studies of this as an effect of the drug, I decided to discontinue its use and see what happened. It was January 2010.

Within just a few weeks my language was back to normal. I still occasionally can't remember a word I want to use (probably due to old age), but I haven't had any inappropriate use of language. I am convinced my problem was related to the medication. It was too much of a coincidence and I don't believe in that kind of coincidence.

I am thankful that, along with being my own advocate, I am also smart enough to research topics affecting my well-being. I don't believe I will be experimenting with new drug therapies again, at least not anytime in the near future. I will take my chances with my disability as is.

Taking a step backward to September 2008, I was experiencing a lot of bladder infections. During one episode while I was in a great deal of pain, I decided to go to the urgent care because I couldn't get an appointment with my regular doctor.

I was in a hurry to leave the office because I had to urinate badly and get to the clinic. I forgot to turn off my chair while waiting for my computer to shut down. Having lost a fair amount of strength in my arms over the past few years, I was unable to move my hand away from my control box, which wasn't a good thing.

One of my staff walked by me, barely brushed against my arm, which pushed my hand forward and sent me full speed crashing into my desk. JR was already there to pick me up to go to the doctor and was standing in my doorway. He managed to get to me pretty quickly, but not quickly enough.

My desk was the same height as my tray and the result of the collision was having my tray pushed into me, leaving me out of breath. My tray sits level with my diaphragm, so it was like getting punched in the gut. JR pulled me back away from my desk and kept asking me if I was okay.

Once I regained my ability to breathe and speak, I was in terrible pain. JR rushed me to the emergency room, which was a bit tricky. I had to recline my chair and couldn't use my shoulder strap without increasing the throbbing. He had to drive like an angel.

We were seen fairly quickly because they were fearful I had ruptured my spleen. Thankfully, that wasn't the case. I was just badly bruised and it would be a month before I was back to normal. However, during the exam, we discovered I had developed a huge kidney stone, which was probably causing all of the bladder infections. One more medical problem for me to deal with, and I still had to pee.

After meeting with a specialist, it was determined my stone could only be removed through surgery, which we scheduled for June 2009. As usual I advocated for myself to ensure everyone was prepared for my unique circumstances.

I'm pleased to say I'm still here, which I believe can be credited to my advocacy. Around the same time, I also found out I am diabetic, and I don't even care for sweets. What's up with that? I am falling apart at the seams. I don't think I like getting old.

As for the diabetes, I must admit I do like my potatoes. I have to take one pill a day and I have really cleaned up my diet. My previous diet wasn't so bad. It's just that with no exercise, I had no way to burn up what I was taking in. I inadvertently lost 6 pounds with my new healthy diet, which was a positive. JR and I are supporting each other through eating healthy and keeping one another accountable.

On February 10, 2010, a month before my second anniversary as chief deputy director, I was appointed by the Executive Committee as interim executive director. The director was suddenly removed in January and I was by default next in line to take over. When I was officially appointed I felt good; they were confident I was the best person, not a default choice.

~~~~

Writing my life story ended up having what I consider to be a four-fold purpose. Initially, my reason for writing about my life was to be a role model for others with disabilities. I wanted them to know anything was possible, even with a severe disability. My hope was this story would give them hope, along with the will and determination to live life to its fullest.

I also believed family members of someone with a disability could learn from this story. My dream was they would see that limiting their expectations wasn't at all beneficial to anyone concerned. I was also optimistic that the friends, neighbors and acquaintances of people with disabilities would learn about the important role they play in the successes and failures in the lives of those individuals.

While writing this book I had a wonderful walk down memory lane. My mind began to open up and go from one experience to another, as I would recall something from my past. Each memory would trigger another and then another and so on.

Things came to mind I hadn't thought about for years. Writing was an excellent brain exercise, and at the same time it was a warm and loving activity, making me feel good all over. I felt as though I had traveled back to my childhood, youth, and young adulthood, almost like using a time machine. That is what this book is for me, a time machine.

While sharing my story to teach others about acceptance and understanding, I learned a lesson myself. Having a disability was actually a blessing for me! My relationships with friends, my parents, my children, and my life's partner, as well as my accomplishments in school, employment, and beyond, can be greatly attributed to my disability. Even writing is linked to my disability.

I can say I am actually okay having been chosen to have a disability and I am thankful for all I have and have done. My life has been good and I have so much more than many who do not have a disability. This throws a light on priorities.

As I neared the end of my life story, I realized I was leaving behind a piece of me, a legacy for my children and my grandchildren, thus another purpose. Even if I wasn't around, they could read and share a large part of my life with me.

I was comforted knowing I would always be linked with them through these words. I know they have their own memories to hang onto, but now they will have my memories as well, which means a lot to me.

However, throughout this book, I have shared a great deal of my very personal and most intimate details of my life and I did so for a reason. I wanted people to know I experienced life as most others, with the same hesitation, exploration and accomplishment in many aspects of living.

As for the walk down memory lane, the intimacy I shared brought back recollections of some of the best times I ever had, memories I had let slip away. I was very grateful to have recaptured those wonderful reminiscences.

The legacy, which I didn't think about until the end of my story, is the part creating the most conflict for me. I want to leave my children and family an inheritance beyond money, an account of my life, but no one wants to know the intimate details of their parents' lives, and for that, I can only apologize for any embarrassment or discomfort those intimacies may have caused them. I hope they understand the motivation I had for sharing such details with the world.

In the end, I want my life story to *inspire* and to *inform*. I have complete confidence in myself and I know that if I set my mind to it, I can do anything I choose.

That is Laurie's Legacy.

CPSIA information can be obtained at www.ICGtesting.com
Printed in the USA
LVOW060301310112

266292LV00005B/3/P